To Tara

God bless you—

Jr Wagner

The first time I met Lori, I was encouraged by her spirit, willingness to follow God's call, incredible smile and joy in life. She has traveled and ministered around the world, spreading the gospel of Jesus Christ and speaking into the hearts of women and men. She has faithfully served in her calling as a female evangelist, writer, mentor, wife, mother, and friend. Thank you for writing this beautiful book, for dreaming with God, and for investing in so many lives: mine included!

—Crystal Schmalz
Chaplain and Founder, Women of Vision Leadership

It is great for women to know that God calls them to a wide variety of places in ministry. Permission is one thing, knowing how is *the* thing. In a practical and systematic way, Lori Wagner has captured what it means to be a woman who serves the Lord in pulpit ministry. Learn and apply these proven principles on how to *Preach Like a Lady*!

—Daniel Koren
Author of *He Called Her*

Lori Wagner has practiced, preached, and taught this exciting compilation of biblical, spiritual, and practical material. It merits the attention of any woman whether or not she has experienced "a calling" in her walk with God. I have worked alongside Lori in many successful literary projects and at national women's conferences. She is sensitive to the leading and move of the Spirit of God. This book will challenge and strengthen you both naturally and spiritually.

—Gwyn Oakes
Former Ladies Ministries President, United Pentecostal Church International

LORI WAGNER

AFFIRMING FAITH
Clarkston, Michigan

AFFIRMING FAITH

8900 Ortonville Road | Clarkston, MI 48348 | www.affirmingfaith.com

Scriptures, unless otherwise noted, are taken from the *King James Bible*, Public Domain. Additional Scriptures taken from: *The Amplified® Bible (AMPC)*, Copyright © 1954, 1958, 1962, 1964, 1965, 1987 by The Lockman Foundation. Used by permission. www.Lockman.org

The Amplified® Bible (AMP), Copyright © 2015 by The Lockman Foundation. Used by permission. www.Lockman.org

The Holy Bible, New Living Translation (NLT), copyright ©1996, 2004, 2007, 2013, 2015 by Tyndale House Foundation. Used by permission of Tyndale House Publishers, Inc., Carol Stream, Illinois 60188. All rights reserved.

The Message, copyright © 1993, 1994, 1995, 1996, 2000, 2001, 2002 by Eugene H. Peterson. Used by permission of NavPress. All rights reserved. Represented by Tyndale House Publishers, Inc.

Young's Literal Translation, Public Domain.

Printed in the United States of America

Cover Design: Laura Merchant | Cover Photos: Jonathan Main

Library of Congress Cataloging-in-Publication Data

Names: Wagner, Lori, 1965 -- author.

Title: Preach Like a Lady / Lori Wagner

Description: Clarkston : Affirming Faith. | Includes bibliographical references. | Includes index.

Identifiers: LCCN 2017909836 | ISBN 9780989737340 (hardback)

Subjects: LCSH: Women clergy. | Women in Christianity—History. | Women in Church Work—History. | Sex role—Religious aspects. | Christian women—Religious life.

Dedication

This book is dedicated to women of all ages who are called by God
to preach, teach, and minister the Gospel of Jesus Christ.

Acknowledgements

I can hardly believe this book is finished. So many people helped along the way, and I am very grateful for the tremendous support I received. First recognition goes to the Lord who is the source of every good thing. I honor and thank my wonderful husband, Bill Wagner, and my family. They have faithfully stood beside me through the ups and downs of finding myself and finding my way as a woman minister. Their support and continued affirmation, especially during the writing of this book, have been such a strength.

I want to acknowledge the women ministers who have gone before. Their endurance and dedication paved the way for others to follow in their footsteps. I also offer sincere appreciation to the men of God who have taken time to study the Word, supported women in ministry, and opened their pulpits. I especially acknowledge Rev. David K. Bernard for his steadfast support of women ministers and my District Superintendent Rev. David Trammell. Both of these men had mothers who were incredible ministers of the Word. I also thank Rev. Daniel Koren who quietly slipped me a copy of his doctrinal thesis on women in ministry at a time I needed encouragement. I also thank him for his time reviewing and providing feedback on the content of *Preach Like a Lady*.

Sincere thanks go to Rev. Marvin and Claudette Walker, my pastor and first lady. Their blessings and support inspire me to continue moving forward as the Lord lights the way, and their input and prayer covering have made a tremendous impact on the quality of this book. I also want to acknowledge Rev. Gwyn Oakes, former Ladies Ministries President of the United Pentecostal Church International. She saw something in me when I was still "wet behind the ears," and I appreciate her encouragement as I launched with shaky steps into the ministry of writing and public speaking.

Great thanks go to my editor, Kent Curry, for fine-tuning and ordering this work in so many ways. Thanks also to Rev. Carla Gray Weiser for sharing her extensive research study on women in ministry, and to Crystal A. Napier, Archivist at the Center for the Study of Oneness Pentecostalism, for her assistance plowing through historical documents. I appreciate Dr. Beth Jan Smith who provided very helpful editorial assistance and Kathleen Newman who helped proof parts of the manuscript. Thanks also to those who gave feedback on segments of the writing: Rev. Linda Brown, Rev. Lindsay Coppinger, Jan Dorman, Isabel Mendoza, Rev. Nate Maki, Rev. Carolann Parker, Rev. Mildred Robinson, and Rev. Darla Staten.

Lastly, I want to thank all those who prayed for me and this project. I felt those prayers and support throughout the research, writing, and editing process and was strengthened and encouraged. God bless every one of you.

A called woman of God brings a unique benefit to the church.
Her contributions in the pulpit and in organizational leadership complement
the work of others and bring balance to the body of Christ. The church benefits
when it optimizes her capabilities and intentionally encourages her to use
every gift she has been given for the kingdom and the glory of God.

Contents

Foreword

F ew people are aware of the intense struggle some women go through after being touched by God and receiving a call to ministry only to be told, "You can't do that because you are a woman." There is guilt when a woman's call is suppressed. There is frustration, perhaps at times even anger, with those who have denied her call. And there is deep sorrow at being considered forever barred from answering that call.

Knowing God does not frustrate the desires of his making, a woman in this situation is left to agonize over the question, "Is my call from God or is it a personal desire?" Not only has the author provided encouragement and guidance for women called to ministry, she has outlined the beginning steps and guidelines for finding God's will. A handbook for women called to ministry is long overdue and, thankfully, is now in your hands. A broad range of topics leading to a successful ministry is clearly outlined. While many writers have addressed the biblical affirmation of women, few are able to articulate how the process really works. In her book, *Preach Like a Lady*, Lori Wagner describes the steps that lead to a solid and wise approach to the daunting challenge.

For a lady, her success starts and ends with God. It is energized by her faith in God and a sense of the call she feels from the Almighty. Women ministers are constrained by a feeling that they can do no other than what God has called them to do, and yet in their faith are able to accomplish far more than they ever imagined possible. As Lori has written, Scripture provides numerous examples of women who rose above the limitations of their gender to accomplish amazing works for God because they were compelled and empowered by their calling.

Preach Like a Lady is a handbook to get you started and guide you along the way. It is well written, a journal for the journey, and a candid "how-to and how-not-to" approach to ministry. Read it, study it, and then use it as a checklist. Affirmed by its presentation of biblical facts, you can now go forward in confidence, with character and conduct becoming to a woman who wants to *Preach Like a Lady*.

—Dr. Janet Trout
Dover, Delaware

Introduction

I did not want to write another book. And that would go double for a book on women preaching. After years of inner wrangling, my doubts had been laid to rest. My peace had been made, but the Lord kept pressing me with a silent, holy haranguing—a lingering feeling that I was not alone. God dropped this project in my heart and it was not going to leave. So the work began.

Preach Like a Lady was written to affirm and equip women called to ministry. It is written in two parts. Part I: Helps and How-tos offers encouragement and guidance for women called to ministry and covers a variety of topics from practical to spiritual. Part II: Records and Rationales provides a biblical and historical investigation of the roles of women in ministry and a woman's authority to preach, teach, and lead.

Throughout the writing, I have navigated away from terms like "equality," "rights," and "biblical feminism." Ministry is serving and should never be about anyone demanding rights or dominating others. At the same time, true disciples of Jesus should sincerely seek the Lord's intention for his people, which does not always align with cultural or even church paradigms.

As with any single doctrinal viewpoint, positions on women in ministry should agree with Scripture as a whole. As we look to the Word, let us rise above the human inclination to peek through the lens of our belief systems for supporting verses and seek to find God's heart on the matter.

If you are a woman who feels a call to preach, it is your responsibility to be certain before acting solely on an inner prompting. Take your burden to the Lord in prayer, talk to your spiritual leadership, and study for yourself to confirm that the whisper in your soul harmonizes with the sacred Word of God. As you journey into the pages of this book, I pray the Lord will give you his blessed assurance that a woman may with grace and authority *preach like a lady.*

PART 1

Helps and How-tos

Encouragement and guidance for women called to ministry

Section 1

The Call and Beginning Steps

the Call

Ye have not chosen me, but I have chosen you, and ordained you.
John 15:16

Acceptance of women ministers differs from church to church. Some are very open to it, while others have reserved particular ministry roles exclusively for men. Today, churches of varying denominations are opening doors for women that had previously been closed. As we examine the topic of "can she?" the point should be made that just because a woman *can* do something does not mean she *should*. Anyone, for instance, can join the circus—but is that what you should do? What I should do?

Every believer has a place to serve (see 2 Cor 5:18), and countless opportunities are available to women who will never speak from a pulpit. A calling to a public speaking ministry, however, is personal and unique. It's not a choice to make, but a call to be answered that must be sacred, certain, and sincere (see Eph 4:1).

If you feel God is leading you into public ministry, don't feel you need to "prove" your call. Gifts and godliness are the true standards for Christian ministry. Your job is to prepare yourself and perform the tasks the Lord brings your way—to develop the gifts you have received from God and consecrate yourself to godly living.

Remember, a call does not come from a person, but from God. Jesus said to his followers, "Ye have not chosen me, but I have chosen you and ordained you that ye should go and bring forth fruit" (John 15:16). No job title, business card, or cutting-edge website will validate your ministry, but fruitfulness will. The late Merrill F. Unger said, "There are many ways in which the call may come—directly or indirectly through circumstances. But come it must. A preacher is not a Christian who decides to preach. He becomes conscious of a call."[1]

God's call is to serve. That means following Jesus's example and giving your life away for the sake of others. It involves exchanging your vision for your life for the Lord's vision for your life. You trade your dreams for his. And it begins with three simple words, "Here I am." When you say, "Here I am," he answers, "Here I am." He is *Jehovah-Shammah*, the Lord with you.

Saul had a "ministry." In it, he devoutly and fervently persecuted Christians until the day the Lord arrested him on his path. God certainly changed this man's vision and ministry. The Lord chose Saul to know his will, to see him, hear his voice, and be a witness to all (see Acts 22:14–15). Saul heeded the call, and with a transformation that changed his name and identity, he walked into the purposes of God. His mission consumed and possessed him. On the other hand, Jonah ran from God and found himself in perilous circumstances until he chose to agree with God's plans. It's your choice to run *to* or run *from* a call of God.

If God chooses you to serve in ministry, he will not only make the calling sure, you will never be satisfied until you answer, "Yes." Life will just seem "not right" until you do. Although feelings of inadequacy may plague you, they may well be the earmarks of a humble heart—the kind of person God is looking to use. Even if you initially resist, God's call should trump any feelings of inadequacy when your confidence is in him. Questions may fly in a million directions, but your heart will know when you are in his will. God's call is so much more than an option or an elective to choose. It's a burning ember that will not be quenched.

Clawing for the Calling

One sure way to know you are misinterpreting a perceived call (or premature in your timing) is a frenzied or obsessive drive for power or position. Even with right motives, spiritually immature Christians can make wrong choices to fulfill what they believe to be the will of God. The Lord strips away excess and carnality to prepare his servants. Consider Moses and how he killed the Egyptian. In his zeal, the man called to be Israel's deliverer was unaware he was not yet ready to lead God's people. When he attempted to operate in his own way and timing, the result was murder and a subsequent wilderness season that consumed one-third of his life. Moses's methods had to be refined by God through a process, and those called by God will endure their own unfolding.

As Moses gazed upon the burning bush, he received confirmation that his call came directly from God. His response, however, expressed his feelings of unworthiness, inadequacy, and fear of rejection (see Exod 3). He said, "Who am I? But, behold, they will not believe me. Oh, my Lord, I am not eloquent" (Exod 3:11; 4:1, 10). It took forty years, but God used the desert to transform a brash, self-confident man into the meekest man who ever lived (see Num 1:23). The Lord told Moses to go in his name. Armed with his call and the name of God, Moses led the people out of bondage.

Similar to Moses, Jeremiah was called by the Lord before he was born, yet he experienced some of the same concerns. He said, "Ah, Lord GoD! behold, I cannot speak: for I am a child" (Jer 1:6). Jeremiah believed he was too young and would be rejected by the people, but God said, "Say not, I am a child: for thou shalt go to all that I shall send thee, and whatsoever I command thee thou shalt speak" (Jer 1:7).

Gideon was personally called by an angel, and yet he hesitated to respond. Several aspects factored into his reticence: The nation's dire circumstances; the lack of the miraculous in his generation; his lack of family background; his lack of experience and age; and the frustration of being under enemy rule. These factors caused Gideon to hold little confidence that God would help Israel in any manner, let alone use him for any great work (see Judg 6:11–16). Nevertheless, armed with God's battle plans and accompanied by the Lord himself, Gideon led the people to victory.

Like these men, Esther hesitated when she was chosen to intervene on behalf of God's people. After speaking with her cousin Mordecai, however, she courageously accepted her responsibility. Her intervention caused Haman's wicked plan to annihilate the Jews to be thwarted. The people were saved when she answered her call (see Esther chapters 3–7).

Each of these reluctant deliverers battled his or her circumstances and doubts, but in the end, each was used in a miraculous way. God uses those who offer themselves to him—regardless of their fears and feelings of inferiority. The Word tells believers to cast down "imaginations, and every high thing that exalteth itself against the knowledge of God" (2 Cor 10:5). There are too many men and women called by God who allow low self-esteem to take a ruling position in their thoughts. This, in essence, means they are giving their thoughts higher credence than the Word of God and what it declares them to be.

God so often works in ways opposite those people would choose for themselves. He used an ignorant fisherman to lead the educated Jewish converts who were trained in the law of Moses. He sent brilliant, educated Paul to the ignorant heathens who knew nothing about Moses and the Law. He called Daniel, a Jewish captive, to reveal his sovereignty to heathen world conquerors. If what God has called you to does not make sense, that does not mean it isn't his precise will for your life. Your intellectual abilities and education levels are no match for—and place no limits upon—the call of God.

Your Personal "Call Story"

Author Gordon MacDonald said, "A 'call story' is a history of whispered words and events that capture the soul and make us aware God is speaking."[2] Your "call story" may not look like someone else's, but it is yours. Own it. Walk in it.

If you are the recipient of a call to minister, your first qualification is your devotion and obedience to the Lord. Embracing the one who calls is the key to any ministerial success in the kingdom of God. Regardless of your personal function in the body of Christ, to succeed, you and your ministry must be rooted in God—in your love for Jesus. Your intimacy with the Lord and your faithfulness and devotion to him are of the utmost importance.

A calling is not based on age, gender, background, or race. It comes at the discretion of the God who made you, who loves you, and who has good plans for your life (see Jer 29:11). Regardless of your age or level of spiritual maturity, the Lord will provide for his plan in your current situation. Timothy was young and relatively new in his ministerial experience, but Paul encouraged him to keep his head up and not allow what others might think to deter him from the work the Lord had called him to. When God is ready to use you, he will use you. And he can use you right now.

A call can come in many ways. Yours may be different than what someone else experienced. That doesn't mean they weren't both straight from heaven's throne. You may have had a dramatic experience—a *shazam* moment you will never forget. Or your call may simply unfold as you progress in your walk with the Lord. Sometimes a call comes as an unexplainable sensation that lingers with you—a constant awareness that God has more for you.

Whatever method the Lord uses to speak to you, there seems to be a common denominator when he is about to bring change into a life. He "stirs up nests" so to speak. Like a mother eagle awakens, stirs, and lifts her young ones from the comfort of their home, God flutters over you. He moves on you and encourages you to spread your wings and learn to fly (see Deut 32:11-12).

An eaglet learns to fly over a period of weeks. It begins by taking small hops in the safety of its nest. The young one opens its wings to gusts of wind that gently lift and then deposit it safely back in the nest. As its strength and confidence grow, the eaglet begins to jump to nearby branches where it continues to hop in the wind before venturing on a first flight to a nearby landing. Throughout the process, the young eagle's parents are nearby. They watch as their young one practices and develops in a safe learning environment until it is able to fly on its own.

> If the Lord is unsettling your nest and sending breezes your way—if you hear him whisper, "Stretch out your wings and fly," you do not have to fear. Go forward in faith knowing your heavenly Father will protect you as he trains you.

At some point in time you must settle the question of your calling once and for all. God confirmed Gideon's fleeces when he had serious doubts. He will make your call plain for you. It's God's desire, after all, that you learn to discern his voice. This is one of the most important facets of ministry. As you mature, you will learn that God often speaks in the same specific way to you. For me, he gives mental pictures that bring insight into situations, or he gives me an impression in my spirit—a phrase or concept. He speaks to people using different methods, but he will most often be consistent so you can learn to trust his voice.

As you seek the Lord, you may not get incredible tangible feedback like Gideon did with his fleeces, but if you have been baptized in the Spirit, you have the Holy Spirit resident within you. You must learn to trust the discernment God gives you about people and situations. When you know deep in your core that your call is from the Lord himself, you will have something sure to fall back on when obstacles and opposition come. And they will come.

The Cost of the Call

When Jesus called, Peter and Andrew immediately left their business as fishermen and followed him (see Matt 4:18–20). Likewise, James and John walked away from their business and father to follow the Lord (see Matt 4:21–22). Have you ever wondered what they saw in Jesus to elicit such a drastic and quick response?

When the Lord calls, the one called must respond without turning back. God may take you from your comfort zone and radically change your life, but like the disciples, he can move in your life in wonderful ways and make you a "fisher of men." The cost of the call will be different for each person, but it is God who is in charge and God who sets the price.

From my experience and observation, it seems there is not always one singular call that happens in a person's life. There may be many calls and commissionings in the course of a person's lifetime. Each of us is in a progressive, developing relationship with Jesus. As he trains us and we mature, he leads us to new places. "The steps of a good man are ordered by the Lord: and he delighteth in his way" (Ps 37:23). The word *way* in this verse means "journey," and a call is certainly a journey, not simply a destination. The Lord promised to direct our paths when

SIDENOTE
from Gwyn Oakes

A calling begins with a burning desire to rise above the average. When you are called of God to do a special work there must be an attitude of submission to both God and his Word. Job said, "I esteem his word more than my necessary food."

God's plan for your life will not automatically come to pass. There must be a time of preparation (that never ends) where you learn how to walk by faith and how to stay focused on what is really important. In order to do that, priorities must be established and maintained. It is easy to lose focus in the hectic lifestyle most of us follow.

Do you know what your priorities are? The Bible clearly identifies the number one priority for every human being whether or not there is a specific call: "But seek ye first the kingdom of God and his righteousness, and all these things shall be added unto you" (Matt 6:33). The Lord himself gave us the foundation.

Outside of a divine calling from Christ, there are things a woman who is called to minister must do to develop her ministry. *Webster's Dictionary* says to develop is "to cause to grow gradually in some way, to unfold or evolve gradually." Notice that Webster used the word "gradually." You do not wake up one day instantly transformed and find you have suddenly grown wings and the glory of God shines through so much that people will ask you to wear a veil.

A call from God comes to each of us in a very personal way. Actually, when it hits it may feel like a bolt of lightning. But that is only the beginning. There are many things to learn. Don't worry. God will help you. You may not understand what the Lord wants you to do at first, and what you are doing at the time may seem insignificant. But believe me, it's not. If it's important to God, it's important! We become vital to the ongoing work of the kingdom of God when we are born again of the water and the Spirit.

—Gwyn Oakes
  Former Ladies President, United
  Pentecostal Church International

we trust in him (see Prov 3:6). Notice the word *paths* is plural. There is not one direction or purpose for your life. We serve a multifaceted God who does not limit people to just one area of service.

Making it Sure

"Wherefore the rather, brethren, give diligence to make your calling and election sure: for if ye do these things, ye shall never fall" (2 Pet 1:10). You have a role to play in preparing and pursuing the call of God in your life. Be diligent about what God has spoken to you. Refuse to settle for less than what he has placed in your heart. There are those who have been called to one office and settled for another, but to do so would mean compromising for convenience or comfort. (Although I can't imagine it's truly comfortable to settle outside God's will).

When David decided to stay home instead of go out to battle with his men, he placed himself in the way of temptation, and it ended in a bad situation. At the time it may have looked to David like he had chosen the easier path, but betrayal, adultery, and murder were the fruit of his decision. Staying in what seems comfortable could lead to a very uncomfortable conclusion.

Be busy doing what you already know to do. God most often reveals his will by steering us as we are in motion. It takes considerably less effort to redirect a ship in motion than to launch a great vessel from a static position. Decades ago, as I stared out an eighth-floor hospital window, the Lord impressed me with a similar thought. From my vantage point I watched a bird take flight from the sidewalk below. The hardest part was the lift-off, but once the bird was in the air, it reached a point where it took very little effort to keep moving or adjust course. The will of God may never come if we wait for it in our easy chairs; but as we go about our days moving in the flow of the Spirit, he will lead and direct us in the ways we should go.

Confirming the Call

If you feel a call to ministry, God will often send someone to confirm what you are feeling. Although it may not happen right away, a true call of God should ultimately be recognized by the church and approved by church leadership in a way that enables you to minister and serve. The Bible gives an example of this with Barnabas and Paul. These men were called by God, and they were recognized and authorized by the laying on of hands by the church. You may be called, but that does not mean you are immediately and authorized and/or ready. Your spiritual leadership should be involved in monitoring your development and launching you into responsibilities that match your maturity.

If you feel called, but your pastor or spiritual leader has not yet acknowledged it, understand it is your pastor's responsibility to ensure any person elevated to a ministry position is seasoned and qualified. Don't begrudge your shepherd's careful protection of his or her flock. At the same time, if opportunities arise to minister outside the church in areas like nursing homes, prisons, or shelters, with your pastor's

> **SIDENOTE**
> *from Mildred Robinson*
>
> Pastoring a church will not come overnight. God will equip you along the way. You may start preaching in a nursing home or even a prison. Others may evangelize or assist a pastor for a few years. All of this will take time until one day God says, "You have passed all of my tests and you are now ready to lead my flock."
>
> —Mildred Robinson
> Pastor; Beaumont, Texas

permission, run with it. Serve with excellence in your church. Volunteer in your community. You may even want to take a short-term missions trip. God will make a place for you to serve if you will make yourself available.

Some people may not understand your call, especially at first, but it is a sacred gift from God even when it may take you down a lonely path. Other people may perceive your call before you do. Those closest to you should see God's leading in your life. Your leadership may invite you to step out in areas of ministry. When that happens, serve where you are asked, even if it stretches you. It can be tempting to talk yourself out of what God has called you to, but a child of God must surrender to the Lord's leading.

Recognizing your abilities and interests may help as you define or refine your call; however, the Lord may ask you to do what you would prefer someone else did. The Lord enrolled me in some tasks for long seasons I would never have chosen for myself. They stretched me. They grew me. They taught me that I could do things I never imagined. And they also taught me to sacrifice and serve where there was a need even when it was outside my area of giftedness (see Rom 12:1). It's good to look to our natural strengths and weaknesses—perhaps even take a spiritual gifts, aptitude, or personality test such as the Myers-Briggs Assessment (www.mbtionline.com). Understanding your strengths and weaknesses may help guide you in your development as a Christian and minister, but regardless of what you discover about your natural or spiritual aptitudes, be ready to say yes when the Lord calls you to any assignment. He has his kingdom purposes, and we must trust him.

Today and Tomorrow

God has a long-term plan that requires many short-term steps. It's only natural that you have questions on your journey, but according to the apostle Paul, you don't have to wander aimlessly. You can understand "what the will of the Lord is" (see Eph 5:17). The trick is to avoid getting "lost in the looking." You don't have to know all the details of where you are going to take positive steps in the right direction, and be careful not to allow the dilemma of "which choice" to lead you into decision making paralysis.

God's Word will light your way as he unfolds his plan.

I believe the Lord has a perfect will, but I also believe we have many opportunities to fulfill that will. If we miss one, and repent, we can be comforted that the Lord hasn't changed his mind about our gifts and callings (see Rom 11:29). You can follow the light the Lord is shining on your next step and move forward even if the step after it is unknown.

"Take heed to the ministry which thou hast received in the Lord, that thou fulfil it" (Col 4:17). Know who you are and conduct yourself with a sense of purpose and unshakeable commitment to God and your call. The Word of the Lord says, "Faithful is he that calleth you, who also will do it" (1 Thess 5:24). Once God calls and you respond, you can be assured that he will help you prepare and provide the right resources and opportunities.

In 2004, I was asked to serve locally as a volunteer for an organization that coordinates annual prayer meetings across the nation. Honestly, I didn't want to do it. I said no without speaking to my husband or the Lord about the offer. The next year I was asked again, and this time specifically asked to pray about it, I did, reluctantly. After praying and speaking with my husband and pastor, I agreed to take the position. As I did my best to serve at the local level, over a ten-year period I was elevated through the ranks from being a city coordinator to a county coordinator, then a tri-county coordinator, then assistant to the state coordinator, and finally the state coordinator. I didn't seek any of these positions, but the Lord used them to promote my ministry locally, statewide, and to a level of national recognition within this respected organization.

The Lord used this experience to train me for future positions that I have subsequently been appointed to within my church denomination. As I served, the Lord was at work in me building my leadership skills and my confidence. So I encourage you: Don't despise the tasks God asks you to do, even if they are not what you would choose for yourself. You may not have his master plan in view. His ways are higher than ours. He sees the end from the beginning, and you can trust his call to every appointment.

While you are developing, be diligent about everyday spiritual disciplines. Be faithful to your personal devotions and spiritual growth and remember that your calling is not from someone else, for someone else, or like someone else's. Refuse to be frustrated, and instead be content with where you are in the process. You are a candle in a candlestick, and you shall give light to your house (see Matt 5:15). You will learn to give light from the position you are in right now.

As you progress and meet new opportunities, make sure to keep in contact with your spiritual authority and operate under that blessing and covering. Walk in the light you have without worrying about the decisions the future will bring. God is preparing, and the little part of the plan you are in today is part of his eternal picture.

Dreams, Vision, and Finding God's Will

But rise, and stand upon thy feet: for I have appeared unto thee for this purpose, to make thee a minister and a witness both of these things which thou hast seen, and of those things in the which I will appear unto thee.
Acts 26:16

The Lord said in the last days his people would receive his Spirit, and when they did, they would prophesy, dream dreams, and see visions (see Joel 2:28). He specifically included his daughters (young and old) in this promise. The opportunity to experience divine dreams and visions has been available to the church since the day of Pentecost (see Acts 2:17). That means that as a Spirit-filled believer, you can expect to hear from God any time, any moment, in any place.

The terms "dreams" and "visions" are sometimes used interchangeably. While dreams include "night visions" received while a person sleeps, they are not limited to them. God gives prophetic dreams and visions to his people. He causes them to see and feel things that inspire them to speak and act according to his direction. While they can be received while sleeping, God's dreams and visions often appear during worship, prayer, or meditation, and they are more than images in your mind. They are perceptions, revelations, divine

> Whatever method the Lord uses to impart a divine communication to you, that perception, revelation, or picture is your dream and your vision for future action.

communications that come as pictures, oracles, or prophesies.[3] In this chapter, both dreams and visions refer to the revealed plan of God for your life.

God gave people the gift of dreaming. However, because dreams can emanate from you, God, someone else, or even a late-night snack, determining the source of a dream is vital. Did it come from your mind, or did God's Spirit reveal it? Did a false spirit whisper into your subconscious, or did someone speak something into your life from their own perception or desire for you? Always evaluate the source of any vision or dream. If you dreamed it or someone else dreamed it about you, when it is from God, you will have a witness in your spirit. It will line up with the principles in his Word, and your spiritual authority and mentors should be in agreement with it as well.

When God plants something inside of you, it simply cannot be forgotten. Even if you have not spoken or acted upon it, something stirs deep inside when you think of it although often you have no idea how it could ever come to pass.

People have their personal hopes and dreams for their lives, but God at times asks us to switch our plans for his. When the Lord spoke to Saul (later known as Paul) in a vision, he stopped him in his tracks and gave him his God-vision for his life (see Acts 26:16). David was tending his father's sheep when a prophet came to his home with an unexpected call to lead God's people (see 1 Sam 16:1-13). Betrothed to Joseph, Mary's dreams for her future were forever altered by an angelic visitation (see Luke 1:27-28).

When God imparts a dream, it may not only change your plans, it can be terrifying. Job said, "Then thou scarest me with dreams, and terrifies me through visions" (Job 7:14). Yes, I took literary license pulling this verse out of context, but it certainly does apply. When God gives a vision, it can cause your spiritual knees to knock. He can terrify you with big plans that require huge risks or take you beyond yourself. God's dreams rarely allow those he gives them to "to play it safe." Dreams can mean danger and require daring acts on the path to your destiny.

Nehemiah led a team on a mission to rebuild the temple. Because of the great opposition they faced, the people worked with a trowel in one hand and a sword strapped to their sides in case of enemy attack. When Ruth's dream for her family died with her husband, she faced many obstacles as she traveled to a new land to pursue a life of faith with God's people. The New Testament records Jesus's followers (male and female) who worked and suffered to launch the Lord's vision of disciples in every nation (see Matt 28:19-20). Today, you and I are part of God's dream. And as we unite with his vision and serve, we, too, will face opposition and struggles.

Dreaming is for Doing

God doesn't give people dreams to simply fill their minds and have no effect on their day planners. He gives dreams for people to act on. That said, ministry dreams aren't usually instantaneously fulfilled the moment they are imparted. They require a period of development. David, for instance, was anointed king many years before he ascended to the throne. I'm sure David was frustrated at times, but God's dream kept him while he was hiding in caves from a would-be assassin. Throughout the process David fixed his heart on God and maintained a sense of purpose and destiny that was greater than the situation he found himself in.

God not only wants you to remember your dreams, he remembers them as well. You may feel forgotten or in a hopeless situation, but consider Joseph. It was only after suffering rejection from his family, slavery, false accusations, and imprisonment that he saw his God-given dreams come to pass. The memory of those dreams may well have kept him in the darkest moments of his prison cell. The hope of your dreams can keep you stable and focused in your times of waiting and even persecution.

Dreams and visions require hope. Dreamers, while they may see obstacles, see opportunities that are worth the challenges and difficulties. They have vision beyond the moment and are kingdom minded. J. Oswald Sanders said, "Eyes that look are common. Eyes that see are rare." Keep looking. Keep dreaming. Focus on what God speaks to you and the path he unfolds before you. And with that vision in mind, keep working.

As retired four-star general Colin Powell said, "A dream doesn't become reality through magic; it takes sweat, determination and hard work."

"Faithful is he that calleth you, who also will do it" (1 Thess 5:24). God is absolutely trustworthy and dependable. He will bring his purposes to pass; and while you are on your journey, he will guard you, watch over you, and protect you as you walk in your call.

As called women of God, you and I cannot rely on the "magic" of the Holy Spirit to see his will accomplished in our lives. We must walk in faith, agree with the vision he has given, and believe the Lord will provide all that is needed to bring his purposes to pass.

Have faith in the Lord and in the dream he placed in you. It's a seed planted by the Holy Spirit that you must nurture. Give it your time. Speak it out. Refuse to let doubt kill it. Fight your fears with faith.

Spiritual vision is believing with eyes of faith the things you have only seen in your spirit (see Heb 11:1). Paul wrote, "But as it is written, Eye hath not seen, nor ear heard, neither have entered into the heart of man, the things which God hath prepared for them that love him" (1 Cor 2:9). So many times people look at that verse from a wrong perspective—with an expectation of new things not yet revealed. Paul, however, followed those words with these, "But God hath revealed them unto us by his Spirit" (1 Cor 2:10). God has revealed things to his people by his Spirit. If his Spirit lives in you, so also dwell the plans and purposes of God, great and mighty things which you would never have seen, heard, or considered without Him.

Tips for making God's dreams for you come true:

- Be positive. When God gives a dream (even an impossible dream), respond like Mary did when she said, "Be it unto me according to thy word" (Luke 1:38). When you do, you are positioned for a miracle.
- Recognize that sometimes "God dreams" require dying to self—saying, "Not my will, but thine, be done" (Luke 22:42).
- Record the dreams God has given you (see Hab 2:2). Keep them where you will see them regularly.
- Ask the Lord for the specifics—"What would you have me do? What is your plan, God?" (see Acts 9:6).
- Keep your focus on the future. "Forgetting those things which are behind, and reaching forth unto those things which are before, I press toward the mark for the prize of the high calling of God in Christ Jesus" (Phil 3:13–14).
- Work your dreams. Remove distractions that hinder productivity and use your time well. "For a dream cometh through the multitude of business" (Ecc 5:3).

- Be prayerful. "Grant thee according to thine own heart, and fulfil all thy counsel" (Ps 20:4).
- Be positive. Jesus said, "If thou canst believe, all things are possible to him that believeth" (Mark 9:23).
- Be persistent, patient, and trust his timing. "And let us not be weary in well doing: for in due season we shall reap, if we faint not" (Gal 6:9).
- Be open and flexible. "I can do all things through Christ which strengtheneth me" (Phil 4:13).
- Make sure your plans harmonize with "God first" principles (see Matt 6:33; Prov 16:9).

Finding God's Will

The Lord has unique, specific purposes for each of his children. In searching for the "perfect will of God," we ask questions. Some questions, however, are already answered in his Word. David K. Bernard said, "Ninety percent of doing the will of God is doing what you already know to do." The Lord shows us how to live, how to walk as children of the light in goodness, righteousness, and truth "proving what is acceptable unto the Lord" (See Eph 5:10). It is our responsibility to search the Scriptures and rightly divide them so we can know how to live (see 2 Tim 2:15).

Every Spirit-filled believer has a guide living inside. While audible confirmations are wonderful, as you mature in Christ you will learn to trust the discernment of the Holy Spirit. The Spirit of God gives inner promptings that so often come without words but will guide you in the way you should go. You can have confidence as you seek direction that you are sailing in the current of his will.

I was talking with a young lady recently about a decision she was making whether or not to continue her education. I told her that even if her path went an entirely different direction, it was not a waste of time to try something she had never done before that could train and develop her in new ways. Every life experience is part of the process that will take you where you are supposed to go. Every lesson you learn brings something to you in the now that is part of your future and even eternity. Today, after all, is part of eternity; and eternity includes today. Your ministry includes today.

Before I had written a book or spoken a message other than to the Junior Sunday school class or the church girls club, I accepted a part-time job helping a man with disabilities manage his public speaking ministry. Working for him, I earned a little pocket money. But more than that, I learned things that helped me launch my own speaking ministry, including writing and publishing my first book. God does not waste our experiences, they become part of who we are.

If you have serious questions or doubts about God's direction for your life, speak to your spiritual leadership, your pastor, your closest family members. They most often know you best and have your best interest in mind. They are able to step back and see the entire picture. If you feel strongly about one direction, but all the people you have loved and trusted your whole life are lifting caution flags, I would be hesitant about proceeding. Whatever you believe God has spoken to you privately (or even through the "prophetic ministry" of others) should ring true in the spirits of other mature, Spirit-filled family and ministry.

SIDENOTE
from Daniel Koren

The most important thing is to find your role and fulfill it. Whatever the Lord calls you to, remember this: your calling is not the most important thing that ever happened to you. Jesus is.

If Jesus has called you, he will open the doors for you. You do not have to force them open by human means. At the same time, do all you can to fulfill your ministry. You cannot push your way into a pulpit, but no pastor will forbid you from winning souls.

—Daniel J. Koren[4]
Author and Pastor; Neosho, Missouri

Section 2

The Character and Conduct of a Minister

Anointing and Authenticity

Now it is God who establishes and confirms us
[in joint fellowship] with you in Christ, and who has anointed
us [empowering us with the gifts of the Spirit].
2 Corinthians 1:22, AMP

Anointing connects a person to God for a purpose of God and often brings with it a position and degree of honor. The Hebrew word for anoint means "to smear or rub with oil."[5] Anointing oil was used in the Old Testament in sacred rites that consecrated people to function in specific titled positions. Throughout Scripture the concept of "anointing for a purpose" replays.

In the New Testament anointing is used metaphorically for the Holy Spirit.[6] The two most common Greek words rendered "anoint" are:

1. *Aleipho:* a general word that signifies "an anointing" prepared from oil and aromatics
2. *Chrio:* "to smear or rub with oil," and by implication, "to consecrate for office or religious service."[7] *Chrio* is further described as "confined to 'sacred and symbolical anointings.'"[8]

Beyond the hygienic and personal use of household oil, *Smith's Bible Dictionary* specifies all official, ecclesiastical, messianic, and spiritual anointing oil was either physical oil or represented the anointing of the Holy Spirit.[9] In Scripture, *anointing* and *oil* are at times used synonymously. Chosen people were anointed to fulfill special purposes or calls. Kings, prophets, or recognized ministers of God were anointed. It is important to note that men did not arbitrarily anoint people of their own choosing. God moved on one person, usually a person of office, power, or great gifting, to anoint another. The act of being physically anointed sets apart a person as one authorized to minister. At the same time, there is nothing in a bottle of oil that will release an anointing upon a person God has not ordained and called to ministry.

A true anointing directs attention to the Anointer, not the anointed. The Holy Spirit selects and empowers people to serve as his conduits to fulfill the ministry of Christ, the "Anointed One." Jesus began his ministry with this proclamation, "The Spirit of the Lord is upon me, because he hath anointed me to preach the gospel to the poor; he hath sent me to heal the brokenhearted, to preach deliverance to the captives, and recovering of sight to the blind, to set at liberty them that are bruised, To preach the acceptable year of the Lord" (Luke 4:18–19).

On the day of Pentecost the Lord released his Spirit upon the earth in a dynamic, prolific way (see Acts 1–2). From that moment on he has anointed and called every born-again believer to serve as his witness and minister of reconciliation. He has placed his oil on you and me to give us what we need to share his love and healing in our generation. But there is a separation and call that goes beyond for some—a special anointing upon those the Lord has chosen for ministry.

A call to ministry brings with it a greater need for the anointing of God to flow in and through your life. Anointing oil is created by crushing olives and spices. Christ, the Anointed One, suffered the cross before he could release the anointing of his Spirit. Although it is not the method we would choose for ourselves, to be an effective minister and leader of God's people requires a crushing or brokenness that releases fragrant oil in our lives.

When you receive the true anointing of God for ministry, your heart unites with his purposes. His priorities become yours. You are called to sacrificially serve the people around you. You are anointed to serve.

In Scripture, anointing has been likened to mantles. These were outer garments, loose fitting cloaks or robes made of animal skin, worn by prophets that signified position, power, and the call of God. Those wearing the mantles of God were his anointed servants designated to serve in specific functions and bear responsibilities in his kingdom. A mantle was symbolic of God's hand upon a person. God places his hand with his call. However, we see times in the Word when God withdrew his presence as a consequence of disobedience.

The sacred anointing oil used in the Old Testament era was holy. It was unique. It was made according to an unalterable pattern. It was exclusively used for the Lord's vessels and priests (see Exod 30:23–33). Anointed priests could not leave the tabernacle (see Lev 10:7). They had to function as God called them in their seasons. As Nadab and Abihu discovered the hard way, the authority of the anointing must be handled with care, or judgment is a dangerous probability (see Lev 10:1–2).

You and I need to be aware that unrepented sin could cause God to withdraw his anointing from our lives. And if our conduct should lead him to do so, we would be in dire straits indeed. Faced with two choices, we would either continue to "minister" without his anointing and approval, or walk away and bring reproach to the kingdom of God.

Anointings and appointings are sovereignly determined by the Lord. When a woman is chosen to serve (anointing indicates being chosen), her God-given anointing should be recognizable and undeniable to those around her. The challenge so often, is this: Will she and/or her spiritual leaders trust God with the anointing he placed on her life?

> God anoints for a purpose. If he has anointed and gifted you to preach, it is a sacred call.

Like the oil that flowed from Aaron's beard down to the hem of his garment, anointing always flows down. When you stay in agreement with God and his leadership, and flow with the anointing as he gives it, your ministry will establish itself. When you walk in your calling—whatever that may be—there is an anointing that abides with the call. As you live out the anointing in you, the glory of God will work through you to light your world with the love of Jesus.

Authenticity

Even the most beautiful and valuable diamonds have imperfections. Flaws verify a stone's authenticity. Flaws prove it was not a laboratory creation, but formed from carbon over time by the temperature and pressure of the earth. You may find a stone that sparkles, but deep inside—beyond the superficial—flaws reveal a gem's true origin, identity, and value.

Being real is not about being perfect, and that's a good thing because no one would qualify. As a matter of fact, if a minister presents herself as perfect, she self-proclaims her fakeness with a façade that will hinder the work of God. Jesus certainly did not go to Calvary to establish an unwinnable war between people and perfection. It is his sacrifice alone that reconciles imperfect people with a perfect God. Be careful that you do not set perfection as your goal. If you do, you will destine yourself and others to live in an endless loop of failure—wallowing in a cesspool of "not good enough."

Authentic Ministry

As a minister, your job description does not include impressing people with your high-level spirituality, your consecrations, your education, or your disciplines. People need to know you are a human being so they can feel good about being a human being, too. Knowing the Hope Diamond is huge but imperfect should inspire all of us little solitaires of the world. And recognizing every person has flaws to deal with can help us extend grace to others, as well.

Many years ago I wrote a simple song with a chorus that goes like this:

> *I choose to see the good in you, please see the good in me.*
> *We each have faults and imperfections of our own.*
> *But I choose to see the good in you, please see the good in me.*
> *We're all just people on our way to meet the Lord.*

Yes, we are all just people—people on a journey. We are people growing as we are going, each of us with personal faults and flesh to cope with. When I minister, I want people to feel they are hearing from a person just like them. If I am secure enough in my relationship with God to be real with them, they will feel safe enough to let their guards down and allow the Word and Spirit to penetrate when I speak with them.

I have struggled with worry wondering if the real me could be good enough for God and ministry. There will always be someone who prays more, who fasts more, who gives more—who seems to sparkle more, give off more brilliant light, be of greater value. There have been times I listened with wonder to a revelatory message and thought, "Now *that* is a message." I have watched as people ministered with anointing and God used them to perform miracles and thought to myself, "See, that is what real ministry looks like." But while those nagging questions come, the truth is, I've delivered a good message, too. God has performed miracles through my ministry as well. Not every message or service is the same—and neither is every ministry.

Hopefully the heroes we look up to are the real deal. Whatever they may be, they are not the real you or me. God uses each of us in unique ways, and instead of wishing I was someone else, I have learned and am still learning to embrace the unique call and person God had in mind when he made me. That is authenticity.

We should not attempt to project ourselves to be what someone else is. Certainly, examples of successful ministers impress and inspire us, but they can also intimidate (especially those younger in their ministries) into a state of lethargy or paralysis. I remember one time I was on a conference call with some highly esteemed evangelists. I know I'm part of the group, accepted as one among them, but I often perceived myself as the "notetaker"—someone learning and observing from the "real" evangelists. My self-perception caused me to hold back from speaking with authority whenever I made a contribution to the call. But on this call, I felt a boldness well up in my spirit. When it came time to share, I spoke up and said, "I have a word from the Lord." What I shared confirmed and built on what God was imparting on that call, and it ended up in a spontaneous concert of prayer. God moved. He used me to encourage ministers known world-wide as mighty men of God, and only God knows how that could impact their ministry as they travel the globe. When you are authentic, your words and ministry can make a genuine impact.

> My ministry—your ministry—may not look or operate exactly like those of the great "powerhouses" we esteem others to be, but every person is a person just like you and me. God can use us when we confidently deliver what he gives us in the places he calls us to serve.

The truth is this: No person could ever be good enough for God to use. It is his grace alone that allows us to approach his holiness. But that is his desire—that you and I would draw near, hear his voice, and share his life-giving words with others.

Authentic ministries must be more than well-scripted facades. If we are not authentic and offer only an illusion of lofty spiritual living on a plane of the impractical, what impact will we have in the real lives of real people? Instead of encouraging our brothers and sisters, presenting an "aura of perfectness" can discourage and weigh others down. Jesus condemned the religious leaders of his day who lay crushing burdens on other people's shoulders they themselves could not carry (see Matt 23:4).

The very thing you have struggled with could be the key to unlock a prison door for someone else. For instance, I have a message the Lord has given me on being free from shame. Yes, that includes the shame of the things we have done, but it also includes shame for anything done to us. Every congregation includes people who have been victimized in their past. In their innocence boys and girls, men and women have been forced to do things they wanted no part of and yet they carry guilt and shame. When I share about my personal experience of being freed from the shame of what was done to me when I was young, it gives hope to others who have been victimized. I have shared this message (The Scarlet Letter) many times, and because I include my personal testimony of rejecting the label of victim and the accusations of shame from the enemy, men and women across the globe have experienced tremendous healing and freedom.

That said, it can be scary to be open and vulnerable. It takes courage to be real; but when you are, you will be empowered and effective. I am not advising that you share all your problems publicly and in detail, but what you hide to protect your image doesn't help anyone. Your transparency and authenticity can impart hope to those around you. Showing people your humanity will help you connect with them more deeply when you minister the Word.

Impartation will never flow from imitation. While we look to those who have fruitful, powerful ministries for encouragement and instruction, we must bring our talents and giftedness to the fore without being driven by competition or vying for position. The Lord has gifted each person in specific areas. He has given you the talent he wants you to have for a specific reason.

Several years ago I accepted an invitation to speak at a conference in Colorado. Not long after, I was notified that an incredible, powerful woman of God, Vesta Mangun, was also going to be speaking at the same conference. I had never met this lady, but I was terrified. I knew I could never minister like she does. Why, her voice fills an auditorium. Her tiny frame is a dynamite-filled package, and her words bind the enemy, loose the power of heaven, and bring people to the throne of God.

My first reaction was a mingling of pleasure and excitement. It was an honor, after all, to be speaking as well. As I began to think of myself speaking on the same platform and ministering to the same group of women, my emotions quickly turned to fear—followed not long after by maniacal laughter: "Oh, God," I prayed, "this must be a joke. I can't do this. Everyone will know I am not a powerful woman of God like Vesta Mangun."

Feelings of inadequacy ran amuck at the thought of standing next to this spiritual powerhouse. I spiraled into a knee-knocking coward. Thankfully I had enough sense to take my concerns to Jesus. The Lord was so gracious. He answered my school-girlish prayers by impressing these words in my spirit, "I don't need another Vesta Mangun. I have one of those. I need you to give the message I have given you with your gifts and personality."

Wow. Was that ever liberating! I realized I didn't have to minister in the same way as this precious woman to be in the perfect will of God. The Lord will use each of us in unique ways, and each of us can be in his perfect will.

Be you. Be the real you—not a cookie-cutter version of someone else you admire. Be true to the person God made you to be and the work he called you to do. Bring your talents and abilities wherever he sends you in your own unique way to encourage, equip, and bless his people.

> **SIDENOTE**
> *from Cindy Miller*
>
> It took a long time for me to even consider myself a preacher. "I'm a preacher?" That was just so odd to me. I didn't even think of myself as that. I think that was part of the struggle. Knowing that I had this calling. Knowing I had this desire to bring God's Word and yet trying to find out how I was going to do that as a woman. The more comfortable I became with "who I am" just as a woman, then the more comfortable I could be finding my place in the pulpit.[10]
>
> —Cindy Miller, PhD
> Professor, Urshan Graduate School of Theology; Pastor, Wrightstown, New Jersey

A Legitimate Lady

Being a woman in ministry includes ministering as the woman God made you to be. Regardless of your position or authority, as a woman you will often think and operate differently than a man. That is not a hindrance. Bringing your feminine skills and attributes to the church will bless and strengthen the body because you provide insights and strategies from a different, often complementary perspective.

Spiritual authenticity develops in your life as you live in agreement with the Word, the authority he has placed in your life, and who he has called you to be. It comes as a result of worshiping in spirit and truth with all your heart, soul, mind and strength.

> The Holy Spirit and prayer are the fuel sources for ministry, but without a functioning vehicle, you will go nowhere. The ministry vehicle is you; the real you. It is your real self, living your real life, and it includes your character, personality, consecrations, and disciplines—even your struggles and trials. Your *make* is "Christian," and your *model* is "Authentic-me."

Consecrations

The lifestyle of a minister is marked by intimacy with God. Only those who are consecrated and dedicated to the Lord can truly serve him and minister to others on his behalf. It's about making a personal choice to commit and dedicate your ways to him. When you do, God notices.

The word *commit* means "to roll, roll away, roll down, roll together." We roll ourselves— we roll our ways into God's ways; his manners, habits, character, path, and course of life. When we do, our dedication to him and desire to please him unite and work together for good. The psalmist said, "Commit thy way unto the Lord; trust also in him; and he shall bring it to pass. And he shall bring forth thy righteousness as the light, and thy judgment as the noonday" (Ps 37:5–6).

Committing your way to the Lord's way means possessing yourself—your "vessel"—in holiness. Some read Psalm 37:5 and consider their "way" as a path, destination, or career; but this passage refers to a person's character and lifestyle. The Lord said, "Come out from among them, and be separate," and when we do, the Lord responds, "I will receive you. And will be a Father unto you, and ye shall be my sons and daughters" (2 Cor 6:17–18). Paul followed this quote from the Lord with these words: "Having therefore these promises, dearly beloved, let us cleanse ourselves from all filthiness of the flesh and spirit, perfecting holiness in the fear of God" (2 Cor 7:1).

Holiness can seem like a gelatin dessert at times—hard to nail down when it comes to practical application. But God is holy, and God is good. So holiness must be good. God calls all believers to partake of his holy nature. Holiness is an attribute of God and can never be confined to a checklist, but it does include some dos and don'ts.

In attempting to define holiness in ways that apply to everyday living, some people can veer to extremes. In a stand-off between legalism and liberalism, I choose *lovalism*.

What is *lovalism*? It's a Wagnerism—a word I created that explains my personal philosophy on living life God's way, rejecting the extremes of legalism and liberalism. *Lovalism* means my choices are not based on rules or rights. It means I choose to do what pleases God because he loves me and I love him. God's Word is clear. He calls us to be holy—separate *from* things he deems potentially harmful to our relationship with him. He calls us to be separated (set apart) *unto* him. The Lord is concerned with our inner persons as well as what we do and how we present our outer persons.

With this subject in mind, it is interesting to note that the stones used in building the temple of God were not cut at the building site. No hammers, chisels, or other iron tools rang out near the temple (see 1 Kgs 6:7). The work on the individual stones took place at the quarry, a remote place away from the building location. And so the Lord works on his daughters today. At times you may feel isolated and the "impact" of a spiritual chisel and hammer. Woman of God, you are a lively stone, being made ready. There is shaping and preparation that must be done in secret by the hand of God—an inner holiness that comes through prayer and the washing of the Word. It purifies the heart and prepares the earthen vessel for the work of the Spirit.

There are times the Lord calls individual followers to higher levels of consecration. Though Samson gets all the attention, in Old Testament times both men and women could make Nazirite vows. These personal, solemn commitments were vows of consecration in which men and women yielded themselves completely to God (see Num 6:1–21). Manoah's wife took such a vow during her pregnancy with Samson (see Judg 13:4).

In the New Testament we find a parallel concept for today's believers. "I beseech you therefore, brethren, by the mercies of God, that ye present your bodies a living sacrifice, holy, acceptable unto God, which is your reasonable service. And be not conformed to this world: but be ye transformed by the renewing of your mind, that ye may prove what is that good, and acceptable, and perfect, will of God" (Rom 12:1–2). In the Old Testament and New we see God's plans for his people have always included consecration and separation from immorality practiced in society—to live selfless lives of holiness. This is how we truly "commit thy way unto the Lord" and accept his ways that are higher than ours (see Isa 55:9).

Holy lives are the result of consecrated hearts and minds. Anointed lips are the result of pure hearts—and that requires regular cleansing. A silver platter tarnishes while it sits on a cupboard shelf. It just happens as a result of the oxygen in the environment. In the same way, simply living in the atmosphere of our world brings a sullying to our lives that needs to be regularly cleansed by the Word and Spirit.

The Word of God sets the standard for holiness—even when the values of those around us are quite different. The example of Daniel and the Hebrew children lets us know God's people can remain steadfast and maintain their integrity even as captives in a pagan land.

Remember, however, as you seek holiness that separation from worldliness does not necessitate disconnecting from all the people of the world. If we do, how can we reach them with the good news? Jesus walked among the people of his day without partaking of any corrupt, sinful customs in the society in which he lived. At the same time, he impartially ministered to people regardless of their culture, background, or social standing. Any consecration we make should be done to draw closer to the Lord, not alienate ourselves from unbelievers or fellow Christians who are at different stages in their walks with God.

Brokenness

Oh, the irony of God. He uses the broken to heal the broken. The pathway to the pulpit is lined with sacrifice and suffering. It unfolds differently for each person—but at some point (and continuing points) along the way, a true servant of God must share companionship with the Lord in suffering and weakness. Dr. Leonard Sweet said, "We bless others naturally through our strengths. But we bless others supernaturally through our weaknesses ... and Scripture makes this clear: God's power is made perfect in weakness."[11]

> Pearls are the products of a recovery process that begins only after an oyster has been intruded upon. Many of the "pearls" of your ministry will be formed in your times of recovery, as well.

Each of us comes to the Lord incomplete and wounded by sin. But when we enter his presence and experience his healing touch, his hope, his grace, his love—we become whole. We can then "break off" a bit of ourselves and extend that to others. Picture the disciples serving the broken loaves and fishes, Mary as she broke her alabaster box, Jesus when he allowed himself to be beaten and nailed to the cross. Each breaking was followed with a giving—a release that ministered to the people around them.

Brokenness and healing will always be components of true ministry. Take a glimpse into the New Testament and you will see the apostle John ready to call down fire from heaven (see Luke 9:54–55). He was full of zeal, but his greatest revelation from God came as the result of his imprisonment and isolation on the Isle of Patmos. Peter was ready to slice and dice men on the Lord's behalf, but it was after his fall and restoration that he was truly ready to feed the Lord's "sheep" (see John 18:10; 21:16–17).

The spikenard in Mary's alabaster box was valuable (see Mark 14:3). It was expensive and luxurious, but it was of no real use until Mary broke her box. As you walk closely and carefully with the Lord, you will experience loss and brokenness that you will be tempted to tuck away inside yourself. Like Mary shattered her box, you must be willing to suffer brokenness—to become more Christ-like and to give more of yourself as you minister to others.

I vividly remember the time of my greatest sorrow. I can still see myself crumpled on the rug on my living room floor. I was crushed, and in the crushing, I came to understand how a person of frail health could die from a broken heart. The pain was that great. The loss came after a wonderful achievement in my writing ministry. A book I had written became a best seller in my church fellowship. In six weeks it went to reprints, and then again in just three months. The book broke sales records for the church's distribution center and was a tremendous, unexpected success ... followed by a personal blow that felt like a semi had parked on my chest.

I will never forget that day. I lifted myself off the rug, wiped my eyes, and reached for the phone to dial my publisher.

When she answered, I asked the question, "Can I start the next book?"

I didn't have it in me to take on such a task, but I knew I couldn't let this defeat stop me, and so I determined to do what I could. I could write another book. I could do my part to equip and educate others and perhaps help someone else who was struggling. Instead of wallowing in my pain and feeling like a failure, I determined to move forward and began the second of what became a four-book discipleship series that has been translated for missions work and used around the globe.

At the Last Supper, Jesus broke the bread and said, "Take, eat: this is my body, which is broken for you: this do in remembrance of me" (1 Cor 11:24). Yes, this is in the context of remembering his sacrifice for salvation, but it gives another lesson as well. When believers allow themselves to be broken, they truly commune with the Lord, and in remembrance of his giving, they give themselves for others.

Consider Job. It is not his brokenness that encourages believers as they read his plight, but the hope found in his healing and restoration. It is only when you know for yourself Jesus heals the broken and binds the wounded you can with confidence and compassion deliver that word to others who desperately need healing in their lives (see Ps 147:3).

Christian Character

Walk worthy of the vocation wherewith ye are called.
Ephesians 4:1

Ministers act as God's representatives. They deliver his Word to people in every state and station of life. While no person qualifies as a perfect vessel, a messenger of the Gospel should be a person of excellent character. Your conduct outside the pulpit affects your ministry in the pulpit. As carriers of the sacred Word of God, when it comes to qualifications for ministry, your character supersedes your capability. It goes beyond giftedness, training, or educating your mind. Novalis, a late 18th century French poet, said, "Character is a perfectly educated will."[12] It's a will that knows what to do and is the result of an educated mind that chooses to do what it believes to be right.

Character is not one "thing" or trait. It's a blend of your conscience, morality, courage, faithfulness, and reputation that manifests in your life choices and conduct—in private and in public. Character includes your internal voice and convictions as well as your willingness to sacrifice for your beliefs rather than serve your own self-interest.

People of good character accept responsibility for their actions. They refuse to be emotion-driven, play the victim, or blame others for their mistakes or life situations. Compelled by conscience to do what they believe to be right, people of character build their lives on godly foundations.

A true minister must be a Christian first. Everything else—every role, title, or position—flows from a relationship with the Lord. Your priorities are extremely important. God first, and then family. If you are married, a call to serve the Lord does not excuse you from your responsibilities to your husband and children any more than a man's call excuses him from his responsibilities to his family.

The wisest man who ever lived said, "A good name is rather to be chosen than great riches" (Prov 22:1). If you lose your good name due to poor character, you will more than likely lose your ministry as well. Like a river, character has boundary lines. People who operate in proper boundaries have the ability to function as a channel of God. Those who attempt to operate outside godly parameters will often realize damaging results.

"There is nothing more important in ministry than character. It begins inside of you. You can't lead people past the quality of their character." My husband actually said that. And I agree. E.M. Bounds had even stronger thoughts concerning the effect of a person's character on ministry. He said, "Dead men give out dead sermons, and dead sermons kill. Everything depends on the spiritual character of the preacher."[13]

In the same way your character grows incrementally, conversely, when it is neglected, it slowly disintegrates. Along great coastlines the silent, subtle effects of erosion consume great bluffs one strike at a time. In the same manner, character and integrity crumble when one poor choice follows another. F. B. Meyer, a British pastor of days gone by said, "No man suddenly becomes base."[14] We may not see erosion's subtle effects on our character until after a moral collapse, but what happened in a moment began with a "bending" of boundaries.

An activity may seem harmless, but if your participation necessitates a bending of conscience, it could be the beginning of a slow demise. The gap between virtue and vice grows greater with each indulgence, and what was once built on rock can slide into sinking sand.

Character cannot be compartmentalized. It influences every area of your life. That includes your home and social settings, in finances, in spirituality, and in ministry. Every aspect of your life should be regarded as part of the whole and lived with as much excellence as possible. Do what is right, even when it isn't easy, regardless of personal penalty or sacrifice.

If you are a woman called to ministry, your good name validates you as a person worth listening to and learning from. Your character is like an invisible stamp that authenticates your ministerial credentials and inspires others to excellence. Your character is what people will remember about you after you leave the room—or the planet.

Some components of character to consider:

Integrity

A key component of character and closely related to it is integrity. Integrity includes:
- adherence to moral and ethical principles
- soundness of moral character
- honesty
- the state of being whole, entire, or undiminished
- a sound, unimpaired, or perfect condition.[15]

Integrity means you do not live by a double-standard. Your words and actions harmonize—they fit together. You are consistent. Your convictions are authentic. Your conduct doesn't change with the company you keep, rising and falling according to the group's standards. There is a "wholeness" that transmits trustworthiness in your sphere of influence.

The apostle Paul acknowledged his ongoing struggle between the things he wanted to do and the things he did (see Rom 7:15). Like Paul, your natural instincts and carnal desires will always be part of a lifelong tug-o-war between integrity and dishonesty, but as a minister, you especially must govern your private and public life as consistently as possible. When you do, the Lord, who sees your faithfulness in the small things and in secret, will reward you openly (see Matt 6:18).

John G. Lake, a leader in the Pentecostal movement in the early 20th century, said, "What the Christian world is suffering for more than anything else is a lack of Christianity." The world is suffering from a great deficit of trustworthy leaders, and professing Christians must lead Christian lives.

Some women take great pains to present a perfect image while a lack of integrity gnaws at them from the inside out. Eventually who you are will show up in public. And for those in ministry, a disclosure of a lack of integrity could cause a reproach that not only affects you personally, but turns people away from their only hope of salvation—the Gospel of Jesus Christ. It's disheartening to see ministers fail. Not only are churches damaged, but a minister's fall hinders the church's witness to the world.

Even if you are acting in good conscience, it's important to heed Paul's advice and refrain from activities that might be misinterpreted by others. "Let not then your good be evil spoken of" (Rom 14:1). Use wisdom. There are times to be bold and courageous in the places you go and the ways you reach out, but be discreet in your day-to-day choices of where to go, what to do, and with whom. A little caution can go a long way in maintaining people's confidence in you as a minister.

Honesty

Closely related to integrity is honesty. In fact, integrity depends on honesty. Some may consider small falsehoods acceptable in today's world, but truthfulness is always *en vogue* for a woman of God.

Jokes have been made by some about "speaking evangelistically"—stretching the truth or exaggerating stories. People speak tongue-in-cheek to add color to messages or make points, but be careful not to exaggerate in any way that would discredit your word. Verify testimonies before repeating them. Fact-check before sharing any information. Always be truthful.

Trustworthiness is honesty's close cousin. If you are dishonest, it goes without saying you are not trustworthy. However, it is possible to be honest-intentioned and fail to follow through on your word. People simply must be able to depend on a minister's word. Any inconsistencies between what you say and what you live will hinder your effectiveness.

Compassion

A minister's character should be Christ-like. James said "true religion" was more than seeming religious. It includes visiting orphans and widows in their afflictions *and* keeping free from the blemishes of immorality (see Jas 1:27).

Jesus's compassion moved him to minister to the needs of others. He truly cared enough to listen, pray, and touch people's lives. Your ministry should exemplify compassion, and one of the biggest indicators of sincere compassion is taking the time to "be there" for others.

Perseverance and Patience

Women of character are stable. They hold up under adversity. And when they do, people notice. Enduring trials and making right decisions will make you more like

Christ and inspire hope in others. In fact, how you respond to adversity and stress reveals the "real you."

When Shadrach, Meshach, and Abednego survived the fiery furnace, King Nebuchadnezzar went from full fury *at* them to full of blessings and positive decrees *for* them (see Daniel 3). Character testing happens. It often comes unexpectedly. But when God's people persevere, they may find themselves elevated to new positions of influence and authority.

Reputation

As a Christian minister, your reputation should be considered more important than any rhetorical finesse or wordsmithing abilities. In fact, because you are a minister, you will be held to a higher standard than the average church member.

One of the realities of public ministry is public scrutiny. At times you will feel eyes on you, but even when you are unaware, be mindful that people are watching. They are watching you in person, online, and on social media. Be careful about the pictures you post on social media. A lack of discretion could do irreparable damage to your reputation. The way you conduct yourself in the privacy of your home does not need to be broadcast for public viewing, especially if it presents you or your family in a manner you would never present yourself in public.

With today's technology, any public moment could be broadcast and publicized to the world with the tap of a button. And those observing your life, however it plays before them, will most likely not be able to separate your message from your mess— so keep your reputation clean. D. L. Moody said, "If I take care of my character, my reputation will take care of itself."

Peacemaker

Some people confuse peacemaking and peacekeeping. Jesus never said, "Blessed are the peacekeepers." Peacekeeping is "policing" others or, on the other side of the spectrum, refusing to speak or stuffing emotions to "keep the peace." Peace*makers* will be called the "children of God" (see Matt 5:9), and a peacemaker is someone who is willing to intervene for the cause of peace. "Making" involves personal creative effort. Although Scripture clearly teaches that believers should live as peaceably as possible with others (see Rom 12:18), being a peacemaker doesn't mean you should avoid all confrontations. We must be willing to put feelings aside and face issues that need to be resolved for the the unity and health of the church.

I confess. I love peace. When my children were young and my birthday rolled around each year, they would ask, "Mom, what do you want for your birthday?" I would say, "Just one day of peace, love, and kindness." When I was young, my three sisters formed a neighborhood club. I don't remember all the trouble their club shenanigans got them into, and I will tell you why. It's because I didn't participate. I may have felt left out at times, but I also missed out on a lot of trouble and its repercussions. I love peace. But as an adult I learned that "peace at any price" is too high a price to pay and doesn't result in real peace at all. I prefer to avoid confrontation, but there are times to lay emotion aside and dive into the duty of peacemaking.

Faithful

Ministry requires faithfulness. At times, that means saying yes. Other times faithfulness means saying no. Whatever decision you face, faithfulness will keep you on the right path when an easier one presents itself with just a small compromise. Being faithful means keeping God as the final authority in your life, and that's a way of living that will keep you stable at every stage of development and in every position on your journey.

Character Development

The Bible gives stark illustrations on the lack of character development in the lives of men like Samson, Gideon, and King Saul. These stories give us an important principle. Gaining prominence for accomplishments or being given quick promotions to leadership can happen out of synch with a person's character development. While the "in the beginning" stories of once "good guys" provide fodder for inspiring messages, their collapses into idolatry and iniquity give us strong reminders of what happens when success is accompanied by a lack of integrity.

Character is not imparted, it is developed. That should give every "Woman in Progress" hope. First Lady Eleanor Roosevelt said, "Character building begins in our infancy, and continues until death." Wherever you are, you can grow in character. You can become more and more like Jesus.

King David prayed that God would reveal his blind spots, and certainly everyone has blind spots. David said, "Who can understand his errors? cleanse thou me from secret faults" (Ps 19:12). If you have a glaring issue, or the Lord is ever-so-gently bringing something to your attention, be courageous enough to face it. When you acknowledge, confess, and devote yourself to making godly, biblical choices, the Lord can help you get right what you got wrong. The first step is to invite Jesus to speak to you—to grant him "all access" into every part of your life. Next, ask him to develop your ability to hear his voice. As you make progress discerning his voice in an area you may have previously closed off, you will find his Word is still well able to renew your mind. He will revive your spirit in such a way that your conduct and character begin to again be molded into the image of Christ.

In Hebrews 1:3, the Greek word *charaktēr* is translated as "express image." The writer of this passage testified that Jesus was the express image or character of God. This word used only once in Scripture, means "the instrument used for engraving or carving" or "the mark stamped upon that instrument or wrought out on it."[16] The definition can include "the exact expression (the image) of any person or thing, marked likeness, precise reproduction in every respect."[17]

Embossing is an example of *charaktēr*. It leaves behind the exact image pressed into it. Embossing happens when the pressure of a stamping tool creates the same image on another medium that is on the face of a die. The way the writer of Hebrews used the word *charaktēr* reveals that Jesus Christ was not just the tool God used to save the world, he was an outward manifestation of the character of God.

The stamp of God (the Spirit of Christ) presses upon his people to mold their character. As you allow the Lord to work in you, he will reveal the secret condition of your heart. When he does, pay attention. Work with the Spirit, "Being confident of this very thing, that he which hath begun a good work in you will perform it until the day of Jesus Christ" (see Phil 1:6).

While you are allowing the Lord to develop your character, you may be challenged at times to compromise the foundations of your faith or apostolic identity. Most often these temptations present themselves as "opportunities" for what is perceived as an advancement. It may sound cliché, but in times like these, ask yourself, "What would Jesus do?" What he would do is what we should do to the best of our abilities. We are, after all, his representatives acting on his behalf.

The pace of your character development must keep track with the pace of your ministry development. As ministry responsibilities grow, do your best to maintain your personal devotions. Don't take on more than you can handle and still thrive in your walk with God and in your relationships with your family members. When presented with new opportunities, counsel with your spiritual advisers and leadership. Consider godly feedback on your readiness and the "rightness" of any opportunity as it relates to your ministry call.

> One of the most important things you can do to advance your ministry is focus your efforts on developing Christian character.

The apostle Paul affirmed the importance of anointing over convincing sermons. He said, "And my speech and my preaching was not with enticing words of man's wisdom, but in demonstration of the Spirit and of power: That your faith should not stand in the wisdom of men, but in the power of God" (1 Cor 2:4–5). Every minister wants to deliver a rousing message, but your words will never speak as loudly as the message your life preaches. You are a living epistle read among men (see 2 Cor 3:2).

The anointing you desire for your ministry will come only as a result of consecration and character. A pure life is a conduit for the pure power of God, and this world needs access to the pure power of God. A. W. Tozer said long ago, "The world is waiting to hear an authentic voice, a voice from God—not an echo of what others are doing and saying, but an authentic voice."

The Flesh Factor in Character Development

Throughout the process of building character, you will face battles between your carnal and spiritual natures. The key to living in victory is to feed your spiritual nature. After all, what you feed will grow, and you want your spiritual nature to dominate.

God created Adam and Eve to be governed by their spirits that enjoyed unbroken communion with God. When Adam and Eve disobeyed God, their spirits disconnected from the Lord and they began to be influenced by carnal appetites and understanding. Their emotions, thoughts, and actions were elevated to higher positions than God intended; and they received corrupt, sinful natures that you and I inherited.

Whatever your struggles with the flesh may be, the sin dilemma in your life comes from your inherited carnal nature. And that carnal nature will remain a part of your human experience until you pass on into glory. That is why you shouldn't be surprised when a sinful thought crops up in your mind or carnal longings run through your flesh. We've all done things we knew we should have left undone. We've all said words we shouldn't have spoken. And we knew right when we were doing or saying those things we were in the wrong. Paul affirmed his personal struggle with carnality when he wrote in his letter to the church in Rome that even when he wanted to do good, "sin dwelleth in me" (Rom 7:20).

The tendency to sin is as natural as water flowing downstream. If you want to go upstream, however, you have to resist the current. If all you had was a paddle and your own energy, you could make progress for a time, but you can only paddle as long as you have the strength and willpower to continue. Sometimes we get weary and drop our paddles. We might lose a bit of progress now and again, but there is good news. We can set a sail and catch the wind that will take us where we want to go.

Progressing spiritually should be a priority for every minister. When contemplating the subject, it is worthwhile to consider how avoiding carnality affects spiritual development. Its importance cannot be overstated. A strong commitment to consecrated living can protect you from harming your reputation and ministry. Sideswipes with sin are damaging enough, but a high-speed collision could wreck your life and result in a devastating pileup that injures innocent bystanders.

It is up to you to overcome the sin that so easily ensnares and entangles. It would be wonderful if we could have a "once and done" victory, but instead overcoming our sin nature is a day-to-day, challenge-by-challenge way of life. In most cases, "the devil made me do it" isn't the reason people cave to carnality. And it's wrong to expect someone else to pray a powerful prayer over you that "casts out" flesh like an evil spirit. You must continually bring your carnal nature in alignment with God's Word. You must choose to resist the enticements your flesh and your enemy present and invite the Lord to search your heart. Ask him to reveal any areas you may have been deceived into accepting wicked or hurtful ways or habits (see Jer 17:9; Ps 139:23–24).

Is This a Sin?

When John Wesley was preparing to enter college, he asked his mother to define sin for him. In her letter written in 1725, Susanna Wesley gave a tremendous answer.

"Take this rule: Whatever weakens your reason, whatever impairs the tenderness of your conscience, whatever obscures your sense of God, whatever increases the authority of your body over your mind, whatever takes away from your relish for spiritual things, that to you is sin, no matter how innocent it is in itself."[18]

Sin is never satisfied. The Bible gives an illustration in Proverbs 30:11–14. In this passage Solomon described a generation who cursed their parents and yet considered themselves pure in their own eyes. Their self-appraisal, however, did not line up with God's evaluation of their condition. Despite their claims of purity, the Lord said they were not cleansed from their sin and were in fact greedily devouring others. This was a rough group of sold-out sinners whose actions demonstrate to us not only the insatiability of humanity's carnal nature, but how it errantly proclaims itself righteous.

Eugene Peterson paraphrased the verses immediately following the above scenario this way, "A leech has twin daughters named 'Gimme' and 'Gimme more'" (see Prov 30:15–16, MSG). In context this implies that sin acts like a leech that latches on to its host. When that happens, the leech releases an anesthetic that prevents its detection at the same time it keeps the blood flowing. Sin's bloodletting weakens and impairs. It drains. It can kill. You cannot allow sin to "latch on" in your life.

One of the greatest perplexities of our day is a belief that the Bible (which teaches believers the ways of God) mandates nonjudgmentalism. This "theology" misapplies Scripture. It is based on moral relativity that allows people to justify their actions by their own convictions without holding them to the lens of God's unchanging absolutes.

There is a right and a wrong; and because the Lord is good and upright, he instructs sinners (you and me) in his way. He leads and he teaches the humble what is right; and his paths are loving and true for those who keep his covenant (see Ps 25:8–10).

Journalist Sidney Harris said: "I am tired of hearing about men with the 'courage of their conviction.' Nero and Caligula and Attila and Hitler had the courage of their convictions—but not one had the courage to examine his convictions, or to change them, which is the true test of character."[19]

As a minister, you must deal with the areas of carnality that assault your mind and spirit. Women may struggle in different areas than those men most often battle, but you must say no when your senses demand their way. Sin's siren call compels

God's children to leave the Father's house for pleasure that would lead them to spiritual poverty. If only people could see the end from the beginning surely they would not take the first step from devotion to depravity. (See the prodigal son parable in Luke 15:11–32.)

The way you live will affect your ministry, and in turn the lives of the people around you. The more carnality you tolerate in your life, the more your ministry will decrease in effectiveness. Your level of fleshliness, high or low, will either repel or attract others to the message of salvation. Our world needs true apostolic, consecrated ministers.

The times people feel overcome by sin or Satan are most often the times they choose to please themselves with self-defeating disobedience. Ironic, isn't it? And so often the end-result of choosing to please self is imprisonment to the very devices that previously offered pleasure and escape.

> "The devil has no conscience and the flesh has no sense."
> —Frank Bartleman
> Writer, Evangelist, and Missionary

Personal Matters

God's Word lights the way for his children, and his Spirit speaks to our hearts. At times the Lord gives a personal conviction to one person that is stronger or different than he gives to someone else. When it comes to personal consecrations, your conviction about an activity or behavior may not be identical to those held by members of your own church. There are times the Lord will deal with you about an issue not because it's sin, but because he wants you to set yourself apart. He may call you to deny yourself to prepare you for a deeper walk or a heightened ministry.

On the other hand, there may be times you witness a minister who is not living high level consecrations and yet appears to be successful—even operate in the gifts of the Spirit. Although it's hard to accept and understand, the Lord may allow a person to be used for a season even when he or she isn't living right. But the poor choice another person makes does not excuse you or me from holy living (see 1 Pet 1:16).

Scottish philosopher and social commentator Thomas Carlyle said, "Conviction is worthless unless it is converted into conduct." You have authority over the works of Satan and need not succumb to carnal desires. God's great power is in you to overcome temptation. When you fall short (and everyone does) the Lord will graciously extend to you one of his most wonderful gifts. The gift of repentance.

The key to victory over carnality is choosing to live in agreement with God's Word. When you conduct your life this way, the devil has no point of entry, and your spirit-man will dominate over the pull of the flesh.

True repentance is more than a feeling. It's a combination of sorrow and faith that leads to converted conduct. Repentance is a beautiful gift that brings healing and restoration, and it will always play a great part in the development of Christian character.

Becoming, Change, and Choices

*This will continue … that we will be mature in the Lord,
measuring up to the full and complete standard of Christ.*
Ephesians 4:13, NLT

Every believer is a work in process. You are not who you were, yet you are not who you hope to be someday. Who you are is who you are, and that is a wonderful new creation with a new identity in God. "Therefore if any man be in Christ, he is a new creature: old things are passed away; behold, all things are become new" (2 Cor 5:17).

Being born again doesn't mean you have become a "renovated reprobate." Through spiritual rebirth you experienced a real and instantaneous spiritual birth into the family of God. Scripture speaks of adoption. It is interesting, however, the Greek word *huiothesia* translated "adoption" refers to more than being included in a family: "God does not 'adopt' believers as children; they are begotten as such by his Holy Spirit through faith. 'Adoption' is a term involving the dignity of the relationship of believers as sons; it is not a putting into the family by spiritual birth, but a putting into the position of sons."[20]

Paul's use of the word *huiothesia* referenced a practice well known in the Roman Empire of elevating a non-blood relative to a position of sonship. This was done to provide an heir or successor. New Christians receive the "spirit of adoption," but that "adoption" or "elevation" will happen in the future (see Rom 8:15, 23). When you were born again, your spirit became new, and your soul began the process of being made new. Someday, your physical body will be made new (see 2 Cor 5:1–5). Until that time, you will continue to learn and grow into the woman you were born and reborn to be.

Being a new creation in Christ doesn't make a person instantaneously mature, and that can at times be frustrating. While spiritual development is ongoing, the Lord wants you to see yourself as he sees you. And when he looks at you, he sees the righteousness and image of Jesus. He sees you changing into his likeness from the inside out.

The times you feel less than glorious—more like a worm than a winner—encourage yourself in the Lord. When you were saved, God deposited a new spiritual genetic code in the eternal part of you (see 1 Pet 1:23). Butterflies give us a natural example of this spiritual concept. The DNA of a caterpillar that morphs into a butterfly is the same before and after its transformation. The identity of the insect is stamped internally whether it is in the shape of a caterpillar, a larva, or a butterfly.

When you were baptized in Jesus's name and filled with the Spirit of God, you were stamped and sealed (see Acts 2:38; Eph 1:13). You will discover who he wants you to be as you journey with him and come to a greater revelation of his nature—the nature that springs from the spiritual DNA he deposited in you. As you discover more of him, you will learn more of who he wants you to be.

Being as You Are Becoming

God has glorious plans tailor-made just for you, but your life is not like a board game that begins with the same opening resources as every other player. You and I are not equally equipped and gifted. Yes, by grace we have equal access to the throne of God, but my talents and resources are not the same as your talents and resources. If you believe someone got better stuff than you, the inevitable conclusion is that you got the short end of the talent stick. We forget that some elusive, universal "talent stick" is not the measuring stick God uses to determine our spiritual progress. God judges you by what you are doing with what he gave you. In fact, the Lord most often judges the invisible, hidden person—not the visible. He looks at the "fruit" in the basket, not the "fruit basket." (See the parable of the talents, Matthew 25:14-30.)

Part of becoming is releasing—letting go of false expectations and disappointments. Forgive yourself. Forgive others. Give yourself some grace. Keep your focus on the Word, your today, and your future.

Stretch.
Grow.

Remember, you don't have to be a perfect person to be in the perfect will of God. As you are faithful to what God has revealed to you in his Word, he will reveal his personal will for your life. Walk in his Word, and you will walk in his will! The prophet said, "He will teach us his ways, And we shall walk in his paths" (Isa 2:3). He is showing you the way to live and teaching you to be the best "you" you can be.

In *Developing the Leader Within You*, John Maxwell said, "You only become what you are becoming right now."[21] And as you are becoming, allowing the Lord to work in you, he will work through you, as well. He connects his people in the body of Christ to serve one another in their God-determined places with their varying gifts and strengths (see Rom 12:5–8). And while you are growing, be assured that he loves you as you are every moment along the way of your transformation process.

Change

Change is often preceded by an abundance of questions. The Lord stirs up internal inquiries that motivate his children to investigate and explore something in them or an opportunity before them. Without explanation, the feathers in your nest can be ruffled by the Holy Spirit—an experience frequently accompanied by a sense of urgency or dissatisfaction.

If the Lord has you in a season of change, you already know change brings anxiety. The fear of the unknown can paralyze even when everything in you is crying out to make a move. These are the times you learn how much you trust the Lord. You learn if you truly trust that he is working all things to your good and that you are hearing his voice. If God is dealing with you to accept a change or a call, knowing others have successfully made that transition should give you confidence.

Surely Rosa Parks experienced some anxiety when she kept her seat on the bus that fateful day in Montgomery, Alabama. She said she acted as a private citizen "tired of giving in." No doubt emotions and questions had stirred within her for some time. What is not commonly known about Rosa Parks, however, is that she was a secretary for the Montgomery chapter of the National Association for the Advancement of Colored People and had recently attended activist training. She did more than just make a decision in the moment, she had been considering her situation for some time and made herself ready when the time came to act.

Like Rosa Parks, God may inspire you to make a change as an impetus to affect a transition in a situation or organization—even a society. Rosa Parks did suffer for her stand. She was fired from her job and received death threats for years afterwards. She was also honored during her lifetime and after. She was the third private citizen in United States history to lay in state in the nation's capitol.

Change is not always as drastic as that Rosa Parks faced, but it does require flexibility, courage, and soul searching. Prayer is essential. And in those times of prayer, you may find that before the Lord can build something new, you must tear down—or allow him to tear down the old. When you respond to God's invitation to change, you welcome him to disassemble or strip away anything in your life that didn't originate with him or isn't part of his current plan. Be prepared, and don't allow the comfort of the status quo to hold you back from new opportunities. On the other hand, be sure any change you make isn't being undertaken simply for the thrill of a new adventure.

When God inspires a change that looks different from what you hoped for, try to look at your new path from God's point of view. His ways are higher than ours. In fact, looking at life through our human perspective could be considered devilish. Consider the time Peter rebuked the Lord. Jesus had revealed some things coming in his future, but Peter rejected them. The apostle was looking from his human viewpoint, and Jesus responded with strong words. "He turned, and said unto Peter, Get thee behind me, Satan: thou art an offence unto me: for thou savourest not the things that be of God, but those that be of men" (Matt 16:23). The Lord made the point that seeing things from a merely human point of view is a dangerous trap that can keep the Lord's people from fulfilling his will.

One of the greatest mistakes in ministry is giving in to a fear of change—an angst fueled by new opportunities for failure. You are on a faith walk with God that will bring you to many doors and opportunities. Give each one serious consideration and prayer and seek wise counsel. Then move forward as the Lord leads. Be receptive to new ideas. God is still a Creator. He is still doing new things—amazing things.

Sometimes it's tempting to look at the "charmed" lives others live. It can appear as if God gave some people instantaneous breakthroughs that lifted them from one place to another in an invisible sanctified escalator. That can happen, but intensive prayer and preparation usually precedes what onlookers perceive as overnight success. Most often, these "overnight successes" paid high prices in secret. They were willing to be used. They were willing to change.

Growing people are innovative people, and growing ministries are the result of willingness to adapt your methods without compromising God's message—to be flexible. Because growth equals change.

> Not every move is necessarily an improvement. People make mistakes, but rejecting change will always result in a lack of improvement. To become who God wants you to be requires change.

Choices

The Road Not Taken is perhaps Robert Frost's most famous poem. In it he addressed a choice his path forced on him when he came to a fork in a road. I can picture the poem's setting in an autumn wood, and I wonder what path I would choose.

While some people struggle with change, others would love to exuberantly trip down every path they stumble upon. In today's world that is simply not possible. There are too many choices. Reality forces us to choose, and as Robert Frost said, our choice "will make all the difference."

When we look back in life's rearview mirror, we can see God's hand at work directing our lives. Even when we make wrong choices, the Lord factors those in and makes all things work together for good to them who love him and are called according to his purpose (see Rom 8:28). His goodness is often easier to see in hindsight than when we are staring into "the wild blue yonder."

God is gracious, a God of restoration and hope, but we must remember that while forgiveness is real, our choices sometimes bring real consequences, and some decisions can never be revisited. There are times you won't get a "do-over." Frost expressed it this way, "Knowing how way leads on to way, I doubted if I should ever come back." Way leads on to way. One step follows another. If you make a misstep, course correct and keep moving forward.

Depending on your temperament, decision-making may be harder for you than others. There are times choices come easy. God's will simply unfolds and you step on the path he lights before you. In the times life's choices are not as clear, it is wise to evaluate your emotional and spiritual stability before making them. One wrong, irresponsible choice made in a state of distress or heightened emotion can forever derail your dreams and those of the people dear to you. The shrapnel of a bad choice could wound innocent bystanders for life.

The most important factor in any decision is God's will. The first place to find it is in his Word. If his Word and will are your highest values, they will help you make the decisions that will impact your todays and ultimately set the course of your life.

Not choosing is a choice—and often not a good one. Not choosing will set you on an aimless path. If you avoid making choices, you may find yourself relating far too familiarly with a scene depicted on the cover of a 1961 *Brother Juniper Strikes Again* book. In the illustration, Brother Juniper is standing at a fence painting circles around arrows he shot into the wood. The caption reveals his not-so-sage advice to his fellow priest, "It's easy! First you shoot the arrow, then you just take your paintbrush and...."[22]

Blindly shooting arrows at a targetless wall and then claiming you shot bullseye after bullseye may create an illusion of success for others, but there is no true victory in it. If your target is a divine destination, your God-dreams require that you are careful and intentional about the choices you make. Stephen Covey said, "Proactive people are driven by values—carefully thought about, selected, and internalized values."[23] Be proactive, not reactive (driven by internal feelings or external circumstances).

At times, life presents crazy choices. You may find yourself in a Jael predicament where you have to decide to do something out of character—something bold (see Judg 4). Wherever life takes you, over and over you will face the decision to evaluate what God has placed in your hands and choose to use whatever that may be for his kingdom purposes (see Exod 4:2). Moses had a rod. Jael had a hammer. Samson had a jawbone. David had a sling. A boy had loaves and fishes.

The Lord has placed in your hand what he wants you to use. This seems to be his regular starting point. He has vast experience taking the implements of everyday life and consecrating them. His anointing makes your common things sacred, powerful, and effective when you offer them to him.

If your hands look empty, ask the Lord to reveal to you what he has placed in them. Stretch them out before him, and as you open your hands to Jesus, he can fill them and use them to release miracles and wonders in your world (see Acts 4:30).

Overcoming Obstacles

Thou therefore endure hardness, as a good soldier of Jesus Christ.
2 Timothy 2:3

Henry Ford said, "When everything seems to be going against you, remember that the airplane takes off against the wind, not with it." Sometimes the "wind beneath your wings" is not a person supporting you, but a challenge to be overcome that lifts you to new heights and takes you to new places. We see this replayed throughout the New Testament. The apostle Paul in particular painted a picture of ministry that included rejection, opposition, and pain intermingled with great joy.

If you are called to apostolic ministry, obstacles are part of your job description. Nothing great is achieved without overcoming challenges. When I think of the Wright brothers, I recall the famous picture taken of their first successful flight. Before that picture was snapped, the brothers worked many years and faced many setbacks as they developed new plans, built new machines, reworked them, and tried again. The famous picture taken of the first flight was snapped before the plane began pitching and then struck the ground breaking the front rudder's frame after only 59 seconds in the air. But the Wright brothers succeeded. Their pioneering work and great investment of time and resources opened a door to travel in a new dimension.

Ministry works in the spirit dimension. And as we serve, we will deal with hazards and obstacles as surely as the Wright brothers or Henry Ford met and rose above theirs. In ministry, there is a real adversary who opposes the work of God, but be encouraged. Often when things get hard, it's an indicator you are on the right track. My pastor's wife Claudette Walker has often said, "If you're walking with God and come face-to-face with the devil, you know you're headed in the right direction."

Enemy forces will come against you and throw monkey wrenches in your workshop. When you hit a hindrance, God can give you the lift you need to hurdle the obstacles in your path—or the grace you need to keep walking until you are safely on the other side.

Tests and trials are part of every Christian's journey. Some have said they come into our lives so God can know what is inside us, but God already knows what is in you and in me. He wants us to know who we really are so we can see where we need to reexamine, retool, and repent—to build something that will take us where God wants us to go. Andy Stanley said it this way, "Character is not made in crisis; it is only exhibited."[24]

Peter was bold. In his estimation, he was ready to go to the ends of the earth for Jesus. He did indeed have a special call of God to a place of leadership in the church, but Peter could not fulfill his destiny until he first passed a test—a test he failed. Peter's failure stripped him of his ego and brash self-confidence. He thought he had lost everything, but God gave him a second chance, and at his first opportunity, Peter ran back to Jesus.

We can learn much from Nehemiah about dealing with setbacks. This man had a God-given goal,

> Whatsoever can be shaken will be shaken. If you are shaken and take a fall, imitate Peter and return to Jesus as fast as you can. God can still use you. After all, he doesn't have any perfect people to work with.

the blessings of his leadership, a plan, and a team. The book of Nehemiah is filled with advances and setbacks Nehemiah experienced as he attempted to rebuild the walls of Jerusalem. Particularly in chapter 4, we see Sanballat and other rough characters oppose Nehemiah and his mission.

When you read the story of this great leader you will see that Nehemiah didn't take confrontation as a personal attack, nor did he attempt to retaliate. Fighting critics is most often not the best approach. In the end, Nehemiah triumphed and became a great example of how to handle opposition: Pray. Work. Be diligent. Don't act in haste. Keep your focus on the Lord. Refuse to be distracted.

Igor Sikorsky, the man who built the first working helicopter, was a man who invested in what others thought impossible. He is attributed with saying, "According to the laws of aerodynamics, the bumblebee can't fly, but the bumblebee doesn't know the laws of aerodynamics, so it goes ahead and flies." On his journey to build a working helicopter, Sikorsky invested time in a craft that didn't work. He eventually disassembled it. He recognized that his design and lack of resources wouldn't produce a successful helicopter, but he determined that his failure would not define his future. With the goal of creating a life-saving, vertical lift flying machine, Sikorsky, a man of faith, tried and tried again until he succeeded.

Nehemiah and Sikorsky both faced opposition. People. Resources. Missing information. If you have a project or a God-given purpose, you will more than likely face a "Sanballat" opposer or a lack of supply. You may have needs to fill and mountains to climb. Others may never support you, but walk by faith, not by the short-sightedness of negative people.

> ## SIDENOTE
> ### *from Janet Trout*
>
> I found that to focus on my calling and its fulfillment redirected my emotions toward positive things. By reinforcing my resolve to minister, in spite of the resistance, I moved forward without giving in to a wounded spirit. I practiced no retaliation; I ignored those who rejected me. I focused on positive emotions and did not participate in a "poor me" attitude.[25]
>
> —Janet Trout, PhD
> Board Chair, Urshan Graduate
> School of Theology,
> Author and Pastor

Overcoming the Obstacles of Criticism and Offense

A wise person considers criticism and grows from it. Not every critic is against you, and there may be an element of truth to critical words even if they are delivered harshly or unfairly. Listen to your critics with humility. Ask the Lord to reveal to you any truth in their words, but then also evaluate the source. Sometimes these words come from a true critic, who loves what you're doing as much as you do and simply wants to help you excel. If they came from someone who forever and always looks at life through a jaundiced lens, recognize that person operates from a negative mindset and push forward with God's plan. This approach helps most of the time—unless like King David you are faced with the pointed end of a javelin. Like David, who was anointed and called, there may be occasions in which, for safety's sake, you must step away from a situation until the timing is right.

Offenses come to everyone, but they could be considered occupational hazards for ministers. The Bible, however, promises great peace to those who love God's law and who choose not to be offended (see Ps 119:165). When you refuse to be offended, you keep the door closed on the enemy. One of his favorite tactics is to ensnare people with offenses.

Being offended is a choice, and when you experience an occasion to become offended, you also gain the opportunity to develop godly character. In fact, being a virtuous woman means being a woman of noble character (see Ruth 3:11; Prov 31:10). People of noble character have substance, strength, and integrity displayed on a marquee of unpleasant situations.

As a female minister, opportunities for offense may come innocently. When that happens, we need to be careful not to be oversensitive. I can't count the many times an invitation has come in my mail for the "minister and wife." Language that has been used benignly by good-intentioned people for decades takes time to change. And in most cases changes are made incrementally, one small step at a time.

Use the correct terminology without disparaging those who have not yet updated theirs. I noticed after doing some work for a leader hosting a "ministers and wives" event, the language on his promotional piece was changed to "ministers and spouses." To some this may seem a small matter. To my husband, although he is extremely supportive and not easily offended, it shows respect and courtesy. When we read materials that imply he is my wife or he should go to a ladies' luncheon while I attend a minister's meeting, we laugh. We choose to *not* be offended over words. Paul gave Timothy good advice when he told him to keep reminding the people and charging them before God not to quarrel about words. Wrangling over words is a valueless waste of time and energy and can actually ruin the people listening (see 2 Tim 2:14).

When others present you with an opportunity to be offended with unkind, inconsiderate, or injurious words or actions, choose to forgive. That doesn't mean you should act like nothing happened and continue to trust at the same level. Instead, it means you release people from the consequences you feel are due to you as a result of their actions or words. The heart of God is always for reconciliation and restoration. Jesus certainly exemplified offering mercy and forgiveness to those who offended him. He was verbally insulted and remained silent. He was struck, but never raised a hand in retaliation.

If we love God, we will keep our victory over offenses. Jesus said, "And then shall many be offended, and shall betray one another, and shall hate one another" (Matt 24:10). Who was Jesus talking to? The "many" in this verse refers to those who allowed their love for God to wax cold (see Matt 24:12). Notice how loving God's ways stops offense. And when that happens, the one who could have been offended staves off a lurking side effect often experienced by those who hold on to offenses: a mangled ministry. Rev. Art Wilson expressed it this way, "Holding on to offenses is a 'potential-killer,' and it has wrecked countless lives and ministries."

Overcoming the Obstacle of Temptation

Another obstacle to overcome in Christian ministry (and life in general) is temptation. Everyone deals with temptation, and everyone who is still human gives in to temptation from time to time. Nobody is perfect. You and I will likely lose our tempers again before we stand at heaven's gate. We will choose selfish ways and say and do things that are not Christ-like—things we will wish we could take back or do over. That's why every one of us should be thankful for the grace of God and extend grace to one another. We are all recipients of grace, and all hopelessly lost without it.

But tripping on your journey is not the same as choosing to continue in the way of sin. A minister simply must not live in a habit or lifestyle of sin. Remember, the only power temptation has is the power you give it. It's unrealistic to entertain temptation, invite it in for a visit, and then expect to be unscathed by the encounter. If you sleep with your head in Delilah's lap, don't be surprised if your sacred vow is cut off. As much as possible, stay out of situations that cause you to be tempted.

When I was a new Christian, I began committing Bible verses to memory. The second verse I memorized was a long one:

> "There hath no temptation taken you but such as is common to man: but God is faithful, who will not suffer you to be tempted above that ye are able; but will with the temptation also make a way to escape, that ye may be able to bear it" (2 Cor 10:13).

I've stumbled in my walk with God, like everyone else does, but committing this verse to memory has helped me many times overcome temptation.

When a temptation comes your way, you can know you aren't the first person or the only person to have faced it and won. In fact, God not only made "a" way of escape, he made "the" way of escape. Jesus is the way. When you face temptation, run to Jesus.

When it comes to sexual sin, we would do well to learn a vital lesson from Samson. Samson was unaware the power of God had left him after the string of poor choices he made. And it was all because of his desire for Delilah. The day of his capture by the Philistines Samson "awoke out of his sleep and said, I will go out as at other times before, and shake myself" (see Judg 16:20), but he didn't know the Lord had departed from him. He was captured, blinded, and enslaved in the grinding house. It is possible to fail in the area of sexual sin and still attempt to minister without realizing the Spirit of the Lord has departed.

If you are married, one of the best ways to avoid sexual temptation is to stay madly, passionately in love with your spouse. Nurture your relationship with your husband above all others. Men may walk into my life, and opportunity may come my way to be unfaithful, but my love for my husband turns my "radar signal" down to stealth mode. I just don't respond to signals or give off signals to others that I am in any way interested in anything close to an inappropriate relationship with any man other than my "hunk-o-husband" Mr. Bill Wagner.

Overcoming the Obstacle of Discouragement

Everyone experiences discouragement from time to time, but thankfully there are strategies we can implement to decrease their impact. One is to release the burden of self-imposed, unrealistic expectations. Having realistic expectations of yourself and others can keep the pressure cooker of life from blowing up. People are wired differently. They have varying levels of commitments to relationships, responsibilities, and excellence. There will always be people on the periphery, people in the core, and those floating somewhere in between.

This may seem a trivial matter, but on a personal note, I love to be on time (or a few minutes early), but some other folks I live with (who shall remain nameless) consistently run late. This has been an ongoing point of contention. Arriving at church angry because someone else made me late has never enhanced my ministry. I have learned that if I really need to be early, I have to communicate that information with a little cushion time or let others know I will have to drive separately if they aren't ready by a certain time. This defuses the situation in advance and takes the pressure off me. Over the years I have had to alter my expectation that others are as motivated as I am to be at church early.

A second strategy to overcoming discouragement is to refrain from all-or-nothing thinking. Too many times people set themselves up for downward spirals by evaluating their lives and situations this way. Then when something happens that doesn't perfectly fit their ideals, negative thinking overshadows and shrinks the positives in life until they are hardly noticeable. I have struggled with this. Because I want to do things with as much excellence as possible, I get disappointed in myself when I make mistakes. But mistakes happen, and calling myself "stupid" doesn't feed anything positive, and it's not true, to boot. Don't allow feelings of failure to rule or lead you to jump to dark conclusions about yourself. And by all means, don't label yourself as a failure.

When thoughts come flying at you, whether from the enemy or your own mental replay of discouragements, hold them to the light of truth. Refuse to accept every negative thought that comes your way. Put them on the witness stand and cross-examine them with the Word of God. *What does God say about me? About setbacks? About overcoming?* Rehearse the Word of God and let it build your faith. Let it triumph in you. Write Bible verses on note cards and post them around your house. Invest in Scripture art for your home or work environment. Set your screensavers and computer background images to things that encourage you.

In a lecture entitled *The Minister's Fainting Fits,* influential 19th century preacher Charles Spurgeon said, "Before any great achievement, some measure of the same depression is usual."[26] By "the same" he was referring to those he had mentioned previously:

- Elijah who fled from Jezebel after the fire had fallen in great victory (see 1 Kgs 19:1–4)
- Jacob who wrestled all night, but then limped in the morning (see Gen 32:22–32)
- Paul who was caught up in the third heaven, but bore a thorn in his flesh (see 2 Cor 12:2–9).

Spurgeon confessed his familiarity with depression calling it a "prophet in rough clothing"—a black cloud that came over him whenever the Lord was about to prepare a larger blessing for his ministry.

Sometimes success brings with it an open door for discouragement. It could be as simple as Monday blues after an anointed breakthrough Sunday, or the backlash of the enemy after an incredible project or campaign. Be aware, and realize that once a pinnacle has been achieved, a subsequent lack of focus can also lead to discouragement.

Discouragement can result from the sometimes unpleasant aspects people experience working in ministry. The loneliness of ministry, a lack of rest, an increase in challenges, and the sedentary lifestyles of study and message preparation can affect your mind and spirit and impair your coping abilities. Recognize the source when you feel discouraged. At times there are seasons that require more of us than others. For instance, writing a book! I have exhausted myself working into the night, but knowing it is only for a season and for a great reason, I can push through any discouragement. It will be worth it all some beautiful, happy day!

Overcoming Impatience

Waiting can sometimes be as challenging as obstacles in your path. If today you feel you are waiting, I want to encourage you. God never wastes waiting time. In it, he works in you or for you—or both. In the times you feel you aren't making progress, wait with expectancy. Trust in the Lord. He *is* directing your path. If you are about your Father's business, he is using you right now.

I remember a moment the Lord gave me such an encouraging word in this area. I was at an annual minister's conference in Louisiana. The power and presence of God were thick, and I turned and knelt at my seat in prayer at the end of the message. I sobbed into my hands crying and praying, "Use me, Lord. Use me."

I never heard a word, but what I experienced touched me deeply. I had been working on a message called "Here I Am." It was an exploration of the calls of God to people in the Bible and their responses. Abraham said, "Here I am." Isaiah said, "Here I am." Jonah did *not* say, "Here I am." He said, "Here I go!" With that message fresh in my spirit, as I was sincerely praying a deep, fervent prayer to the Lord, he tenderly ministered to me. It was as if he placed a finger under my chin and gently lifted my gaze to his. Then he said, "Here . . . I am."

Lo, and behold, I realized he *was* using me. He knew my heart was to please him at the same time he knew there was more for me to do. But in that moment, he wanted me to be at peace and know he heard my prayer. He saw my heart, and he had been using me as I dedicated myself to serving him and others.

Yes, look forward. Yes, seek and work for things to come. While you wait, instead of spending your time longing for some different field of ministry or advancement, look around and see the lives that need his touch, his comfort, right where you are. You live among people who need to experience the love of God you can share with them.

One of the most beloved verses on waiting is found in Isaiah. "But they that wait upon the Lord shall renew their strength; they shall mount up with wings as eagles; they shall run, and not be weary; and they shall walk, and not faint" (Isa 40:31). The waiting in this passage doesn't mean sitting with your hands in your lap. It means to "look for, hope, expect." It speaks of being strong and robust—being tied together like a rope. It means to fix your hope on God, and God is anything but still and stagnant. If you are tied to him in the "waiting," you will be in motion as surely as the wind blows and the rivers flow. Working while you are waiting reveals your faith that God will bring his promises to pass.

SIDENOTE
from Mary Dupre

For my birthday, my great-granddaughter picked out a gift for me that had a saying on it. It read, "Not to spoil the ending, but everything is going to be okay." Learning to wait on Jesus can be difficult if we walk in our fleshly feelings, but when we realize the battle is not ours but the Lord's, everything is going to be okay. Jesus Christ has our back and is fighting for us, going ahead of us, and clearing the way.

—Mary Dupre
Pastor; Marlette, Michigan

My sister married into a family that owns a ham curing business. For four generations family members have worked that business. To prepare the hams, the meat is put through a process that pulls the moisture out of the flesh. This is so it will not spoil. To cure ham, the atmosphere must be perfect. The ham is washed and then sealed with a curing mixture of salt and seasonings. That treatment, however, is not enough. Slits are cut through the flesh all the way down to the bone and salt is packed in the incisions. After all that processing, it's time—time to sit on a shelf. For weeks. If after the standard waiting time the ham is firm, it can be used; but if not, it has to stay in the curing mix until the moisture is gone.

My point in sharing this illustration is this, in our lives there is a curing process. It includes some time just sitting in "solution." As the salt and seasonings do their curative work, they pull things out that could cause rot and decay. As much as we would like to think we are ready for whatever the Lord has in store for our lives, we often must first experience his curing process. And it happens while we wait.

Yes, it's important to wait on God, and it's easy to get restless and frustrated in God's "waiting room." Consider, however, the possibility that sometimes we keep ourselves on the bench. The Lord may be waiting for you to step out in faith on his promises. As you do, he will bring those promises to pass (see Ps 37:5). When you delight yourself in him and commit your journey to him, he who began the good work in you will be faithful to complete it according to his pleasure and in his timing (see Phil 1:6). So you can be fruitful in every good work.

Overcoming Sorrows and Suffering

No sound person would sign up for suffering, yet suffering is a tool God uses to develop people. To teach them compassion. To balance them after achieving great spiritual victory. To keep them humble.

You can only give to others what you have received, and it's in sorrow's school God's children learn much that helps them minister to others. Sorrow is one of our greatest instructors, teaching us lessons we would never learn on the mountaintops. Poet Robert Browning Hamilton eloquently expressed this concept in one of his most popular works:

> *I walked a mile with Pleasure;*
> *She chatted all the way;*
> *But left me none the wiser*
> *For all she had to say.*
> *I walked a mile with Sorrow;*
> *And ne'er a word said she;*
> *But, oh! The things I learned from her,*
> *When Sorrow walked with me.*

The Lord called Job "a perfect and an upright man" (Job 1:8). Job reverenced God and turned aside from evil, yet who suffered more loss than he? Yes, Job had some lessons to learn. He did. He endured the tremendous loss of family, fortune, and fitness, all the while he was right smack dab in the middle of the will of God. If this man God held in such high regard suffered, we shouldn't be surprised when we suffer as well (see Phil 1:29).

The apostle Peter said some believers would suffer for doing well "according to the will of God" (see 1 Pet 3:17, 4:19). When you suffer, you can trust Jesus to keep your soul, and he can use the suffering to bring glory, redemption, and healing to others. Author C.S. Lewis said, "Pain is God's megaphone." The Lord uses the school of suffering to prepare his people to minister to others.

In the times you walk through the valleys, remember the Good Shepherd is with you (see Psalm 23). He is tracking with you and ever aware of your situation. He communes with you in a unique way in suffering (see Phil 3:10). He is near the brokenhearted (see Ps 34:18). And when we share in his sufferings, we learn humility. We acquire new depths in prayer and compassion. The ground of our souls is turned over and furrowed, making our hearts more willing and inclined to grow (see Jas 1:2–4). And when we share in his suffering, we share in his glory (see Rom 8:17).

When you are in the valley of suffering, you don't have to be superwoman. Just take one step at a time as he lights the path before you. Cast your cares on him and know that he cares for you (see 1 Pet 5:7). And remember these words of Paul, "Our light affliction, which is but for a moment, worketh for us a far more exceeding and eternal weight of glory" (2 Cor 4:17).

Sometimes we suffer at our own hands. You and I have made choices in the past we have regretted, and some of those follow us into our todays. Israel suffered a great loss in the Valley of Achor, but two centuries afterward the Lord called that same place a "door of hope" (see Hos 2:15). The place of suffering became the place they sang and danced as they had in the days of their youth. The very place you suffered as the consequence of your own poor choices may become the place of your greatest joy. How many addicts, for example, are now running recovery programs? If you made a mistake, God can redeem it and use it to reach and encourage others.

Your suffering is not just for you. There are people watching, and as you go through a trial, it not only produces hope in you. The people around you will catch some of the overflow as they watch you overcome and walk in peace in the middle of your storm (see Rom 5:3–5).

In Michael W. Smith's book, *It's Time to be Bold,* he recounted the story of a Roman senator who went to the coliseum to see for himself how Christians faced death. He watched as a ferocious lion stalked a girl who stood bravely in silence awaiting her fate. Later the senator wrote of the account in his journal. Just before the girl died a violent death she "did something that changed his life forever. She smiled at him. The Roman was haunted by that smile for days afterward, until he could no longer run from 'the God who teaches men how to die.'"[27] Reportedly, the senator became a believer and eventually faced the lions for his own faith in Christ. This story inspired Smith, and I agree with his conclusion, "There's no better witness to the watching world than believers who stand firm under suffering."[28]

The wounds of suffering can leave their marks on our lives. The topic of scabs and scars is less than appealing, but when dealing with suffering's wounds, both are part of the discussion and the healing process. In the Old Testament, priests were not allowed to minister if they had unhealed wounds. One of the requirements for serving as priest was that a Levite could have no scabs on their bodies (see Lev 21:20). Scabs are crusts—hard layers formed over wounds that aren't fully healed. Scars, on the other hand, are the marks of a previous injury. In his body, Jesus still carries the scars of his healed wounds. He was a spotless lamb who was wounded. Healed now, the scars he bears authenticate his identity as the resurrected Savior. You may have scars from past suffering, but they are not hindrances. They can be marks of authenticity. You once were wounded, but now you are healed. Your scars can offer hope to other wounded people.

The Lord uses scarred people. However, if you are in a state of "fresh woundedness" or are continuing to "pick at the scab" of an old wound, healing must come to you first before you can extend it to others. When people continue to pick at spiritual scabs, they will never serve as effectively as they otherwise could.

Another verse I memorized as a new believer is still a favorite, "For we know that all things work together for good to them that love God, to them who are the called according to his purpose" (Rom 8:28). When I learned that verse I believed it to be true as much as I could, but I came to understand the principle at a much deeper level when I walked through the valley of losing my first husband to cancer. It wasn't what anyone would consider a good situation, but God is faithful. He can bring beauty from ashes, and he has promised to make everything beautiful in his time. Jesus can take "not goods" and make something useful, even beautiful.

That season was one I never want to live through again, but one of the lessons I learned in it is that trials come to everyone. They are part of life. Our trial didn't mean my husband was in sin, I was in sin, or that we were missing the will of God. We did learn much through that time that drew us closer to him, but we were just as saved going into the trial as we were on the other side.

Through that time of suffering, I learned that life doesn't always play out the way we expect, plan, or hope; but it can still be good, because God is good and he has good plans for his people (see Jer 29:11). I learned that I can trust Jesus, just like he said. He was with me at every turn. I learned to ask the right questions, not, "Why?" but, "What do you want me to learn from this?" "How should I respond to this?" And asking the right questions can keep you on the right path even in hard times.

I have certainly faced opposition to and in my ministry. And I have purposely chosen not to focus on those situations in this book. I choose to believe those who have opposed my ministry (or all women in ministry) are truly convinced they have the right biblical position on the matter. I have learned over the years that I can choose to not take personally a person's lack of support or even the rare adversarial confrontation. I hope you are able to do the same.

Most people will never know about the conflicts you face in your private world. Hold your head up and do the will of God. Don't feed the fury and fervor of combatants to your call with social media posts, pity parties with others, and (heaven forbid) from the pulpit. It's normal to feel a certain sadness with rejection, but rise above it, and preach like a lady.

Tips for Overcoming Obstacles

- When you are tempted to be offended, ask yourself why you are upset. Sometimes you must release and forgive, but other times you may need to address a situation.
- Learn to release hurts and disappointments, especially those that come from "friendly fire" or jealous assaults. Let go, and go on—move forward as a stronger, better, more compassionate person.

- Keep your eyes on Jesus and the task he has given you. He will keep you walking down the middle of the road so you can safely avoid falling into a ditch of self-pity on one side or a pitfall of pride on the other.
- Be persistent—as proactive as possible—and realize some things aren't problems that can be fixed. They are realities to deal with.
- In those times you feel trapped, don't expend all your energy swinging wildly. Slow down and find the right tools and strategies to take care of the situation at hand and continue on your journey.
- When the enemy is fighting you, don't be discouraged. Be encouraged. He must see something in you he is determined to stop.
- Face your problems one at a time. Author Richard S. Sloma said, "Never try to solve all of the problems all at once—make them line up one by one."[29]
- Walk in faith, and as much as possible remain calm under pressures.
- Stay optimistic. When the three Hebrew men survived their fiery furnace, they were promoted

SIDENOTE
from Janet Trout

Notes from a session at General Conference 2017: *Life in Balance* There is a time to stop striving and struggling. Don't retreat to somewhere you have already been. Know the season of your life. This is a sign of maturity. Review your seasons and rebalance if necessary.

Order and structure offset chaos and confusion. Are you organized for what you pray for—or what life dropped on your doorstep? Reorganize for your current season. You have to think about the weights you carry. Be balanced. Plan, think, strategize, look ahead. Everything is not your thing to do. If something isn't a fit with the trajectory of where you are going, let it go. Discipline yourself. Say no. If it has nothing to do with who you are and where you're going, let it go.

Find your avocation and make it your vocation. Don't spend your energy in the wrong places. Live your life by a compass, not a calendar or a clock. Set your face to Jerusalem. Set your

GPS, or waste time and energy driving in circles. You set your direction.

Place all your energy on where you are going. Some things have to be cut off, and some added on. You can't change people by chasing them—pouring into buckets with holes. Don't waste your time studying other people's motives. "As for me and my house...."

You need fresh priorities for current circumstances. You can't afford to do nothing. You are stronger when you bring balance into your life. Choose what you allow in your life. Arise and go. The problem isn't what you lack, but how you handle what you have. Show God you aren't a high-risk investment. Acknowledge changes as you go through the different seasons. Trust God. Have an encounter with God. Now is the time. Jesus knew his decision would take him to the cross. The mission is greater than you. Invite your destiny to take charge of your destination. Sir Edmund Hillary said, "It's not the mountain that we conquer, but ourselves."

—Janet Trout, PhD
    Board Chair, Urshan Graduate School
    of Theology; Author and Pastor

(see Daniel 3), and your "fiery furnace" can elevate you.

- Sometimes "problems" stem from our own lack of expertise or ability. Don't make excuses. Recognize your flaws and deficiencies. Find mentors. Develop where you can. Pray. Read. Consult. But also use wisdom. Delegate. Build an obstacle-hurdling team of supporters and/or co-workers.

Finally, overcoming obstacles includes taking risks. Spiritual ministry requires moving into the realms of the Spirit. We risk when we witness, when we speak challenging words, when we move in the altar and pray with people. We risk when we operate in the gifts of the Spirit. But risk we must. If God calls you to step out and move in a new area, take a God-risk and follow that prompting of the Spirit. You may not get it perfect, but that doesn't mean a perfect God isn't working with you and training you.

There are times I can scarcely bear to listen to my own messages and hear my tongue trips or misspeaking, but that doesn't mean the anointing of God wasn't in that service ministering to the people. And as I watch, I learn where I can improve.

We grow by doing, even spiritually, by trial and error. Be courageous. God is bigger than your mistakes.

Serving in ministry necessitates taking risks and leading others to take risks alongside you. You may fail even after being prayerful and faithful. Failure can come not only as the result of taking a risk, but from being too cautious. And being too cautious can lead to stagnation. The Lord has called his people to be bold and courageous pioneers willing to take chances to advance the work of God.

Courageously Confident

Cast not away therefore your confidence,
which hath great recompence of reward.
Hebrews 10:35

ntimidation. Its prefix *in-* means to enclose. The root word *timid* means lacking in self-assurance or courage; fearful or shy. The suffix *-ation* indicates an action, state, or condition. Put it all together and you get:

InTIMIDation:

- being enclosed in a condition of a lack of self-assurance or courage
- being confined in a state of fear or shyness
- being restrained by forces that dominate—forces from without and forces from within.

At some time in your life you will face intimidation. Elijah, one of God's boldest prophets, ran for his life when Jezebel threatened him after a great victory (see 1 Kgs 19:2–3). Sanballat and Tobiah mocked and intimidated Nehemiah when the Lord sent him to rebuild the walls of Jerusalem (see Neh 4:3). The Lord called Gideon a mighty man of valor, but Gideon's focus on his low situation filled his mind with doubts and questions (see Judg 6:12–16). The apostle Paul acknowledged his personal struggle with intimidation when he said, "And I was with you in weakness, and in fear, and in much trembling" (1 Cor 2:3).

Unreckoned intimidation can keep you from functioning fully in your call. The devil has not changed his *modus operandi*. He still uses his time-tested tactics—shifting your focus away from what God has spoken and on to your thoughts, feelings, or desires. Intimidation may scream or whisper, but its message is the same. "You aren't good enough. Who do you think you are? You can't do that. What will people think of you? You are going to fall flat on your face. You better sit down—back off."

I have certainly had my share of face-offs with intimidation. Some of the most challenging have occurred close to home. Would I stand, or would I shrink back? Many times I have been asked to pray at public events in which I felt pressure to omit the name of Jesus. Sadly the pressure most often came from professing Christians. I understand choosing to abstain from being purposefully offensive, but praying is a matter of faith, and my faith is in Jesus. If someone is asked to pray, they should be given the freedom to pray according to their faith. If not, why ask them to pray at all?

Praying in Jesus's name is not an option. It's a biblical mandate. And so while I have felt some awkward stares, I have also received positive feedback as well.

On a wider scale, I once tried to resign from a volunteer position I held with a national organization that had stepped back from taking a stand for praying in Jesus's name at their events. These people loved God, and their position was not adopted because they felt it was unimportant, but because they didn't want to be offensive. I love peace. I didn't want to make an issue of it, but the Spirit would not allow me to remain quiet.

I prayerfully wrote my letter of resignation and outlined my position: that the foundation for prayer was repentance, and repentance must be proclaimed in the name of Jesus. That Jesus's name is more than a tag-line on the end of our prayers. It gives the prayer the authority of the name of God. It unifies the prayer with the heart of the Father through the only mediator between God and man. Jesus is the reason we can approach the throne of grace, and believers are commanded to do all things in his name. Without his name, we carry rifles with no ammunition into a very real battle.

I let them know I was not offended, and neither was I giving an emotional response, but in reality, at a Christian event, there should be no restriction. And any decision to avoid using the name of Jesus was not going to change the hearts of people who opposed us. There will always be those who are offended at the name of Jesus, but it is my belief a Christian organization should boldly proclaim the name of our savior.

Intimidation tackled me as I wrestled with my position that challenged godly people I respected. Just tapping the send button on the email required some determination, but the courage of my convictions won. Shortly after, I received a reply from a leader asking me to participate in a conference call on the subject. If I had been intimidated before, I was certainly intimidated then. Who was I to stand in defense of the name of Jesus before all the top-level leadership of this national organization? You can only imagine I had people praying for me. I was shaking when I picked up the phone. But after making my case and hearing the words, "Lori, you're right," I was overcome with an amazing sense of God's pleasure and peace. They changed their position. They amended their prayer and website. And the name of Jesus was declared at thousands of events all over the nation, including the White House.

A spirit of antichrist is among us, and God's people must stand against it. So often it's acceptable to pray in our society … just as long as it's not done in Jesus's name. But that is caving to the intimidating antichrist spirit influencing our world. This is just one example of facing intimidation that can come from many sources. I didn't want to make that stand. It created conflict in my heart. It could have ruined relationships and my reputation, but my reason for holding back (pride) was not weighty enough to stop me from standing for the Word and name of God. And when I stood for Jesus, he stood with me.

Pride is intimidation's core fuel source. When people are too afraid to take a God-inspired risk because they might fail, they are protecting themselves. That is pride. Pride focuses on self. If pride is having a high opinion of yourself, how can it control someone with low self-esteem? This may seem oxymoronic for the truly shy or those who suffer with feelings of inadequacy. But the stark reality is this: If you hold your low opinion of yourself in a controlling position, higher than God's Word, you have a pride problem. You could dress it up and call it humility, but it's a "high thing" that has exalted itself against the knowledge of God. It must be brought into captivity and obedience to Christ (see 2 Cor 10:5).

If you have a "high thing" in your life, you will bow to it. You will obey it. You may despise it, but your actions will show you esteem it more highly than the Word. That is a form of duplicity—double-mindedness that will make you unstable and ineffective no matter how sincere your devotion to the Lord (see James 1:8.).

The Word says, "Submit yourselves therefore to God. Resist the devil, and he will flee from you. Draw nigh to God, and he will draw nigh to you. Cleanse your hands, ye sinners; and purify your hearts, ye double minded" (Jas 4:8–9). When you are intimidated or afraid of failure, choose to agree with the Lord and tune out the voice of the enemy. The Lord will be near—close enough to purify your heart and remove any double-mindedness.

As your heart is purified, speak in agreement with the Lord. When you audibly confess his Word, you unite your words with God's. His Word is written in Scripture, but it also comes as *rhemas*, those things spoken by the living voice of God into a person's spirit by an unction of God or through another believer.

When the Lord puts a *rhema* "go" in a woman's heart, she must resist letting an instinctual "no" have its way. Refuse to let your feelings take the reins. More than once I have pointed a finger at the woman in the mirror and said, "Emotions, you are not the boss of me." We simply must refuse to let feelings and fears stand between us and the person God has called us to be.

That doesn't always come easy. It means getting your "self" out of the way. I remember distinctly a time the Lord dealt with me on this subject. It was after a church service. Everyone in the congregation had gathered around the altar and we were singing a song: "I give myself away, I give myself away so you can use me." Standing at the altar, eyes closed, singing that song in all sincerity, I received a strong impression in my spirit that literally changed my way of thinking—*How much "self" are you talking about?*

With this probing question, the Lord hijacked my worship. I knew what he was asking. "Self" means more than my time, talents, and treasure. It is who I am—my identity. It includes my visions, my dreams, and my plans for my life. Was I willing to give all that to him? Would I trade my dreams and visions for my life for his dreams and visions for my life? That is what giving "self" away means. And it includes getting your "self" out of the way—including any lack of confidence or overestimations.

This will be an ongoing work, but when we trade our dreams for his, we can have confidence that we are in his perfect will and that he will perform his will in us. Our confidence is not in our abilities, but his. Now that is liberating. That means you can step beyond your "self" and do great things!

> "Our girls need to see the power of God working in anointed women who are doing what the Lord has called them to do."
> —Daniel Koren
> Author and Pastor;
> Neosho, Missouri

In dealing with "self," we must not compare ourselves to others (see 2 Cor 10:12). Doing so can take us from one swing of the pendulum to the other. One moment we feel quite accomplished and proud, the next, like a grasshopper (see Num 13:33).

Whether intimidation whispers or whoops, choose to cast down the high thing and walk *not* in the fear of man that brings a snare (see Prov 29:25). Don't walk in fear, walk in the fear of God. "God has not given us a spirit of fear, but of power, of love, and of a sound mind" (2 Tim 1:7).

Word-Immersion Therapy

If you are dealing with intimidation, immerse yourself in the Word. Rehearse who you are in Christ and revel in the joy of being not only free from sin, but free from shame. The enemy will try to intimidate people with shame from past failures, but there is a crimson stream of blood that washed away every guilty stain when you were baptized in the name of Jesus.

When God looks at you, he sees something beautiful—a beloved daughter cleansed from all unrighteousness (see 1 John 1:9). Rahab was a harlot, but she was cleansed by her faith in God and became part of the lineage of Jesus Christ. Mary Magadalene, a woman possessed with devils, was delivered and became a faithful disciple. Peter failed the Lord. He denied him, yet the Lord filled him with boldness to speak before a great assembly on the day of Pentecost and used him to help found the New Testament church. Like these and so many others, you can dust yourself off from failure and move forward with boldness.

Being confident does not disregard the reality of fear—especially the fear of the unknown. It is operating at a level higher than your fears. It means you trust the God of the universe who created and commissioned you with your todays and your tomorrows. After all, "it is better to trust in the Lord than to put confidence in man," even when the "man" is you (see Ps 118:8). Addie Stephens, a pioneer woman preacher who established three churches and helped write policy for the original United Pentecostal Church International's Ladies Auxiliary in 1953, said, "If we will obey the calling, Jesus is able to take us through."[30]

In prayer one day an image came to me that has helped me overcome cowering to intimidation. I could dimly see God's Word and promises through a veil, but they were not clear. I became aware of a "feathery veil" that had been dropped by the enemy like a screen in front of me. With the veil in place, I could not reach the promises of God I saw beyond it. But I didn't have to stay behind that veil. I could simply sweep it aside. It had no power to keep me from what God had placed within my reach. Before I was able to do that, I first had to recognize the veil for what it was—intimidation. Intimidation is a shroud suspended by the Father of Lies with the diabolical intent to make you think your calling and destiny are out of reach. But that is not true.

The adversary cannot separate God's people from his promises. What real power does he have over blood-bought believers? Jesus, the lion of Judah, thoroughly, resoundingly defeated Satan. Scripture calls the devil a roaring lion. Roaring was the function of the older, toothless lions, and Satan's forces act the same way, making noise to scare their prey to death or drive them into the jaws of sin.

While it is true an old lion may not have many teeth, staying out of paw's reach is still a wise decision. Even a toothless lion can inflict serious damage with a sweep of a clawed paw. We do need to be sober and vigilant, but as long as we are not running with the devil's "pride" and continue to refuse giving him a foothold in our lives, he is no real threat (see 1 Pet 5:8–9; Eph 4:27). He simply holds that feathery veil of intimidation in front of our eyes that keeps us from understanding the real freedom we have in the Lord. We are masked by misunderstanding; but if we will turn to the Lord, he can strip away the veil (see 2 Cor 3:14–16). Then we can see who we are—beautiful women in progress, being transformed into the image of Christ.

> "The most difficult thing is the decision to act. The rest is merely tenacity. The fears are paper tigers."[31]
> —Amelia Earhart
> Aviation Pioneer and Author

Your strength to serve in whatever capacity the Lord chooses should come from knowing you are walking in God's will. Whoever and whatever you are, you are that because God poured out his incredible grace and kindness upon you (see 1 Cor 15:10). Whatever God made you to be, accept that. Come to terms with it. Refuse to wish to be someone else doing something else. God has uniquely gifted and called you.

Tips for Overcoming Intimidation

- As you serve, remember that boldness is not the same as arrogance. Be confident but not haughty.

- As you step out, be prepared to face opposition. When you do, humble yourself and cast your care on the Lord who will exalt you in due time (see 1 Pet 5:6–7).
- Trust the God who called you to fill your mouth with the right words to say.
- Be willing to walk in the dark in the light of the Lord to go places you have never been. Take others with you. Reach where others have not. Blaze a new trail.
- Acknowledge your fear but "do it anyway." *Carpe diem!* Seize the day!
- Recognize there are risks and be willing to take them (see Isa 41:10). A mistake along the way could be your greatest teacher and lead to your greatest success.
- Be careful, not careless, but don't allow "caution" to keep you from action.
- Use wisdom and discernment. Not every opportunity is God's plan for you. Be willing to say no when an offer or idea doesn't fit with what God is asking you to do.
- Don't "own" someone else's problem. Recognize that intimidation from the mouths of others will often accuse you of the very weakness the accuser is dealing with (see 1 Sam 17:28).
- Volume and courage are not the same. Being confident can at times mean being vocal (like Peter) and at other times being silent (like Ahab's chief of staff, Obadiah). Know the difference.
- Courage can be more than leading a charge, it can also include righting wrongs and reconciling relationships.
- Refuse to operate on old programming written in a language of past failures like the Israelites who circled in the wilderness forty years. All things are new. The Lord redeemed even your failures and can use them for his kingdom purposes.
- Don't be lulled into lethargy by the necessities of day-to-day life. Awaken to the unrealized possibilities God has for you and rise above any perceived limitations or prejudices to advance the kingdom of God.

Someone once said, "A brave man dies but once, a coward dies a thousand times." When you are crucified with Christ (even your fears), you can truly live (see Gal 2:20). One act of bravery can open doors that would have otherwise remained closed. David's brave stance against Goliath slung him into a position of national renown. In Andy Stanley's book *Next Generation Leader,* he said, "Killing Goliath did not make David a leader, but it marked him as one.... What people saw in David had been there all along."[32] God has already deposited in you what you need, but you have to have the courage to use and activate the gifts. One act of courage can make a great change in your life and the lives others.

Over a decade ago I had the opportunity to experience the blessings of bravery. It was not fun. It was challenging. I was pressed and stressed and torn. In public, I smiled; in private, I cried.

As a local representative of a national organization on prayer I was faced with a challenge. The municipal government denied my request to use public property for a peaceful gathering. The same property had been used for ten years for the same gathering, but the request was denied because it was identified as an expressly Christian event. Knowing the First Amendment guaranteed equal access to the public property and could not impede the public exercise of religion, I politely challenged the decision. A two-month contest ensued that made national media, but in the end, the city government acquiesced to the law of the land. The local paper ran a story with a headline stating the municipality had received a lesson in civics.

That was one scary time. I was under severe public scrutiny. I was

SIDENOTE
from Rosalynn Austin

Some may never set out to be a leader; however, when following God, that can be exactly who you end up as. When God called me to lead, to serve, to preach his Word, I just simply said, "Yes." After the Lord placed on my heart a call to pastor, I prayed about it. Simultaneously my husband answered his call, and without hesitation said to me, "You will pastor also."

We are husband and wife, parents to two amazing children, best friends, preachers and now pastors. We know in order to be effective we have to have balance in our marriage, home, and external ministries. My husband (a preacher, worship leader, and pastor) is not intimidated by the path God has me walking. Instead, he supports it, prays for me, and encourages me to continually say yes to God moments and choices.

> We both founded One Church in Parkville, Missouri, and we both pastor it. We bring different strengths and abilities and maximize those as we are serving in God's kingdom. Our passion to serve God is our guide.
>
> —Rosalynn Austin
> Co-Pastor; Parkville, Missouri

misquoted in the newspaper. My intentions were misjudged and my character maligned. I was accused of prejudice and discrimination. Although I was prepared and poised to litigate, it was never my intention to do so. You can imagine my relief when after two months and four meetings the city council finally voted to approve my request.

There were times I was shaken. Before one council meeting in particular, a local "minister" flanked by supporters attempted to manipulate me in the hallway. The air was so thick with spiritual opposition the intimidation felt tangible. As a result of the conflict, my name was splashed all over the internet, including a pagan website, and since has been published in Harvard law studies on pluralism. This all happened because I stood for the right of Christians to peacefully gather and pray on public property.

Yes, the experience took a huge personal toll on me and my family, but it brought together a group of people in the community who drew a line in the sand and stood together for the exercise of our religious freedoms. The event that had previously maxed at 200 attendees had over 500 participants that year and incredible news coverage to boot. Resources flooded in for balloons, programs, and publicity. The conflict brought my name before the leadership of the city and also the organization in which I was involved. It eventually led to being offered a position in the organization as a state coordinator and as a speaker at their national leadership conference. In the political arena, I have been blessed to offer the invocation at many public gatherings, including giving an invocation on the floor of the Michigan Senate. Each of these opportunities came as the result of facing conflict. And in them all, I pray the name of Jesus was glorified. It was certainly lifted. Praise God.

God's Course Requires Your Courage

Stephen Covey said, "All things are created twice. There's a mental or first creation, and a physical or second creation to all things."[33] The Creator dreamed you up. You were in the mind of God before you were in your mother's womb. Allow yourself to dream God's dream for you, and have the courage to accept God's creative plan for your life.

When God gives you his dream, have the courage to decisively move forward—not focusing on the "ifs," but the "hows." In times of indetermination and when you lack expertise in an area, acknowledge your uncertainties and commit yourself to finding answers.

If you feel something big inside you, pray, seek wise counsel, and then confidently step across the threshold. King David said, "On the day I called, You answered me; And You made me bold *and* confident with [renewed] strength in my life" (Ps 138:3, AMP).

A called woman of God cannot seek refuge in what has been convenient or comfortable in the past. Neither is a church benefited that remains content with roles and organizational structures for the same reasons. Individuals, local churches, and organizations should be willing to step into the uncomfortable zone for the cause of Christ.

The international ministry of Janet Trout has exemplified one in which a called woman of God was willing to stand, work, do the uncomfortable, and address legitimate issues with character, strength, and grace even when decisions didn't go the way she hoped. A missionary, church planter, pastor, bible school and Christian college founder, songwriter and singer, chair of the board of Urshan Graduate School of Theology, Janet Trout knows the value of the input of each of God's people, and at the same time the incredible importance of the unity of the body of Christ. In her book, *The Journey of Women in Ministry,* Rev. Trout said, "I can be productive in ministry without having to create turmoil in the culture of the organization."[34] We can stand, speak, and serve, but let's do so with grace. The Word is clear, after all, on God's sentiments about those who sow discord among the brethren (see Prov 6:19).

Intimidation seeks to control. Christian minister and author John Bevere said, "An intimidated person honors what he fears more than God."[35] In *Breaking Intimidation,* Bevere went so far as to call intimidation a form of witchcraft that must be confronted. With the weapons of spiritual warfare, in the name of the Lord, and with his authority, believers can boldly confront intimidation (see Eph 6:11–18). Empowered by the Holy Spirit, you can find the strength you need to face intimidation

SIDENOTE
from Angela Overton

Whatever your ministry—writing, teaching, medicine, preaching, music, administration—God wants you to be confident in the talents and calling he has gifted to you. It's time to push beyond past failures and insecurities to have unbounded confidence in yourself, your calling, and God's plan.

—Angela Overton
   Co-chair of The Deborah Project

and fulfill your destiny in God (see Ps 27:1). Even in the midst of fear, God can keep you strong and you can maintain good courage (see Deut 31:6).

General Omar Bradley defined courage as "the capacity to perform properly even when scared half to death."[36] Know God. And when you do, you can be strong and do exploits (see Dan 11:32). Like Daniel in Babylon, your environment doesn't determine your destiny. With God, you can accomplish striking and notable deeds. And when you do, your achievements can build bridges that influence and inspire others.

You are destined for victory, but courage is required. As you seek to do his will, you can trust the Lord's provision. He grows his faithful chosen ones into places of greater ministry and influence. The Lord has given women something worthwhile to share with the body of Christ. When you answer his call to ministry, you will not always feel like you "fit in." Don't be intimidated. Don't cower behind the comfortable, but walk with confidence in the path God has called you to.

On your journey, maintaining a right attitude is one of your most important responsibilities. It is not, however, always the easiest thing to do—especially when doors aren't opening as envisioned or planned. If God has given you a gift to preach and minister publicly, he will provide the opportunity when it is time. Until then, keep your spirit Holy Spirit sanctified, your mind renewed by the Word, and serve where you are with a smile on your face. "As every man hath received the gift, even so minister the same one to another, as good stewards of the manifold grace of God" (1 Pet 1:10).

Imagine how Joseph felt. He was sold into slavery by his brothers, falsely accused of misconduct when he had remarkably maintained his integrity, and then wrongfully imprisoned. Emotionally, he got down; but he never compromised his honor. He continued to treat people respectfully, and in time he received both position and power.

Throughout Joseph's trials and disappointments he didn't allow himself to become hard or bitter. When after many years he was reunited with his brothers who had severely mistreated him, he wept. He drew them near to him and kissed every one of them (see Gen 45:15).

One of the most remarkable lessons we can learn from Joseph, who was both a great leader and public servant, is to keep the right attitude even in rough circumstances. Joseph exemplified a key principle for success. If you keep a right attitude, it will keep you headed in the right direction even when serious detours crop up along the way. Joseph could have been crushed when life turned out so differently from the dreams he had received from God, but instead he carried the prophetic visions God had given him deep inside until he saw them fulfilled.

Attitude Bolsters and Buoys

- Keep focused on your call. Don't depend on outward circumstances to make you happy.
- Make sure your zeal comes through as spiritual fervor, not resentment, antagonism, or anger. Sometimes passion can come off as "attitude."
- When you are discouraged, do not allow yourself to trip into the bottomless pit of self-pity. Remind yourself of the blessings of God in your life.
- Hold tightly to the promises of God and release the pain of disappointments. They can make you bitter.
- Discussion is one thing, but avoid trying to prove yourself right at the expense of rejection and fostering wrong impressions. Avoid being argumentative or defensive, but speak the truth in love (Eph 4:15).
- There are times situations will be out your control. As much as you are able, "live peaceably with all men" and foster peace (see Rom 12:18).
- Bless them that curse you. Shake the dust off your feet and move forward.
- Let go of ministry failures. Judas failed sitting under the best pastor, teacher, leader, and friend imaginable. It happens. Learn and grow.
- Start every day at ground zero. There is no mountain of past achievements or valley of failures that can stop you from moving forward today.
- Prepare yourself in advance for mixed messages. Some men and women who

profess support for women in ministry may not accept your ministry. Don't take it personally.

- If you feel like a "problem" or the "elephant in the room," think of yourself as a blesser instead. You may be different, but you bring something unique to the table.
- Try to maintain a positive self-image. Know who you are and who God called you to be.

SIDENOTE
from Rob McKee

God knows the score, and he keeps accurate records! Barak fought most of the battles of Deborah but was just a footnote in the "Song of Deborah" (see Judges 5). Most of the song's praise went to Jael, the woman who killed Sisera.

Almost 1,100 years later, the 11th chapter of Hebrews records the heroes of the faith. Omitted from the list: Jael. Included: Barak.

Don't be discouraged. God sees your every service and sacrifice. Keep serving God's kingdom in humility. God's "well done" is worth more than the world's songs of personal praise.

—Rob McKee
Pastor; Katy, Texas

Singleness, Dating, and Marriage

I have learned, in whatsoever state I am, therewith to be content.
Philippians 4:11

In my first book, *Gates & Fences: Straight Talk in a Crooked World,* I wrote, "Dating is not a recreational activity. Putt-putt golf is a recreational activity. It is not a game to play with people's emotions—including your own."[37]

If you are single, beware of dating for entertainment's sake or simply because you are lonely. Waiting for God's best will help you avoid potential dangers in a "dating trap" that can lead to compromising a beautiful future for short-term pleasure. That's not a good trade. If you are single and getting a little "long in the tooth," it could become tempting to slip into "evangelistic dating." "Flirt to convert" is not a wise practice, especially for a ministry-minded woman. You want to partner with a man who is spiritually mature.

In Paul's letter to the Corinthian church, he wrote, "Don't team up with those who are unbelievers. How can righteousness be a partner with wickedness? How can light live with darkness?" (2 Cor 6:14, NLT). No matter how others choose to live their lives, a Christian woman should view any potential romantic relationship through God's perspective. If you are in a relationship and you know it's not "the one," let it go. Even if you're unsure of what's next.

I have experienced being single when most of my friends and peers were not. I grew up in Kentucky and girls married young, often right out of high school. Twenty-five seemed like an old maid. I found love and married a wonderful man, but he died before we celebrated our seventh anniversary leaving me a widow. I know what it's like to feel lonely, but I want to encourage you not to be disappointed if you don't have a husband, fiancé, or boyfriend. Trust God. Thrust yourself into the work of God.

Here are some companionship considerations for when you are evaluating a life-long commitment:

- Does this man have his own relationship with God that is independent from yours?
- Does he have a prayer life?
- Is he active in church?
- Does he share your like, precious faith—holding the same doctrines and lifestyle choices you believe are biblical and life-ordering?
- Does he accept responsibility for his actions or make excuses for them?
- Does he treat you like a lady?
- Does he treat his mother and other women with respect?
- Does he have a good work ethic?
- Is he faithful to the house of God?
- Is he a good steward of his finances?
- Does he keep confidences?
- Is he supportive of God's call on your life?
- Does he have a complimentary or non-conflicting call?
- Is he intimidated by you?
- Is he needy? It's one thing to enjoy companionship, but another to be demanding of time and attention that could create conflict down the road.
- Is there a trail of "exes" in his past that would indicate a problem with commitment, loyalty, or faithfulness?
- Are there children from previous relationships? As a woman who was widowed and remarried, I can testify that blending a family is harder than you might think. Be prepared.
- Is he encouraging you to violate God's sexual boundaries? Premarital sex is extramarital sex. It takes place outside marriage. If the person you are dating is willing to compromise God's word on sexual boundaries before marriage, there is no guarantee he will keep them after you are wed.

You don't have to answer every one of these questions affirmatively, because there is no perfect man, but knowing what you are getting into is a good idea, and only you can answer what is a "deal breaker" issue for you.

Of course, the above questions are all about considerations that affect you. In fairness, you should ask yourself how your prince charming would answer comparable questions about you. Would you be a "good catch" for a godly man? That is something to consider.

In a conversation several years ago with a young man who had been disappointed when a godly young woman didn't reciprocate his affection, I asked the young man if he was the kind of man he thought the girl *should* be interested in. I was not unkind or cutting, but I wanted him to think about what he would be bringing into a relationship with the goal of marriage. Was he stable, godly, faithful, and prayerful? Was he the type of spouse a godly woman would be looking for?

If you are single and looking for a relationship for what it can give you, you are probably not ready to be in a healthy relationship. In marriage, like Christianity, we give ourselves, our lives, and our rights to another.

Singleness

The Bible promotes both marriage and singleness. Most women marry, but some do not. Your marital status should not be a determining factor in your call to ministry any more than your gender. Not all men are called to preach, neither are all women. Not all married women are called to minister in one capacity while

single women serve in other ways.

You certainly don't have to be married to minister. The apostle Paul was single, and many of the women ministers discussed in this book were unmarried or widowed. I was widowed at the age of 32. Since my first husband's passing, my ministry activities changed dramatically. I remarried, and I am thankful the Lord gave me not one, but two good husbands. Having a supportive spouse is wonderful, but should you be single or find yourself single, your servant's heart and call from God are your most important ministry factors.

When the Lord does a thing, he does it just right. If marriage is in your future, trust the Lord to bring the perfect companion just for you. Until he does, and as long as he has not, remember that Jesus is your bridegroom and serve the Lord with gladness.

SIDENOTE
from Brenda Bowley

When God calls an individual, he calls a vessel, not a male or female. Along their ministry journeys, some women find themselves "spiritually single." Some husbands may not follow the ministry path God calls their wives to walk. If that is your situation, you can still go and do what God has planned—even with an unsaved spouse.

I pastor a church without my husband. When I was praying about getting licensed, I said, "Lord, if this is what you want me to do, talk to my husband and tell him to let me go and do what you have asked me to do." That is exactly what happened, and he was very supportive.

My husband was not always a support throughout my ministry, but forty years into my walk with God, I baptized him in Jesus's name. I'm still believing he will receive the Holy Ghost. In the meantime, he backs me in every way he possibly can, and I am careful to include him as much as possible in things around the church like carpentry, maintenance, and repairs. This gives him a part of the call even though he is not yet fully serving God. If you find yourself in a similar situation, "love the devil right out of him."

If you need help, talk to godly men and women in your life. Go to your pastor, sectional presbyter, or district superintendent in matters you need support. Listen to those over you. You are called for a purpose, and God has a perfect plan as you follow his direction. You can do it! Preach the Gospel! Obey God! Pray for your husband and see the salvation of God. May the Lord give you favor to faithfully complete the work of your calling.

—Brenda Bowley
Pastor; Madison, Maine

Marriage Roles and Family Life

Be kindly affectioned one to another with brotherly love;
in honour preferring one another.
Romans 12:10

In the book of Ephesians Paul penned instructions to believers regarding the relationships in their homes. His intentions in writing were clear. His desire was that people of God would be wise, "understanding what the will of the Lord is" (Eph 5:17). Each individual point the apostle made was a part of his comprehensive teaching on the subject and should be regarded in context with the whole.

In our world today it is common to see what I call a "Sesame Street" teaching approach. Concepts flash one right after the other with colors and sounds. While that may work well for learning A-B-Cs and 1-2-3s, it does little to foster concentrated thought on complex issues. Both Paul's and Peter's writings on order in the home and church require more than sound bite analysis. We need more than excerpts to comprehend the whole of the biblical teaching on order in the home.

The Bible includes instructions for every believer. Paul taught that every Christian (male and female) should submit "one to another in the fear of God" (see Eph 5:21). This verse is immediately followed by instruction directed to married women, "Wives, submit yourselves unto your own husbands, as unto the Lord. For the husband is the head of the wife, even as Christ is the head of the church: and he is the saviour of the body" (Eph 5:22–23).

In this passage it seems clear the Lord established oversight in the home to the husband. The point should be made, however, that the husband-wife relationship in the home is distinct from other relationships—those in society and the relationships between all men and all women in the church. A godly woman yields to her husband's leadership in the home, but she is not positioned by God beneath the authority of every other man in the church or out. Spiritual authority in the church is an entirely different matter than spiritual authority in the home and is based on callings and gifts, not gender.

The word "head" used by Paul to establish a husband's leadership in his family at times indicates authoritarian rule. In the home, however, in the marriage mutually entered between husband and wife, the woman chooses by her free will to yield to her husband's loving leadership. For this yielding to be biblical and in agreement with the full teaching in Ephesians, it should be two-sided. A husband's leadership should exemplify the leadership Christ provides his church. Jesus was not domineering with those who loved and walked with him. He was empowering, encouraging, and equipping. In fact, he launched people into ministry.

What Paul put forth as a conduct for the home is exemplified by the flow of authority in the church. The disposition of oversight requires two base components: a wife choosing to live agreeably with a husband, and a husband who lays his life down for his wife. Neither seeks his or her own way over the other. Each prefers the other in love and works together for the common good of their family and the kingdom of God.

It's a believer's choice and responsibility to yield to the power delegated by God in the home the same way the church owes its allegiance to Jesus. Wives are to comply with their own husbands, and those husbands are to love and give themselves sacrificially for the betterment of their wives. Note the words "their own" in Ephesians 5:24 which emphasize this instruction is indeed a household code meant to be applied exclusively between a husband and wife.

I will be honest. The word "submit" is not my favorite word in the English language. (Come to think of it, most people would say that.) I don't reject the application of the word, I just prefer the word "agreement." To me, that is what submission means. I choose to agree with my husband (or the Lord or my spiritual authority) even if at times that means yielding my preference. Certainly, the biblical picture of submission is not one in which believers cower under authoritarian dictators. A true reflection would be one in which Christians choose to agree with their God-given leadership—men and women placed in positions of authority who themselves should be motivated by love and have good intentions for all.

In Paul's letters he affirmed a new standard of relationship for Christ's church that was far more sacrificial and demanding than what had been practiced in the patriarchal ancient world. In fact, at the time of Paul's writing, women had been under male authority for millennia. The apostle's teaching on mutual submission impacted the husbands in a much deeper way than it did the wives. Think about the setting. Paul and his contemporaries lived in a culture where marriage meant little if any sacrifice for men. And women were often seen as property, like animals and land. What we take for granted today is actually revolutionary because it obligated the men to change.

The Lord clearly does not promote domination and control among his people. The way he leads his church is the way a husband should lead his wife, compelled by love. And a wife should love and want to please her husband. I appreciate when my husband does nice things on purpose simply because he loves me and wants to please me. And he likes it when I do the same for him. It makes marriage wonderful.

Paul's instructions to husbands called them to take the lead in serving and giving, and he instructed the wife to reverence her husband—which means to treat him with deference by yielding final judgments in the home to him and treating him respectfully.

A survey of the New Testament reveals the marked absence of the word "obey" when it comes to husband and wife relationships. Children are instructed to obey their parents. Slaves/servants must obey their masters. Women, however, are instructed to respect their husbands, treat them courteously, and allow them to lead. This does *not* mean she should withhold opinions. This does *not* imply that if a woman has a strength in a certain area, her husband should squelch her gifts. Nor should he rule over the house making every decision. At the same time, the woman should not try to commandeer authority in an area her husband prefers to manage. The biblical form of home government is the foundational structure laid by the Lord for the good of all families—even if contemporary society disagrees.

Wise, confident, believing husbands and wives should openly communicate and allow one another to take the lead in the areas of their strengths and according to their abilities. Christian author and speaker Lisa Bevere said, "A woman does not yield to a man because she is weak; she yields because she has found the place, that safe place in which to entrust her dreams, to lend her strengths and find her vulnerabilities protected."[38]

A Beautiful Sight

The way spouses treat one another sermonizes to outsiders in a way no prepared message ever could. While no relationship will be without its blemishes, men are called to represent a sacrificial, loving Jesus to the world; and women are called to illustrate the responsive, healthy relationship the church enjoys with the Savior. As Jesus poured out his life providing for the church's every need; a husband should issue forth love and affirmation for his bride. Like Jesus, he should endeavor to equip her and encourage her to walk in her call. And as he does, he can expect a returning tidal wave of love and respect.

It can be challenging at times for a wife to give love and respect to her husband when there is disagreement. As much as I don't like to admit it, the areas my husband and I collide are the places we need each other the most. I need him to slow me down. He needs me to speed him up. I need him to help me think things through. He needs me to help him step out and take a risk. Those are the places we can butt up against each other, but it serves our family best when we work through any friction and come to a resolution rather than let the sparks ignite a fire. Sometimes I am right. Sometimes he is right. We both have to be willing to admit when the other person has the best answer and work together for the good of our marriage.

It has been rare that we have not been able to come to some understandable agreement. However, in one case I had been invited to minister overseas. The location wasn't the safest place for a woman to travel alone, even though the offer came through a legitimate missionary affiliated with the same church organization I am affiliated with. I was eager to go, but he said he didn't have peace about it. So I declined the offer.

I confess I was disappointed. It was my first bonafide invitation to minister overseas and I really wanted to go, but I trusted my husband's heart. This man loves me more than anyone else and allows me to travel all over the world. He is ministry-minded and a wonderful, supportive husband. I let go of that disappointment, and in the years following have walked through many other open doors of ministry—including invitations to minister internationally. How could I have gone on that trip knowing my husband was not at peace about it? Could I have considered it a spiritual contribution to the kingdom of God when I was out of order in my home and operating outside of my husband's blessing? How could I have expected the Spirit of God to anoint any ministry conducted with a willful, selfish attitude? The kingdom of God does not work like that.

God presented Eve to Adam as his companion. She was created to be with him and lead with him from a position of dignity. In fact, the word "obey" is used most often in Scripture in conjunction with obeying the truth of the Word of God. And that Word proclaims that men and women are to love and serve one another as joint-heirs with Christ.

If Paul got the men's attention when he told them to love and serve their wives, they surely noticed when he called women their joint-heirs (see Rom 8:17). In the culture of the day, women didn't receive inheritance. But in the church (spiritually) a woman is in the same legal standing as any male heir. She has the same status and position. She approaches God on her own behalf. Wow! Talk about the transforming power of the Gospel! Paul upended centuries of inheritance law for the sake of women.

Because of Christ, hearts are transformed, and men and women are to treat one another with honor as equals. A husband and wife together are a divine unity of one flesh (see Matt 19:6). A wife is a part of her husband, not his possession; and he is a part of her, not her commander.

One Body

A woman is "one" when she is single. When she is married, she becomes a new kind of "one" with her husband. When the two become "one flesh," the individuals retain their individual personhood and identity. Together, the two share their lives, their dreams, their joys and sorrows as one family unit. Together, they are one flesh, but they are not one mind.

In 1 Corinthians 7, Paul discussed the physical union of husband and wife. He called their coming together "due benevolence" that is owed one to the other (see 1 Cor 7:3). Immediately following, he said, "The wife hath not power of her own body, but the husband: and likewise also the husband hath not power of his own body, but the wife" (1 Cor 7:4).

Once a man and woman enter into a marriage, they no longer have exclusive rights over the use of their bodies. The vows and consummation of their marriage affect the rights of both partners. In essence, the woman transfers to the man the power over her body, and the man transfers to the woman power over his. This Scripture affirms coequality between husband and wife in their most intimate union.

You may be wondering what this passage has to do with the subject at hand. The Greek word *soma* (translated "body") does not exclusively refer to a person's physical being. Certainly husband and wife who "became" an indivisible, united one do not stay united continually in the flesh. *Soma* refers to "the body as a whole, the instrument of life" and sometimes "the complete man." It's the same word used metaphorically for "the body of Christ, with reference to the whole church."[39]

The significance is that the "power" the men and women transfer to each other represents the same definition the word Jesus used in Luke 22:25 when he said, "The kings of the Gentiles exercise lordship over them; and they that exercise authority upon them are called benefactors." The "power" a husband and wife have over their spouse's body means they give mastery one to the other. Each spouse allows the other to exercise authority. In the most intimate way possible, in the marriage bed, both men and women have the same rights one over the other.

In verse 5 of the same chapter, Paul addressed husbands and wives agreeing to times of non-intimacy. Seasons of celibacy could be initiated by either a husband or wife, and both had veto power over the decision of the other. There are times in marriage one spouse may have a lesser desire for intimacy than the other, but a loving spouse should consider and meet the needs of his or her partner. In holy matrimony, mutual submission is God's ideal. It speaks of teamwork, even when one person is leading the other.

When one considers the application of the "one flesh" premise established by God, the more commandeering and dictatorial a husband treats his wife, or vice versa, the more their marriage is damaged. Ironically, it creates a situation in which the noncompliant or belligerent spouse suffers personal losses of his or her own making. On the other hand, the more a person edifies and supports their spouse, the more blessings he or she receives. Relationships blossom. Marriages are strengthened. This is important to public ministry, because what happens in the home affects what proceeds from the pulpit.

Home Life

New covenant relationships in the church don't negate the order in the home or gender distinctions. Being equal doesn't imply being the same, and being born again into the family of God doesn't obliterate a person's obligations to established order. Traditionally women have most often handled the greater share of domestic responsibilities. Their service to their families, however, doesn't mean they are unequipped to serve in the kingdom of God.

A woman called to preach must be in order in both her home and church. Keeping homes and marriages healthy is foundational to effective ministry. You must ensure *your* house is in order before attempting to minister in the house of God.

While some women are in challenging circumstances with marriages to unbelievers or unsupportive husbands, in general effective ministry is the fruit of healthy relationships in your home. When you honor your husband—which includes not only respect in private, but public praise—people take note. They take note of dishonor as well. Honoring him will bring honor to your ministry and create a conduit for the anointing to flow. Dishonor blocks anointing.

Before I minister, my husband and I pray together. It may happen over Facetime or the phone when I am traveling, but what a blessing it is to me to know I am covered by his prayers and have his blessing. I was once in a conference in Michigan's upper peninsula and realized we had not connected before the service. I pulled out my phone and texted him a message, "Get ready to pray. I'm putting you on speaker." When I took the pulpit I told the women gathered that I didn't minister without my husband praying for me, and he was on the phone to do the job. What a sweet presence of God filled the room when he prayed (and the women loved it).

There may come a time when I am in a remote location and we are unable to connect, but there is an anointing that flows when ministers maintain order in our homes, in our churches, and in our ministries. I honor my husband by asking him to pray. He blesses me, and it releases me to minister with confidence and authority.

Standing by Your Man

- Your love and respect for your husband should be evident to all.
- Honor him as the head of your home.
- Build his confidence and help him feel secure in his role in your life and ministry.
- Encourage him to develop his spiritual gifts and walk in his unique call, even if that takes time from yours.
- Make him feel treasured—every person is of equal value to God.
- Take time for just the two of you to be together and be attentive to his feelings and needs.
- As much as possible, include him—in planning, praying, attending events, and give his input serious consideration.
- Always consult him before agreeing to travel or minister away from home.
- Never argue in public, and never mention disagreements from the pulpit. Degrading your spouse disgraces you and discredits your Christian character.

- Show him (and show others) your sincere appreciation for his support and the sacrifices he makes for you to serve in your call.

Children in the Home

There is nothing more important than family, and since your home life follows you to the pulpit, the health of your family relationships is crucial. Fulfilling the call of God shouldn't be done at your family's expense. Yes, there will be sacrifices, but you shouldn't forfeit your children's needs for your ministry's sake. If a call is from God, he will not ask for a choice between your responsibilities to your family and your service to him. After all, being a minister means being a Christian—and that certainly includes providing for the needs in your own home (see 1 Tim 5:8).

Some thoughts on the special needs of a minister's children:

- Create times just for your family to enjoy some rest and relaxation.
- Refrain from criticizing church members or complaining about situations in front of your children.
- Present ministry to your children as a blessed opportunity rather than a great sacrifice.
- When at times a substantial sacrifice is required, do what you can to bless your children in other ways.
- Do what you can to keep your private life from the public eye.
- Have some down time in a safe place.
- Discipline and train your children. While they won't be perfect, and neither will you, your family should be a good example of a Christian home.

All the Single Ladies

Paul didn't forget the single ladies. In fact, in the chapter we looked at above (1 Corinthians 7), along with the married men and women, Paul addressed the unmarried. He noted it was good for men to be single like he was (see 1 Cor 7:26). He noted in two other verses that unmarried men and unmarried woman have more opportunity than those who are married to care for the things that belong to the Lord (see 1 Cor 7:32, 34).

Paul recognized the same opportunities being single provides to both men and women. He used the same language to describe both men and women caring for the things of the Lord indicating like opportunities to the unmarried regardless of gender.

If you are single, celebrate who you are—as a woman and a minister. If you are married, do the same, but also celebrate your role as wife and the man in your life— the man God made him to be and the blessings of having him as your companion, your co-laborer, and fellow-heir.

Ministerial Relationships

Let us therefore follow after the things which make for peace,
and things wherewith one may edify another.
Romans 14:19

Personally and in ministry, women benefit from healthy, wholesome relationships. Networking with other ministers, especially women ministers, will hone and help you as you develop your gifts and walk in your call.

There are times in ministry only another minister will understand or be able to offer the advice, consolation, or encouragement you need. If you are blessed to know other women ministers, make the most of those relationships. If, however, you have limited access to other women in ministry, reach out to those who have walked the path before you. Experienced pastors, evangelists, and missionaries might surprise you with just how much they are willing to support you. Every Christian should want to see the expansion of the kingdom of God and the baton of ministry pass successfully to the next generation. Save your money and vacation days and go to conferences where you can spend time with others serving in ministry, especially women.

Everyone should read books about other women ministers. We can learn so much when we read the accounts of those who have served in our day and before us. I have been personally encouraged and challenged by the writings of and about women like Nona Freemen and Corrie Ten Boom. Nona was a young, insecure woman called to be a missionary to Africa. Corrie lived through the horrors of captivity in a Nazi concentration camp. There is so much to learn from their experiences if we will take the time to read them.

As your ministry grows—and your circle of ministering friends with it—be realistic in your expectations from other flawed-yet-sanctified human beings. Not everyone will be your favorite person, and although you are surely some kind of wonderful, not everyone will consider you his or her best friend either. The more you get to know people, the more you will see their humanity and the more they will see yours. Extend grace to others and be open and honest about your own shortcomings. As much as you possibly can, live peaceably with everyone (see Rom 12:18).

As you connect with new people, don't allow yourself to get "superstar-itis"— a disabling condition where you believe some particular people are either too far your superior or too far inferior to have a meaningful conversation. While you are talking, be you—not someone you aren't. If you are "Type A," be your outgoing, energetic self (within reasonable social boundaries). If you are "Type B," be confident, but don't try to force yourself into something you're not. The Lord knew what he was doing when he made each of us, and he will lead you to the right connections for you when you're true to yourself.

For those times you find yourself to be the only minister in a skirt, there is no getting around the reality that you are different from the sea of suited men you are swimming among. Pastor Mildred Robinson said of her experience, "At times I felt destined for victory, but at other times I felt like a dinosaur. You see, women pastors were extinct in my area."[40] You may feel alone or awkward, but make it a point to contribute if you have something to offer. Do not, however, feel you must speak unless you have something worthwhile to say.

If you are the only female in a group, you can be relatively certain the cumulative of masculine thought likely did not include what crossed your mind or spirit. You bring something different to the table, and that is healthy to the body of Christ. If you're in a formal meeting following prescribed rules of conduct, be properly prepared to engage in the process of sharing with the right motions, calls, or points—or prepare to be ignored. Most business meetings follow Roberts Rules of Order, and simplified versions are available to understand and learn the process.

Be aware that sometimes your own thinking can box you in. In the times you fail to connect, it can be tempting to blame the composition of the group or throw the gender card on the top of the excuse pile. The reality is, you must speak for you. Most people aren't going to immediately judge your input based on your gender. Acknowledge your God-given call and abilities by stepping onto the field and sharing what the Lord gives you.

Networking Tips:

- Attend networking and fellowshipping events even if you are the lone lady minister. Bring someone along if you can, or encourage another to attend.
- When you have the opportunity to speak, promote what God is doing, not your ministry goals.
- Be sincerely interested in what God is doing in and through others.
- As much as possible, help others achieve their goals.
- Spend time with people who focus on building up, not tearing down. Critiquing for improvement is not the same as criticizing and fault-finding.
- If you find yourself consistently in the company of complainers, do your best to find people to spend time with who will provoke you to be more and do more for the Lord.
- Build relationships with people who focus on solutions instead of problems.

SIDENOTE
from the Author

There have been times I have floundered reconciling who God called me to be with the realities of life. For instance, at a conference, should I go to a ministers' wives session or a minister's session? This can be especially challenging when the leaders specify one meeting is for "the men" when everyone knows it's for "the ministry." There are also times ladies' events break out into "ministers' wives" and "laity" sessions. Where does a woman minister fit in?

Sometimes these situations just happen—people fall back on the language they have used for years and the paradigms they have lived within. For me, being offended is not the issue. It's knowing where I belong. I don't want to be (or appear to be) rebellious or overassertive, but at the same time, I want to be in the session that is most beneficial to my call.

One year in particular I was having a hard time with this. Perhaps it was amplified because I had been confronted and directly challenged more than once at this multi-day meeting about "my authority" to speak and write, and the scripture about "women keeping silence." I am thankful this is not the norm or representative of the body of ministers at large, but I was feeling worn.

I walked down a hallway toward some break-out rooms where ladies' meetings were scheduled to take place. When I entered the beautiful event created with loving, good intentions, my already heightened emotions swirled into a full-fledged pity party. I felt so isolated—like a triangle that didn't fit on anyone's pegboard made for circles and squares.

I turned and left the room, holding back the flood that threatened to break out and splash all over the conference center carpet. The woman greeting people in the hallway that morning knew me. We had spoken at a ladies' conference years before.

"I don't belong anywhere," I said.

She looked me straight in the eye and said,
"You're Lori Wagner. You belong everywhere."

I shook my head and laughed. I know who Lori Wagner is better than anyone. I know I don't "warrant" any special recognition or treatment. But her words brought much needed clarity and affirmation. I realized that wherever the Lord places me, at "that moment," that is where I belong. My ministry may never fit into a "slot." I am thankful networking opportunities for women in ministry are opening, but whatever the future holds, I can be confident that as I trust in him, he is ordering my steps.

Wherever you are, if God put you there, you belong.

Accountability

Obey them that have the rule over you, and submit yourselves: for they watch for your souls, as they that must give account, that they may do it with joy, and not with grief: for that is unprofitable for you.
Hebrews 13:17

In simple terms accountability happens when you give an account of yourself to someone else. Everyone should be answerable to someone. Accountability breeds integrity, and a lack of accountability too often results in corruption—if not of a person's character, then their call. An absence of answerability can result in deviations from your God-given course.

Accountability is more than allowing someone to confront you with issues or concerns. It goes beyond you having a sounding board to bounce your thoughts against. Being accountable gives you feedback on your goals and progress. It provides an opportunity for you to receive instruction from someone who not only has a vested interest in your success, but who may well have walked down a similar path. Being accountable is like holding a "looking glass" in front of you that helps you see yourself better—your strengths and weaknesses. And most importantly, the person holding the reflector in front of you can help you determine if your hopes, plans, and paths are looking smart in the most important mirror of all—the Word of God. At times, we can fool ourselves into thinking all is well when our perception is as skewed as a reflection from a fun-house mirror. There is safety in sharing.

As a female minister this occurs when you willingly subject yourself to report, explain, or justify your conduct to a trusted peer, mentor, or leader. It's never wise to consider yourself beyond answering to your spouse or spiritual authority. When you first start in ministry, accountability should at the very least include your pastor and husband/parents. These vital relationships are the most important in your life, and these are the people who know you better and care for you more deeply than any others. Theirs are the voices that should have the greatest influence in your life.

Whether you are a ministry hope-to-be, a rookie, or a seasoned veteran; you need relationships with trusted people who love you enough to be honest with you. You need a friend who will pat you on the back when you need encouragement, but who also knows when you need a good "kick on the backside." I need someone who loves me too much to let me get away with compromise, with neglecting my spiritual walk and my responsibilities. You do, too.

My sister and I have an informal accountability relationship. In the past she has asked my opinion because she said she didn't want to be in "spiritual fruity land." I always laugh when she says that, but she is right. Having a scripturally solid "sounding board" is an anchor that will keep you from drifting too far out to sea on your own thoughts and tangents.

Character Qualities for an Accountability Partner

Trust is the primary ingredient in an accountability relationship. Nobody wants to share her secrets with a "Delilah"—someone who will expose them or use them against her to her hurt. You must have confidence that the person you are opening yourself to—the one you are sharing sensitive and personal information with—has your best interest at heart.

Following are some characteristics to look for in an accountability partner. One who is:

- "Swift to hear, slow to speak, slow to wrath" (see Jas 1:19)
- Continuing to learn and grow (see Prov 1:5)
- Making wise choices in their companions (see Prov 13:20)
- Not quick to judge, but discerning (see Matt 7:1–2)
- Sincere in their love and care for you as a person (see 1 John 4:21).

Protection

Accountability brings safety. It keeps you from hanging out in vulnerable situations—in places you are susceptible to knuckle under temptation's pressure.

SIDENOTE
from Crystal Schmalz

Mentoring the leaders and ministers of tomorrow is an important part of our calling. I have found both by being mentored and mentoring others it brings encouragement, a support network, affirmation and confirmation of calling, and helps transfer the important doctrine and stories of our tradition. Imagine what our movement could look like in fifty years if we invested in intentional mentoring efforts for the next generation!

—Crystal Schmalz
  Chaplain and Founder,
  Women of Vision Leadership

The safest place is a public place; and the safest of safe places is a public place surrounded by godly people who influence you in positive ways. The accountability factor of positive peer pressure can be a great friend if you make wise choices in the peers you run with.

Whoever you are with, walk in the light. Sin loves darkness. It could be said that sin grows in the dark—even the smoky places of our hearts and minds where we nurture our carnal natures and shelter them with excuses from the light of God's Word. We deceive ourselves if we think our sin will stay hidden. King David said, "If I say, Surely the darkness shall cover me; even the night shall be light about me. Yea, the darkness hideth not from thee; but the night shineth as the day: the darkness and the light are both alike to thee" (Ps 139:11–12).

If you have a habit or activity you feel you must hide, that should be a red flag in and of itself. Look to nature and learn from its example. Flowers, fruit-bearing trees, vegetables, and herbs grow in the sunshine. Even chickens need light to lay eggs. But in the dark, things like fungi and bacteria thrive and colonize. It is in the dark cockroaches and skunks scurry about.

Spiritual growth doesn't happen in the dark, so be careful not to retreat into shady places that stunt rather than cultivate your progress. If you have an area in which you tend to lapse from uprightness, go to someone you have made yourself accountable to and talk to them. Confess it. Pray together. Ask him or her to follow up with you about it. The Bible says that when believers conduct themselves in this way, they can receive healing (see Jas 5:16). God wants to heal you and make you whole.

Avoid situations where you have no accountability. Don't allow yourself to be "alone" with your weaknesses. The Bible instructs believers to flee all lusts. Inappropriate desires flutter through our thoughts, pull on our emotions, and cause our flesh to yearn for what it ought not have. When that happens to you, it is your responsibility to be purposeful and prompt about walking in the opposite direction (see 2 Tim 2:2). If you are single, remember Paul's words to Timothy. Your brothers in the Lord should treat you in the same way they would treat their own sister, with absolute purity (see 2 Tim 5:2).

Plans and Protocols

I recently heard a saying that rang true in my spirit: "Better safe than vulnerable." Keeping yourself accountable to a select safe person or two is wise. You can keep yourself from vulnerability in general, however, by conducting in public any meetings that might be questionable or cause temptation. Being in the public eye encourages everyone involved to be on his or her best behavior. Not only that, meeting in public keeps you from situations that could (not by your own choice) spin out of control.

You never know what someone else will do or say. As a minister, you simply must be careful when meeting with others—at work, in counseling, in ministry, and in your travels. A woman should not meet alone with a man or with a child who is not a close relative. Meeting in public, or having a third party in the mix (or at least nearby), is a protection for all—including those who may be absent from the meeting. If you need to speak with someone on a sensitive matter who doesn't wish to have a third party in on the discussion, you can meet at a location that provides visibility and accountability. If you don't have an office that would accommodate this, use your local library, a coffee shop, or some other public venue. Libraries often have rooms with windows available where you could conduct your meeting privately but still be observed by the public or a third party seated in view.

If you find yourself in an unplanned, unexpected situation that could be compromising, remove yourself from it as soon as you possibly can and let your husband or accountability partner know what happened. I would recommend documenting it somehow. It could be as simple as a note in your journal, but it is a prudent precaution. You may have done nothing wrong and had no intention of wrong, but in our litigious society, these simple protocols could save you from slander. Even a false accusation can irreparably damage your ministry and reputation.

In contrast to the safety a public meeting provides, the place with the highest vulnerability is alone—especially late at night. Alone can be wonderful in so many ways, but some struggle with "aloneness." We must be accountable for our "alone actions" as well as our public conduct.

Through electronic communications and media, you have access in your solitude to people from every walk of life any time of the day or night. Use wisdom and discretion. In addition to talking to your accountability partner about your private world, following are some suggestions to help you keep control of your private domain:

- If social media is a slippery slope, take control over who and what you are connected to. "Unlike," "hide," and "unfollow" whatever and whoever hurtles you on a negative trajectory toward sin. For the most part you can filter what comes to you through profile preference settings. Social media is a tool you can use to speak life into your world, but as much as you are able, don't let it influence you negatively.
- If online content is a struggle, get filters for your devices. Filters are available that connect to home servers and work with all the technical apparatus you might have—computers, phones, and tablets. You can also subscribe or purchase a tracking program that sends a report to someone you trust who will hold you accountable for every website visited.
- Be "password protected." That means sharing your login and password with your husband and/or accountability partner. Some couples even choose to share social media and email accounts for their own protection.
- Regardless of your marital status, be careful to avoid inappropriate emotional intimacy. Opportunities for these types of relationships most frequently present themselves in job situations, but they abound online and through social media as well. Although these relationships may never lead to physical affairs, an emotional affair can be extremely damaging to your spiritual life and ministry.
- While most of us use computers and other devices for work and ministry, we also use them for entertainment. Your entertainment choices are just that— your choices. Refuse to be "alone" with temptation by choosing to amuse yourself with programs and music that feed the lust of the eyes, lust of the

flesh, and the pride of life you are trying to conquer. You shouldn't entertain yourself with anything your spiritual authority couldn't wholesomely enjoy with you. There should be nothing "hide-worthy" in your life.

Personal Protections

If you are a young person just moving out on your own, certainly continue to honor and listen to your parents; but also make yourself answerable to others. If you are married, one of the best proactive measures you can implement for overcoming temptation is a healthy relationship with your husband. Discuss any conversation or incident that made you feel uncomfortable. Establish safeguards and boundary lines before you find yourself in challenging positions. Talk about situations you may have to face in advance and determine a plan of action. Agree in advance with your husband (or accountability partner) on a ready response you can use any time you receive an offer that makes you uncomfortable or would put you in a compromising situation. Rehearse it. Then when you need it, even in an awkward situation, it will come naturally and easily.

You can establish a code that triggers an immediate phone call. I recently read a social media post about an "X-plan" one family implemented. Any time a family member gets in a compromising or uncomfortable situation, they can text an "X" to another family member. The person receiving the message calls and says, "Something has come up and I have to come get you right now," or "Something has come up and you need to come home right away." Even if you are out of town, an emergency, "Something has come up and I need to talk to you right now" could provide a way out of an awkward situation.

When I have been asked to do something that set off an alarm in my spirit, I simply answered with a prepared statement: "I'm sorry, but I have other plans." I don't consider that a fabrication in any way. It's absolutely true. My plans are to never say *yes* to a compromising situation. It's my plan to *not* go where I sense that niggling warning in my spirit. My plan is to flee temptation and walk in the ways of the Lord. I do have plans, and those plans are to let the peace of God rule my decisions and steps.

Any time I am invited to minister—whether it feels right or I have concerns—I always respond, "Let me pray about that, and I'll check with my husband." Although I'm an evangelist, supported by my husband, blessed by my pastor, licensed by my district, officially enrolled in my church organization's Enrolled Evangelist Program with freedom

SIDENOTE
from Cindy Miller

It may be helpful to role-play a scenario you expect to find yourself and rehearse an appropriate response, so when you find yourself in the moment of decision-making you can lean on the script you have developed. Brainstorm numerous ways to respond to difficult challenges. Be prepared with an answer in the hour of temptation.[41]

—Cindy Miller, PhD
    Professor, Urshan Graduate
    School of Theology;
    Pastor, Wrightstown, New Jersey

SIDENOTE
from Lindsay Coppinger

Accountability has a purpose—helping us become who God intends us to be; not just in actions, but in truth, inwardly and outwardly holy for the glory of God.

—Lindsay Coppinger
    Evangelist, Teacher and Missions
    Coordinator; Murfreesboro, TN

to minister wherever I am invited; I still make myself accountable to my husband and pastor. When I first started speaking out, I brought home CDs and DVDs of my messages to my pastor and first lady so they could hear what I was saying. It opened a channel for correction if it had been needed. That accountability made me feel safe and more confident. I wasn't out there ministering alone, unchecked, or unhinged.

Along with tangible areas like media, relationships, activities, and finances, a minister should allow an accountability partner access to the unseen areas of their lives. Moods, attitudes, and thought patterns are not exempt from scrutiny or correction. Sometimes we need to be reminded that our feelings aren't necessarily facts and they shouldn't be allowed to govern our lives.

Allowing accountability partners access—giving them the opportunity to speak words of correction and direction—will help keep you stable in the swirling chaos of this world. It's more important than ever that Christian ministers not just have a form of godliness, but that they walk in apostolic anointing that comes from living godly consecrated lives.

Section 4

Ministering as a Lady

Platform Etiquette and Appearance

Let all things be done decently and in order.
1 Corinthians 14:40

Appropriate conduct on the platform is crucial in setting and keeping the right tone in any service. Because platforms are usually elevated—and always in a position of prominence—being on a platform places a person in a position for constant scrutiny from the shoes up. A minister's appearance, conduct, and mannerisms can uplift, distract, or even offend the people they hope to minister to. If you are privileged to lead and speak on a platform, your personal reverence will inspire reverence in others. Different venues and types of services allow for variation in presentation style—in levity or sobriety; but in general, keep in mind your dress, bearing, and behavior impact the flow of the service and reception of the people.

Appearance

Having a sense of style is fine, but as a minister, you should never want your appearance to be a stumbling block. Conform your personal dressing styles within safe parameters so as not to hinder or distract others. God's messenger should not detract from God's message, and that can happen if we dress ostentatiously. You want the people's thoughts on the Word, not the woman. Will others take you seriously, or will they write you off by your appearance? It might not seem fair, but it is true. People look at the outer person, and how you present yourself is something to carefully consider (see 1 Sam 16:7).

I once went to hear a woman minister I had listened to many times on the radio. I was prepared that she had different views on modesty in dress, and when she took the stage I was not surprised she wore an outfit and adornments I would not have chosen. What I was unprepared for, however, was the light show. As she moved about the stage, bright lights reflected off her sizeable jewelry in a dazzling display. I was so distracted I had a hard time focusing on her message. When I left I made a mental note to be more aware of how my dressing choices could positively or negatively impact the audience I was trying to reach.

Being considerate goes beyond sequins and sparkles. I have a friend who gets dizzy if I sit across from her wearing a busy print. This may affect only a small group of people, but the people across from you (at a restaurant table or on a stage) will appreciate your consideration. Choose clothing that would most likely not cause discomfort or distraction to others.

When speaking, I always take a careful inventory of what I wear. Personally, I prefer to wear jackets because they cover the body well. I feel more at liberty to worship knowing body parts are not getting any extra attention as I move around. Under a jacket I wear a blouse or rounded-neckline shirt. These look nice and soften the look of a tailored jacket. While we are discussing shirts, when it comes to necklines, keep in mind that what is modest on one person may not be on another. And when it comes to style and fit, you must dress the body you actually have, not the one you wish you had. Wear what covers you well, does not inappropriately accentuate womanly curves, and looks best on your body type. And wear appropriate undergarments that effectively perform their functions. If it is cold, be aware of how that affects your body and dress accordingly.

I am not advocating that you dress like I dress, or in a style that doesn't fit your personality. Be yourself (your sanctified self), but I would encourage you to consider the overall effect of your outfit—and from every position. What is modest standing may not be when seated. What is full coverage at the pulpit could create a peep show during altar ministry or worship. Nobody wants that to happen, so make sure you move around as you check your outfits. From every angle, cleavage should be completely covered and your skirts (including slits if your skirts have them) should not rise above the knee exposing the thigh. As you choose your skirts, remember that many platforms are elevated, and you may have to walk up steps. Consider what people will see as you stand on the platform or walk to the pulpit.

Be sensitive to the men around you. Especially when you are ministering, don't be negligent of the ways your conduct and clothing can affect them. God made men to be affected strongly by what they see, and you don't want to purposely distract men from worship or the Word. So while you are in the dressing room checking the mirror, check your motives. Your flesh might persuade you to wear something that would be better left on the rack. When you make your selections, remember to purposefully present yourself as you would like to be received. And also keep in mind the old adage, "Dress for success." Different professions require different outfits. Dress like the minister you want to be and remember that you aren't representing yourself, but the Lord, the church, and if applicable, your husband and pastor. As an ambassador for the Lord, present yourself appropriately. *Appropriate* is a key word when it comes to appearance.

Appropriateness means your hair and dress are not only modest, clean, and neat, but suitable to the particular situation and never gaudy. The English word translated "modest" in the Bible comes from the Greek word *kosmios* which means, "orderly, well-arranged, decent, modest."[42] What you wear at a mall, at a park, or at a formal wedding will vary, but your clothing should always be modest and fitting to the location and activity. The Bible admonishes Christian women to "adorn themselves in modest apparel, with propriety and moderation, not with braided hair or gold or pearls or costly clothing, but which is proper for women professing godliness, with good works" (see 1 Tim 2:9–10). When Paul wrote this passage in his letter to Timothy, the younger man was pastoring the church in Ephesus in a pagan environment where women used jewelry to attract attention and flaunt wealth. According to Paul, a woman professing to be a Christian (especially one who feels a call to ministry, I would add) must be careful to keep her physical appearance suitable and moderate. In *Paul, Women and Wives,* author Craig Keener said, "It is thus relatively certain that the hearers in Timothy's congregation would have grasped Paul's point, had Timothy read the letter to them: 'dress and live simply and unenticingly, but be lavish in your spirit; decorate your heart with purity and humility.'"[43]

To me, dressing and living simply and unenticingly includes hairstyles, shoes, and accessories. I do want to make the point, however, that people notice your shoes, especially when you are on an elevated platform. Whether you get your shoes from the second-hand store or an exclusive boutique, make sure they are polished and in good condition.

Hair should be clean and styled neatly. Some women lean toward more elaborate hairstyles than others. If that describes you, be aware there is a line between lovely and outlandish. You and I don't live in first century Ephesus where the women fashioned their hair in intricate styles weaving in gold and jewels, but we can have our own brand of gaudiness that is just as distracting or showy. Isocrates, an influential Greek orator in the fourth and fifth century said, "Consider that no adornment so becomes you as modesty, justice, and self-control; for these are the virtues by which, as all men are agreed."[44]

I concur with Isocrates. Modesty is admirable. Justice is engaging. Self-control is pleasant and refreshing. Embrace these. Wear them, and you will be one winsome woman. Your best accessory is your smile, and the most effective skin and beauty treatment is being filled with the radiant Spirit of God.

Pulpit Protocol

When speaking out as a guest minister, check with the person who invited you to determine

> If you are not scheduled to be on the platform for a service, it's still a good idea to be "platform ready" in your appearance. You never know when you may be called on to fill in for someone to lead prayer or to testify.

any platform preferences. It's best to go in knowing platform protocols. Don't assume the standards of other churches are the same as in your home church even among churches in the same denomination. Sometimes a simple look around at the other ladies in ministry will suffice (even on a church website or social media). Other times a pastor or event organizer may send a written document outlining expectations.

I was once scheduled to preach a revival in the state of Washington. I didn't know the pastor, and he didn't know me. He found my name in a magazine and asked me to come because he had a woman in his church he felt had a call to ministry and who would benefit from exposure to a woman preacher. (That is a good pastor, in my opinion.) As I made my way across the country, the Lord began to deal with me about taking off my wedding ring. I was thankful I listened and slipped it into my purse before I got off the plane. The pastor hadn't told me his preference, but I would have been the only woman wearing a ring. Believe me, it would have been noticed. When a female minister is invited to speak in someone else's pulpit, she should never want to appear to disregard the pastor's directives to his church, even if the standard in her home church or her personal convictions differ. I always want to err on the side of safety. It may seem a simple thing, but putting aside some freedoms or humbling yourself to take off something you feel at liberty to wear can open doors; the converse can also true. Being insensitive or unconcerned with the local protocols can slam doors shut that, once closed, may never open again.

On another occasion I was invited to speak at a girls conference in California hosted by a church where the ladies wore head coverings in worship. I didn't realize this when I accepted the invitation and was never instructed to wear one, but when we arrived at the church for service and the girls started pinning their head coverings on, I felt I should ask the host her preference. The decision was left to me, and I opted to wear one. I didn't want to take that pulpit as an outsider—to take a liberty that might hinder someone else, cause confusion, or be considered "in error." The people sincerely believed in wearing head coverings for worship. There are times to humble yourself and lay down your rights for the cause of Christ. When you do, that is not caving in or pandering, it is showing respect.

Pre-Service

Pray. Pray. Pray. Pray to prepare yourself, and when possible, pray with the others involved in the service. Create or obtain a service outline, and when it's in your control, meet in advance of service with the people who will also be ministering on the platform. Confirm the order of service, seating arrangements, and each person's responsibility.

If you are ministering outside your home church, you may not be able to have a meeting, but do connect with the person running the service before it starts. At home, predetermine some signals with musicians and other leaders to keep elements of the service starting and stopping as they should. Any announcements made should be brief and as concise as possible. Details can be provided in bulletins, overhead projections, emails, calls, and flyers.

Each church will differ in platform seating arrangement. The service leader is commonly seated next to the minister speaking, but in some churches ministers don't step on the platform until worship is concluded. These varying possibilities are why it's good to have a preliminary meeting, especially when speaking out.

Leading Service

If it's your job to lead a service, make sure you know who is doing what before you begin. Be aware that in any gathering people may join you for worship who have no idea what is happening. When making transitions from one element of service to another, give verbal directions so people know what to do.

If you are assigned to lead congregational prayer, invite the people to join you. You can simply say, "Let's pray together," and then begin. Giving clear direction is always important, especially for visitors.

As much as it is in your control, keep the order of service flowing. Anticipate the transitions from one element to the next. Be in position as soon as possible so people aren't standing around waiting. Be respectful of how long congregants are standing. The elderly and mothers holding young children can tire long before you do.

Having a prepared service outline should not hinder the flow of the Spirit. As the service leader, it's your job to be closely in tune with the Spirit of God at all times. Ministry should be prepared to deviate from the outline if the Lord moves in worship or upon the people and guests. This flexibility doesn't negate your responsibility to come to worship prepared. Do all things with excellence unto the Lord.

The platform is a sacred place of ministry, and even more so, the pulpit. When you take the pulpit to deliver a message, give your thanks and honors as the situation necessitates, but refrain from using too many super-whammy-awesome-like superlatives. If you're introducing a speaker, give a good introduction, but be careful not to exaggerate or make the prologue so flowery the speaker is embarrassed. You want to prepare the congregation for ministry by sharing credentials and character, but then getting out of the way.

Keep the sacred desk sacred. Humor and illustrations can add a human element and impact to a message, but refrain from using coarse humor or anything that could turn the listener's thoughts in a carnal direction or down a needless bunny trail.

In Service

Don't slouch. Stand tall and sit tall. When you're seated, it's usually best to keep both feet on the floor. If this is an uncomfortable position for you, cross your legs at the ankles, not at the knees. When you're at the pulpit, be aware of your stance and movements. Repeatedly shifting your weight from one foot to the other can be distracting.

Be supportive of whatever is happening behind the pulpit. Give the service leaders, singers, and speakers the support you would like to receive. If you are the speaker, join in the worship and prayer. Not only do you have a personal, biblical mandate to enter his gates with thanksgiving, you set the example for the congregation. If you seem uninterested in worship and prayer, even though you are legitimately focused on your upcoming message, worship and prayer can be devalued in the eyes of some in the congregation.

When it's time to give in the offering, be prepared to participate, even if you are on the platform. It's part of your worship and encourages others to give. With digital payments, you may put in just a token, but do it anyway. If you are the one in charge of receiving the offering, give some notice so both the people giving and those collecting will be prepared. If any specific directions are needed, give those verbally.

SIDENOTE
from Jonathan McClintock

I have watched young preachers sometimes who have mannerisms and distractions in the way they project things. I understand over time that they will learn how to eliminate the distractions. For some preachers, kids are out there counting how many times the preacher is saying 'hallelujah' or 'praise God.' These 'crutches' are mainly the result of inexperience. This is also because they are having trouble getting a handle on the human emotions, energy, and passion.[45]

—Jonathan McClintock
Pastor, Teacher and Author;
Saint Charles, Missouri

It's a Package Deal

Appropriate platform etiquette and appearance will always be factors in your ministry. A minister should be modest, and modesty is about more than your dress. It's about refraining from drawing undue attention to yourself in your apparel, grooming, conversations, and in the way you conduct yourself. It includes body language, the way you talk, and even the way you eat. As a woman minister, remember you aren't "one of the guys," and you shouldn't act like one. The ways you move and speak can be both gracious and powerful at the same time. You don't need to be aggressive with gestures or gruff in voice inflection or tone (although squeaking is not pleasant to listen to either). You can stand with poise and confidence without being intimidating or masculine in your mannerisms and motions. A woman preacher may have an incredible message, but if care is not taken, her delivery could repulse the very people she has prayed for and prepared to reach. Being appropriate is not a gender-specific requirement. Every minister, male and female, should strive to be modest, moderate, and appropriate in conduct and presentation.

Bronya Shaffer, a noted lecturer on Jewish women's issues, said in an online interview, "At times we dress with the intent to impress, but we always dress with the intent to express. We have an image of self in mind and that is how we want others to see us. So we dress accordingly."[46] This is a powerful thought. What is your dressing expressing about you? Could it be hindering or helping your ministry?

As a woman in ministry, wherever you are, you represent your status as a daughter and ambassador of Jesus. Having the right blend of respect for yourself and honor for God's house and his people will help you fulfill the call of God on your life with excellence. When you have that right mix of humility and confidence, and you conduct yourself accordingly, you will carry an authority that will announce itself as you enter the room. The power of God in you will shine through.

For women in ministry some things (even some styles of clothing) are simply inappropriate. We must walk worthy of our callings (see Eph 4:1). What others may do, say, or wear, we simply must forgo so as not to bring reproach to the work and the kingdom of God.

Preaching

And he said unto them, Go ye into all the world,
and preach the gospel to every creature.
Mark 16:15

In one sense, preaching is "showmanship"—but unlike the entertainment business, Christian ministry should not put the preacher on display. It should put God on display. That's what Jesus did. He put God on display in his world. In this chapter we will look at the art of preaching, and we will begin with the commencement of Jesus's public speaking ministry. On that great inaugural day, Jesus stood in the synagogue and read the words of Isaiah:

"The Spirit of the Lord is upon me, because he hath anointed me to preach the gospel to the poor; he hath sent me to heal the brokenhearted, to preach deliverance to the captives, and recovering of sight to the blind, to set at liberty them that are bruised, To preach the acceptable year of the Lord" (Luke 4:18–19).

Three times in this passage, Jesus used the word preach. He said he came to preach the good news, to preach deliverance, and to preach spiritual vision. And while he was preaching, he ministered healing and liberty. As Jesus traveled and spoke, he trained his disciples and told them to do what he did—proclaim the good news that freedom from sin is available to everyone.

> Jesus instituted preaching as the means of communicating the love of God, his offer of redemption, and instructions in right living to those who would follow him.

The Bible says, "It pleased God by the foolishness of preaching to save them that believe" (1 Cor 1:21). Isaiah's prophecy came decades before the birth of Jesus, which lets us know it was long a part of God's plan that faith would be imparted to people who heard the preached Word (see Rom 10:17). But as Paul asked the members of the church of Rome, "How shall the people hear without a preacher?" (Rom 10:14).

If you are a woman called to preach, God has placed his confidence in you to reach people in your world with the saving message of the gospel. It's his message, and you are his messenger. As a lady preacher, you deliver that message in your own unique way. Your personality and character impact the way you prepare and present and play a big part in your audience's reception of your message.

Just as some men preach in gentle ways, some women preach with joy and passion. You don't have to fit a certain stereotype or deliver with a specific presentation style to minister effectively as a woman preacher. God uniquely created each of us, and preaching "like a lady" will look different for you than it looks for other female ministers. Preach like the unique vessel God created you to be. Let Jesus shine through you and use your gifts, temperament, and personality.

Preparing the Preacher

We touched on different aspects of leading and preaching in service in Chapter 12, but I want to mention here that before you ever step on a platform to do any type of ministry, do a personal heart check. Before a service starts I close my eyes and imagine myself at the altar of repentance. I say things like, "Lord, I lay myself down before you today. Purify my mind. Purify my heart. Purify my motives. Wash over me. Cleanse me and prepare me to minister your Word today."

Your goal in preaching is not to deliver a word, but to connect people with God through his Word in ways that impact their lives and lead them to a response. Leading people to God begins with your personal journey to the presence of God at the altar of repentance. A preacher should never rush into a sacred place of ministry without repenting—acknowledging his or her personal need for forgiveness and grace.

The Art of Preaching

A call to preach is a sacred privilege, but the art of preaching is learned and requires time and training to become proficient. At times, preaching is a form of sacred storytelling. A good story teller is animated. As you tell the great stories in the Bible, lead the people into a full experience. What did it sound like? What did it look like? How did the people feel? Without taking away from the message with over-dramatization, keep people engaged and interested as you lead them to Jesus. When you tell "God stories" use voice inflection, facial expressions, and gestures to help you convey your message. Throw yourself into your story, look people in the eye, and make the listeners feel a part—move their emotions.

While you preach your stories, always remember to preach the Word. Biblical truths should be included in every message regardless of the audience, subject, or presentation method. The Word itself carries power and authority. Unsheath your "sword" and see what God will do. Be ready at all times, instant in season and out, with a Word-based message that will "reprove," "rebuke," or "exhort with all long suffering and doctrine" (see 2 Tim 4:2). To reprove means to reprimand, and to rebuke means to express sharp disapproval. These negative aspects are part of preaching at times. Clearly Scripture admonishes leaders to correct those in error and is filled with many "if-then" statements that include the potential for disaster and destruction for those who disobey. God's Word, however, is overwhelmingly positive. Patiently build people and teach them the ways and words of God in ways that encourage them in their faith. This should be the emphasis of your ministry. Preachers should be in the building business, not the demolition business. And as Wisdom teaches, we can build with our words or we can tear down with our words (see Prov 1:20, 9:1).

In any building program, the integrity of the materials used is of utmost importance to the structural integrity of the building being raised. When you are edifying (building) others through the preached word, faithfully deliver the truth as it was written, and as best you know how, present it as it was intended to be understood and applied to its hearers by its author. You simply must maintain biblical, sound doctrine. Yes, people need "how-to" information to navigate this life, but of primary importance are the foundations of the faith and the new birth experience. In his book, Preaching: *The Art of Narrative Exposition*, Calvin Miller said, "'how-to' has replaced 'repent and be baptized.'"[47] Saving the lost is the central element of the Great Commission. No one can live a victorious life if they are spiritually dead. Show people the way to eternal life, and from there add precept upon precept, line upon line.

When you preach the Word—even as you delve into Old Testament concepts—always include the gospel message: the death, burial, and resurrection of Jesus Christ.

After all, Jesus is the Word made flesh. The promises of the Old Testament are fulfilled in the New, and the heartbeat of Jesus was and is to seek and to save the lost. An evangelistic thread should be woven into the fiber of every message regardless of the chapter and book the text was taken from.

The Spiritual Aspect of Preaching

Preaching is more than delivering a message. It's a spiritual activity that releases the Word and Spirit of the Lord. Without the Spirit of God active among us, our sermons would be nothing more than lectures from an old book. But where the Spirit of the Lord is, miracles happen. We study, we pray, we structure our messages and prepare to give them as the Lord leads, but God is sovereign. He sometimes leads us beyond our notes into a flow of his presence. When you feel him enter in as you are speaking, be willing to set aside your message and entertain his presence. Your goal in preaching is to connect people with God. If the Lord wants to do that before you finish your message, that should be just fine with you. Trust God's Spirit to anoint you and guide you as you deliver his Word.

SIDENOTE
from J. T. Pugh

God's method of changing situations is to change people. His appeal is to the heart, and that by the gospel. When people are changed, other things take care of themselves. The greatest contribution the preacher can make to society is to preach the gospel that saves from sin.[48]

—J. T. Pugh
Pastor and Author; Odessa, Texas

Preaching Tips

- Have everything prepared to walk to the pulpit organized and ready to go—notes, Bible, props, hanky, and anything else needed.
- Smile.
- Keep personal problems out of the pulpit, and refrain from making the sacred desk a soap box.
- Butterflies may never go away entirely, so harness them and use them to your advantage. They will keep you on your toes.

- Never begin with an apology.
- Set the mood for your message. Take the microphone with confidence in what God has given you.
- Practice.
- Use variety and change things up so you can keep your audience's attention.
- Use quotes and clichés sparingly.
- Speak the truth with love and conviction.
- If someone disrupts a service (accidentally or intentionally) don't be afraid to stop the service. Depending on the circumstance, humor may work—a funny comment and then get back on track. Other times it can be effective to stop and ask the church to pray. This will draw people's attention back in the right direction.
- Interject humor into your messages when appropriate. Laughter relaxes people and opens their hearts. Many ministers start their sermons with funny stories.
- It's not necessary to introduce what you are going to do by saying things like, "Let me tell you a story," or, "In conclusion." When you begin a story, start the story. When you begin the conclusion, start the conclusion.
- While question-and-answer sessions are at times appropriate in teaching sessions, preaching is not the time to open the floor for discussion.
- Before you speak, spend time familiarizing yourself with the content of your message as much as possible, especially when preaching a message you have preached before. Keep things fresh.
- Work on developing timing. Pauses can be powerful.
- Be willing to be transparent. Transparency brings believability. Share challenges you have faced as well as personal humorous stories. Let people see your humanity and the grace of God at work in your life.
- Women ministers can be more emotional than men. When it's time to preach, be sober or be cheerful, but don't be overly tearful. While that depth of tenderness can be effective at a ladies-only event, it may make men uncomfortable.
- Although it's often easier to speak at ladies-only events, minister freely and confidently in mixed-gender meetings. Every assembly deserves the best you can bring.

- The volume of your voice doesn't determine the power of your message. Vary your tone and volume, but be aware constant "loudness" can be just as monotonous as a droning blandness.
- Use your volume and emotion with discretion a.k.a. "keep your powder dry." Soldiers carrying gunpowder keep it dry so their guns will fire as they should when needed. Be prepared and save your resources (your volume and emotion) for the time they will make the greatest impact.
- Learn to balance your volume and tone with the words you are conveying— they should match. Some women tend to giggle when they are nervous or don't know what to say next. Train yourself not to do this. Inappropriate expressions, verbal and non-verbal, can detract from your message.
- Line up in advance any help you may need with props, visuals, or anything else.
- While nobody likes to trip over their words, don't be discouraged if you do, especially as you are learning and developing. A right spirit can do more good than a perfect delivery.
- Speak clearly and distinctly, and try to avoid rushing through your message.
- Gestures and body language give life to a message, and the bigger the audience the bigger your gestures should be. Be aware, however, that motions like swaying back and forth, pacing, and holding on to the podium can distract.
- As difficult as it can be at times, watch recordings of yourself and evaluate where you can improve, preferably with a loving, insightful friend or two.
- Work to fine-tune nervous habits and eliminate repetitive words or interjections.
- Dress comfortably, but appropriately. You don't want to have to fidget or tug at clothing to keep things in place.
- Take Plato's advice: "Wise men speak because they have something to say, fools because they have to say something." Silence can glorify God more than an abundance of man's words.

Among Benjamin Franklin's many pithy comments are these, "Remember not only to say the right thing in the right place, but far more difficult still, to leave unsaid the wrong thing at the tempting moment."

Altar Call

Every message preached should be prepared and presented with a desired response in mind. When you minister, you want people to receive and apply the Word. It's your responsibility to make an appeal to action. End your messages by giving people an expressed opportunity to respond.

How you handle an altar call may vary according to the location or the content of the message. Traditionally, ministers have called people to respond by asking them to step out of the crowd by themselves and coming forward. Today ministers will often extend the invitation to the entire congregation. This practice makes it easier for those who are being tugged by the Holy Spirit to respond without feeling they are the "lonely sinner" in a group of watching saints. Regardless of your approach, the close of your message is critical. Invite the people to respond.

The Lord said through his prophet, "As the rain cometh down, and the snow from heaven, and returneth not thither, but watereth the earth, and maketh it bring forth and bud, that it may give seed to the sower, and bread to the eater: So shall my word be that goeth forth out of my mouth: it shall not return unto me void, but it shall accomplish that which I please, and it shall prosper in the thing whereto I sent it" (Isa 55:10–11). Those who invest their lives in preaching are guaranteed a return. It may not be fortune or fame, but God will bless his Word and it shall do what he intended it to do.

God wants you to succeed. The people in the congregation came to be ministered to, so even if they look staunch, most of them are hoping you hit the ball out of the park. Preaching is a high calling, and those God invites to join him in it are blessed to play an integral part in the most important work in the world—preparing people for eternity.

Ministry Matters

Let no man seek his own, but every man another's wealth.
1 Corinthians 10:24

I n this chapter, we will explore some different skillsets within ministry. As you read you may notice I have not covered every aspect of the five-fold ministry. Because I have not served in every position, I have limited comments to areas of my experience.

Ministering in the Prophetic Gift

In the New Testament, prophetic gifts were used by trusted leaders for course correction, to convey gifts, and to set people apart for ministry. A prophet can be a person who speaks on God's behalf on current day issues, as well as one who tells of events before they happen. They are never fortune tellers; they simply speak the words God gives them, which may tell of things to come (blessings or consequences) as people heed or disregard the Word of the Lord.

While some would not consider the ministry of teaching or preaching a prophetic ministry (even when well studied and well prayed over), there are times teaching has a prophetic aspect to it. For example, once when I was worshiping with my eyes closed the Lord gave me a mental image of a river of water flowing through the church sanctuary. It had detail that developed into a preached message that was a prophetic word for our church.

Considerations when operating in prophetic gifts:

- Be careful and concise, and make an effort to keep from being shrill or squeaky when you speak.

- Speak life, inspiration, and unity as much as possible.
- If you are pointing out where people have strayed, always do so with the purpose of restoration.
- Never publicly single out and correct leadership.
- Keep with the tone and course of the meeting you are in.
- Know the Word.
- If you say, "Thus saith the Lord," be sure you are hearing from God. There are times you may get an inclination or direction from God, and there may be times a person gets a picture or a word but is unsure of its meanings (see Acts 15:28). If the meaning is unclear, share the image, thought, or word, but don't give an authoritative interpretation or application.
- Learn to discern the false voice of the flesh that speaks under its own inspiration, ungodly spirits versus the pure words of the Spirit (see Heb. 5:14).
- All prophecy should be tested and proved against the Word of God. Today's prophecies must not contradict the prophetic word of Scripture.
- Recognize that prophets cannot turn on and off the anointing or flow of a gift. It operates at the will of God, not the will of man.
- Sometimes a prophet can discern the will of a person (what is in his or her heart to do). Be careful you don't misinterpret what you discern from a person's desire and speak about it as if it were the will of God for that person's life.
- If you are gifted in prophecy, be prepared that you may not always be understood by others and may experience some aloneness. The Old Testament prophets often lived in isolation.
- Be more concerned with pleasing and fearing God than men.
- Learn to keep a secret. Not all words are meant to be spoken when they are given, if ever.
- Be willing to take a risk with Jesus.
- While a prophetic word comes from the Spirit of God, use discretion and act considerately in public.

English author and evangelist Leonard Ravenhill said, "The prophet comes to set up that which is upset ... to call into line those who are out of line! He is unpopular because he opposes the popular in morality and spirituality ... there is not a more urgent national need than that we cry to God for a prophet!"[49]

That said, prophets are human beings. Not every word one speaks is an utterance from God. Prophets may "miss it" as they grow and develop in ministry. Growing in the prophetic should be a natural outflow of spending time with the Lord. Rest in him. Pray in the Spirit and seek the Lord. As you do, you will grow in his character and learn to better hear his voice, perceive his visions, and know his desires.

Ministering as an Evangelist

If you feel a call to the evangelistic field, speak with your pastor, especially if you are part of a church organization. Having your pastor's approval will bless any work you do for the Lord. Honoring your spiritual authority releases spiritual authority into your ministry, and leaders who would have you speak to their people want to know you are not a rogue, maverick minister. Being bold is one thing, but being unaccountable and freewheeling can raise legitimate concerns. Pastors, after all, are in a team-building business and they want to bring someone in to minister in their churches they can trust to enhance their team-building efforts.

Considerations for Evangelists:

- When you first begin speaking at venues other than your home church, get your pastor's approval on bookings. If married, confer with your husband; if unmarried, confer with your parents or other trusted counselors.
- Arrive at the location and the pulpit prepared to minister to the congregation, the pastor, and the pastor's family.
- Preach salvation to the lost and encouragement and revival to the church.
- Avoid issues that are areas of personal conviction. Leave pastoral issues to the pastor.
- Evangelists are often given messages for the church at large that they deliver over and again in many locations. When giving the same message in many locations, seek God for his anointing and his purpose in each service despite the familiarity of the message.
- Always leave a church better than when you arrived—no "messes" for the pastor to clean as a result of something you said or did.

- Do what the host pastor asks you to do. If you are given liberty, take it, but always work within the parameters you have been given.
- Be willing to do more than speak in the pulpit. Ministering to the ministry and helping build the church are part of the work of the evangelist.
- If you are asked to go on visitation, go. Be a blessing, but set boundaries on how much time you need to be prepared.
- Always conduct yourself properly. This is especially important for a female minister in a male-led church. Be friendly, but not flirty. Pay special attention to the pastor's wife (if applicable), and greet her first when possible.
- Be conscientious about spending church finances. When scheduling travel, be frugal with expenses. At restaurants, avoid ordering the most costly items.
- If you are staying in a pastor's home, be helpful and gracious to eat what is prepared. It's always a good idea to travel with snacks, but particularly if you have special dietary needs or restrictions. By all means, advise the pastor in advance if you have a serious food allergy.
- Unless the pastor gives approval otherwise, as much as possible keep your contact with church members limited to the pastor's presence. You are there to build the church by pointing people to Jesus and supporting their pastor's ministry.
- Don't listen to church members complain about their leadership.
- When operating in spiritual gifts with individuals, as much as possible speak where the pastor can hear what you are saying.
- If a situation occurs that causes you to feel uncomfortable or one you don't know how to handle, contact your pastor for prayer and advice.
- If you are invited to speak at a church that is outside your church's organization, run that request through the proper channels. Remember you are under constant scrutiny. How you present and conduct yourself will be important to the receptivity of your ministry. You can hinder your message and the work of God if you aren't careful.
- Be friendly. When you arrive, make eye contact with people. Shake their hands. Create an atmosphere where they already feel connected with you as a person before you begin speaking.
- Participate in the worship service.
- After you leave, send a thank you note to the pastor and church family.

- Build a network of preaching contacts. This is the product of building friendships with people wherever you go.
- To increase your opportunity for ministry, attend conferences and meetings where you can make connections. Work in the altar. Worship God. Build relationships.
- "Laying hands" on a man to pray for him is a practice that may vary for you as you minister in different situations. When traveling, examine the culture of the church and respect their custom. Talk to the pastor first. If you have liberty to operate in this manner, be discerning. Walk in the Spirit, but also be wise. If you are unsure how to publicly pray for a man, you can bring a man with you and ask him to lay hands on the person you are ministering to as you pray and speak into his life.

Jesus said, "Lift up your eyes, and look on the fields; for they are white already to harvest" (John 4:35). Evangelists continually look to the field with their ears tuned and their messages ready. If God called you to evangelize, he called you to succeed, and he will open the right doors and opportunities as you learn to hear his voice and follow the leading of his Spirit.

Ministering as an Administrator or Pastoral Assistant

Being an effective assistant presents a unique set of ministry opportunities and challenges. If the Lord positions you as a "number two," your number one priority is to serve the leader he placed over you. More than being a "yes girl," being an assistant means serving your God-appointed leader's God-given dreams and visions—not yours. That in no way diminishes the gifts and brain the Lord gave you to use; however, your job as assistant is to make your pastor or leader fulfill with excellence what God has called him or her to do.

Knowing your leader's vision and heart well will help you fulfill your role, especially in times of his or her absence. Having great communication is a must, but a servant's heart will be the key to your success. Your pastor should give you his or her vision—a clear job description with parameters and authority, specific tasks, and protocols to follow. If you are unsure about a task, it's almost always best to avoid making assumptions. Ask for clarification. This will help you accomplish your job and also reassure your pastor that you are being very intentional about supporting his or her objectives.

In the times you don't have clear direction, be observant. Whatever you see that needs to be done, do it—anything from campus maintenance to ministering to people in need of comfort or counsel. If you have authority to do it, do it.

When you have something to say to your pastor or leader, say it with clarity and confidence. Don't, however, beat a dead horse. Share your ideas, but then step back and allow your leader to have the final say. If he or she should make a mistake—and you can be sure that will happen at some point—any "I told you so" look or comment from you will not help, neither will it elevate you in any positive way.

You and Your Leader

When you disagree with your leader, refrain from dumping your feelings anywhere but to the Lord in prayer. In public, always maintain a united front. Your church will not be blessed or strengthened by knowing you and your pastor are not in synch. If, after prayer, you still have serious concerns, share them directly with your pastor. In areas of difference of opinion, it's your job as assistant to support the leader's vision. If a Christian leader is in unrepentant sin, that is a different matter altogether. You do not have to stay under that type of ministry. The Lord may have sent you to an assignment for a season, and when the Lord releases you, you can remove yourself from the influence of immoral or corrupt leadership.

Although issues at times can be very serious, I often say, tongue-in-cheek, "I don't agree with myself all the time." No two people will ever agree 100 percent of the time. You won't agree with your pastor's every decision, but you can still give your support—not only to the position, but also to the person.

As an assistant, you may find yourself in the position of hearing your leader's frustrations. In the times he or she is discouraged and blows off steam, extend some grace. The same grace you give should boomerang back to you when you need it, and you will.

As we discussed previously, attitude is incredibly important. However close your relationship with your pastor may be, be careful not to expect him or her to be your best friend. It's not your pastor's job to meet your emotional needs. You are there to serve. Resist being offended when ministry seems like a job, because you do have a job to do.

If you have a personal counseling need, go to your pastor first and get advice about the best way to handle any issues of concern. If outside counsel is necessary, your pastor may be able to recommend just the right person.

When the Saints Come Marching In

Be bold enough to speak up when people are gossiping or being derogatory. Try to turn a negatively focused conversation to the positive. Refocus disgruntled members away from your pastor's humanity and to his or her position as leader. Encourage them to pray for their spiritual leaders. Do your best to comfort and kindly refocus critical church members.

Be your pastor's eyes and ears and provide any necessary information. Surprises in ministry aren't usually the good kind of surprises. At the same time you are being your pastor's eyes and ears, also be his or her echo. Say what you have heard your pastor say in ministry, vision casting, and counseling. And remember the importance of not saying what should not be said. The importance of confidentiality cannot be overstated, and a lack of discretion can destroy a church or your ministry. Keep the confidence of your pastor and the congregation.

Business Details

When it comes to the practical and tactical, make sure you make note of what your pastor says to you, especially in regards to any assigned responsibilities. Then follow through and follow up. Handle the details and allow your pastor the freedom to focus on the big picture. As much as possible, be available to help at any time for any need. The unexpected is sure to visit on a regular basis.

After your family, serving as your pastor's assistant should be your number one priority and primary place you minister. Opportunities to minister elsewhere may present themselves, but be careful to maintain your priorities and focus, and be attentive to your leader, especially when in public. As inconspicuously as possible, attend to his or her needs.

If you have been given purchasing power, make sure you get approval before buying anything beyond normal operational expenses. Every pastor appreciates frugality with church finances, and good stewardship is a must. If you make a mistake, don't make excuses. If you get something wrong, make it right if you can, and then apologize and move on.

An assistant should be a faucet, not a drain. Pray. Uplift. Refresh your leader. Be loyal. Be faithful. Be a buffer and a sounding board. Refuse to gossip. Correct whatever problems you can. Ease your leader's burdens; they are heavier than you know.

SIDENOTE
from Diana Reed

The gift of administration is mentioned in 1 Corinthians 12:28, along with many other important gifts in the body of Christ. To see how important this gift is to effective church ministry, one just needs to look in the book of Acts and observe how church leaders came to identify problems or needs in the church and how they looked for individuals, both men and women, who could help bring order to chaos and who would assist leaders in accomplishing their vision. Just as the skeleton of a human body provides the framework for all movement in that body, administrators are the bones of an organization and ministry.

As a young woman I felt the call of God into full-time ministry. At the time, I didn't know where that path would lead, but I was determined to follow it. I was privileged to evangelize in my late teen years. I gained valuable experience while working for wonderful pastors and district leaders. Teaching is my passion and I am thankful for the many opportunities I have had through the years to share the Word of God with others and see their lives transformed. After I married, my life was spent in pastoral ministry which was very rewarding. Woven throughout all of these ministry experiences, administration played a role in my contribution to God's kingdom.

When my husband passed away suddenly at the age of 36 and my life in pastoral ministry came to a screeching halt, I earnestly sought God for his path for my life. I was in new, uncharted waters. My heart's desire was to continue working for God, but how could I support myself and my two young children in full-time ministry? Was this even possible?

I asked God to align his provision for my family, the gifts of administration that he put in me, and a place in his kingdom that needed those gifts. Prayer answered! Currently I am the church administrator of a wonderful thriving church in a metro area. I have been able to support my family while working full time in ministry. I often reflect with humility that God miraculously answered my prayer. The scope of my ministry has grown, and I serve as an associate pastor (with a general ministerial license) all while working as a single mom. The work of the ministry is clearly supported by administrators who know how to understand the vision of a passionate leader and help craft the plan to bring the vision to pass. As a church administrator, I have the privilege of walking alongside pastors and ministers with a great vision for our city, our region, and the world, and helping them execute their vision all for the glory of God. The gift of administration that God put in this lady has truly been a gift to me.

—Diana L. Reed
Associate Pastor and Church Administrator; Cincinnati, Ohio

For additional resources and instruction, visit the Preach Like a Lady website.

Video classes and module training offered will include:
- Practical Helps on Studying, Journaling, Reading, and Writing Sermons
- Spiritual Disciplines of Prayer, Meditation, Fasting, Rest, Giving, and Self-Discipline
- Leadership Issues like Delegation, Ministerial Ethics, Financial Stewardship and the Law.

www.PreachLikeALady.com

PART II

Records and Rationales
A biblical and historical investigation of the
roles of women in ministry

In the Beginning

So God created man in his own image, in the image of God
created he him; male and female created he them.
Genesis 1:27

"In the beginning, God created...."
These powerful words established the record of God's original design for humanity.

Genesis 1:26 and 1:27 are parallel verses. Biblical writers utilized parallel verses to strengthen a point they were making. The complete meaning of both verses is not understood in one verse or the other, but both verses together deliver the complete meaning.[50] When a writer utilized parallel verses, "Verse A" and "Verse B" were not meant to be treated as independent statements even if their structures formed grammatically complete sentences.

As you read Genesis 1:26–27 below, bear in mind these two verses form one complete thought—the second verse strengthening and adding more information to the first.

"And God said, Let us make man in our image, after our likeness: and let them have dominion over the fish of the sea, and over the fowl of the air, and over the cattle, and over all the earth, and over every creeping thing that creepeth upon the earth. So God created man in his own image, in the image of God created he him; male and female created he them."

This couplet reveals God's original plan in making mankind—to be like him. Both male and female were made in his image and both were given dominion over all the earth. In Genesis 1:27, the word "man" translated from the Hebrew word *'adam* refers to "humankind" which comes in two forms, male and female. Both are made in the image of God. Neither alone bears his full image.

The "image of God" indicates resemblance, like a shadow. Since God is a Spirit,[51] he has no physical body. Therefore, we shouldn't consider his "being" in relation to the physical bodies of human beings. Instead, God's image refers to the spirit nature he created in Adam and Eve. As spiritual beings housed in human containers, the Lord made humans to function as his representatives, doing the work he gave them of ruling over the earth and creating life in earth. They worked together—one complementing the other to fulfill the purposes of God.

Our Creator is neither male nor female. The Lord is a spirit, and his essence is reflected in the joint creation of male and female. Although pronouns like "him" and "his" are used by people to communicate about God, the Lord has no gender identity and should not be considered masculine based on a biblical usage of gender-specific pronouns. In fact, the Word talks about God's arms, eyes, hands, wings, and breasts, among other anatomical terms. Before the birth of Jesus, the Spirit of God had no physical body, so how can these anatomical terms apply? There must be additional information to consider.

"Our Father, which art in heaven" is more than just our Father. Scripture calls the Lord "husband" (see Isa 54:5). The same "being" as father and husband can only be rationalized when the Word is approached with the understanding that each description of God reveals a different facet of his nature, his character, or humanity's relationship with him.

It has been said the image of God is a "double image" that transcends gender and has both masculine and feminine characteristics. The Lord "bore" his people like a mother bears a child (see Deut 32:18). He likened the way he comforted his people to a mother comforting her child, and a mother hen gathering her chicks (see Isa 66:13; Matt 23:37).

In Genesis 1, Scripture tells us that Adam was made from the dust of the ground and given the breath of life from God. In the second chapter of Genesis, the Bible flashes back and zooms in on the sixth day of creation. Genesis 1:27 provided an overview. In Genesis 2:18, God revealed an important detail. Up to this point, everything he had made he deemed good, but in verse 18, he said it was *not* good for Adam to be alone. He recognized the longing in Adam's heart, his feelings of "incompleteness" even while living in paradise, and the Lord determined to make him a "help meet." Creation without woman was not good. It was incomplete.

"And the Lord God caused a deep sleep to fall upon Adam, and he slept: and
he took one of his ribs, and closed up the flesh instead thereof; And the rib,
which the Lord God had taken from man, made he a woman, and brought her
unto the man" (Gen 2:21–22).

I believe God knew the longing Adam had because it was an experience he shared
with him. The Lord had no one of his kind, no one "like" him, so he decided to make
one. The Lord scooped up dirt and made Adam and then Eve from the same building
materials—all with an end-goal in view, his bride.

Understanding "Help Meet"

The order of creation never implies a lesser value, capability, or an authoritative
hierarchy (a system of ranking one person above another). The question, however, is
still out for many: What exactly is a "help meet?" Does the use of this word indicate Eve
was "subordinate," "suitable," or "similar" to Adam?

The term "help meet" is rendered from two Hebrew words. The first is `ezer,
which means "aid" and "help." It comes from a root word that's "primary idea lies in
girding, surrounding, hence defending."[52] These meanings certainly do not imply
weakness, but rather strength. In fact, the Lord calls himself Israel's `ezer in Scripture
(see Hos 13:9). He is the help that comes from the hills and the shield about his
people (see Ps 121:1; Deut 33:29; Ps 33:20). He was their military ally. Certainly
no one would propose that when the Lord was identified as Israel's helper he was
subordinate or under Israel's authority.

The second Hebrew word *neged* translated "meet" brings additional clarity to this
compound description of woman. It means "the front part" and "as over against" which
implies things that are alike but are being compared. Specifically, in reference to
Genesis 1:27, the meaning of *neged* is "corresponding to him." In rabbinical teaching
the word *neged* was often used "in speaking of things which are like one another."[53]
Eve was created by God for a face-to-face relationship with Adam.

Adam looked into Eve's face and
saw the image of God.
Eve looked into Adam's face and saw the same.

When Adam first identified Eve in verse 23, he did not give her a proper name, but designated her "kind" and gender. Similar to the way "tigress" is the feminine of tiger, woman is the feminine form of man, or "man-ness."

The use of the word *neged* implies Eve was Adam's spiritual and intellectual equal. She was made of the same substance and essence. She was created to be a strength, help, and blessing, and God placed her right in front of Adam—a "help corresponding to him i.e. equal and adequate to himself."[54] The *Septuagint* (a Koine Greek translation of the Old Testament from the Hebrew Scriptures used widely by the Jews dispersed through the Roman Empire) translates the "helper" Adam could not find in Genesis 2:20 as the Greek word *homoios*.[55] This word means "like, resembling, similar"[56] and signifies equality. In addition, *homoios* not only relates to appearance and form, but "of ability, condition, nature," as well as like in "action, thought."[57]

The Lord presented Eve to Adam in the Garden to transform his "not good" to "very good." She was his friend, lover, and partner. The first couple shared in divine origin, sacred purpose, failure, and prophetic hope.

Adam was overjoyed when he met the flesh of his flesh and bone of his bone. In a sense, he was meeting part of himself repackaged into a similar and corresponding mate—one of his own kind who was neither inferior nor superior. In fact, mankind's first recorded words are found in Adam's loving response to Eve. "This is now bone of my bones, and flesh of my flesh: she shall be called Woman, because she was taken out of Man. Therefore shall a man leave his father and his mother, and shall cleave unto his wife: and they shall be one flesh" (Gen 2:23–24).

God made Adam from the dust of the earth, but then fashioned Eve from his substance. He took the "she" out of "he," separating his image into two distinct beings. Although they were created at different times, they were not truly separate creations, but distinct renderings of the same Creator who has feminine, masculine, and gender-neutral attributes.

Yes, the creation account gives a chronological order of formation, but before the fall in a sinless environment, the Bible does not record a governmental hierarchy. Adam and Eve depended on each other to fulfill the will of God. The Lord gave the man and the woman identical charges—to be fruitful and have dominion. These plural commands were given to both Adam and Eve, who were commissioned to lead and govern the earth side by side.

The Fall

The book of Genesis, although it contains a wealth of knowledge, does not give information "before the beginning." When Adam and Eve came on the scene, the devil was already there. From a human perspective, life could have been easier without the devil on location. But God had his purposes.

In the Garden the Lord planted a tree and told man not to eat from it. Some have questioned why he would do such a thing. Perhaps he placed the tree in the Garden as a reminder of who he was and always would be. He gave mankind authority and dominion, but he wanted them to remember he would remain Sovereign over all.

When Satan approached Eve in the Garden, he made her a poor offer. She and Adam were already reigning together. They already had dominion. They were already like God in essence—created in his image. They already had knowledge of good. What Satan misrepresented as an opportunity for more was actually an offer to know evil.

It is important to note that according to the text Eve and Satan were not the only two on the scene at the time she ate the fruit. Eve "took of the fruit thereof, and did eat, and gave also unto her husband with her; and he did eat" (see Gen 3:6). Scripture seems to indicate Adam was in the Garden during the exchange, but Satan spoke to Eve instead of her husband.

Some have proposed Eve was more vulnerable to temptation than Adam. If that were true, it would seem to be a faulty premise to attribute any alleged weakness to her make-up. Eve was made of the same substance as her husband. If Adam had not wanted what the serpent offered, it seems he would have intervened. Consider that God directly gave Adam the prohibition to refrain from eating from the tree before Eve was created (see Gen 2:16). His instruction was apparently transmitted to Eve second-hand. I would propose that if there was a greater weakness in Eve (a point that could be argued either way), her vulnerability could be attributed to her lack of first-hand knowledge of God's words regarding the tree. The fault may well lay in her education, not essential nature; in a failed communication, not a frail, feminine character.

Addressing the Issue

When discussing the dialogue that followed the fall, it's important to remember that God was aware of everything that had happened. He knew all the details, but when he entered the garden, he called for Adam (see Gen 3:9). Adam, in response, turned the Lord's attention to his wife (see Gen 3:12), after which God directly addressed Eve.

This is an interesting occurrence in light of how life played out in the centuries that followed. By the time Jesus was born, a woman was not allowed to testify or speak on her own behalf. But in the Garden, God (knowing the woman had failed) addressed Eve directly. Adam did not speak for her—in fact, he blamed her in an attempt to deflect God away from him. In the Bible, however, we find no record of Eve being held accountable by God for the fall. In fact, the apostle Paul repeated several times that one person was responsible, and in two places identified Adam as the one who led the human race into sin (see Rom 5:14; 1 Tim 2:14).

Some would withhold ministry and leadership opportunities for women in the church on the basis of Eve's failure, but Adam failed as well.

Consequences of the Fall

Curses. God issued two of them after the fall: one on the earth and one on Satan. Adam was not cursed. Eve was not cursed. Cursing implies a loathing that was not in the heart of God for his people. Disobeying the Word, however, brought severe consequences to humanity.

The curses issued in Genesis disturbed the condition of the earth and the standing of the devil who had presented himself in the Garden as a serpent. The serpent was identified as "more subtil than any beast of the field" (see Gen 3:1). The word subtil means "shrewd," "crafty," "sly," "sensible," and "prudent." Many commentary writers support the position that before the fall serpents were some form of erect creature. The serpent after the fall was "cursed above all cattle, and above every beast of the field" (see Gen 3:14). The Lord said, "Upon thy belly shalt thou go, and dust shalt thou eat all the days of thy life" (see Gen 3:14).

Mankind had been created from the dust of the earth, and as the result of sin, the dust of the earth they would become again. Satan would slither in the dust on his belly at the feet of men and women. Even more significantly, the ultimate defeat of Satan would come through the offspring of the woman he deceived. Jesus, the seed of Eve, would bruise the serpent's head and the serpent would "bruise his heel" (see Gen 3:15).

Banished from Eden, Adam and Eve were about to experience a new, foreign way of life. The Lord addressed Eve first with her consequences. "Unto the woman he said, I will greatly multiply thy sorrow and thy conception; in sorrow thou shalt bring forth children" (see Gen 3:16.) Eve would now suffer in childbearing.

Eve's second consequence affected her relationship with her husband. The King James Version translates it this way: "And thy desire *shall be* to thy husband, and he shall rule over thee" (see Gen 3:16). Note God did not vilify Eve, but defined the results of her sin. From that time forward she would live in a world that would be home to both the creation of God and the penalty of sin.

It might be important to note that "shall be" in the above verse is italicized, which means it is not in the original text. Eve's desire to Adam doesn't appear to be the result of a command of God, but again, a result of sin. This statement could well have been prophetic in nature and was certainly fulfilled. *Young's Literal Translation* renders this portion of the verse: "and toward thy husband [is] thy desire, and he doth rule over thee."

As a consequence of the fall Adam and Eve's relationship shifted. Eve would from thereafter have an increased longing for her husband. A reflection of this increased longing can be seen in the way women often turn to men for affirmation and value. Some women are overly dependent on men. This could be a characteristic of woman's fallen nature, but it does not appear to be her created, original nature.

The last of the Lord's words to Eve were, "And he shall rule over thee." The word translated "rule" is the Greek word *mashal*. It has several meanings. Its first use is found in reference to the sun ruling the day and the moon ruling the night (see Gen 1:16). Abraham had a servant who ruled over all he had (see Gen 24:2). Joseph was a ruler in Egypt (see Gen 45:26). To rule can certainly mean to have dominion, but it also has a gentler side. The sun rules the day, but it provides life-giving light to the world. A steward's role, like that of Abraham's steward or Joseph as governor, was to take good care of someone else's possessions for the benefit of others. This brings to mind the words of the Lord in 2 Samuel 23:3, "He that ruleth over men must be just, ruling in the fear of God."

From the beginning, one of the strongest elements of humanity's fallen nature has been the struggle for control. God's original intention was not a patriarchal order, but that a man would leave his father and mother and cleave to his wife.

Proponents of patriarchy *ad infinitum* often cite creation order as evidence of male supremacy, but this simply does not reconcile with Scripture. Some claim Adam "naming" Eve shows his authority over her, but he did not give her the name *Chavvah* (translated Eve) until after the fall. He merely called her "woman." *Chavvah* means "life" or "living" and comes from a root word that means "to breathe." The meaning of Eve's name has greater significance because it was given *after* the fall. Even in the face of their judgment for sin and impending deaths, Adam gave his wife a name that held a prophetic meaning. Life and breath would come through his beloved. Humanity would continue and victory would come (see 1 Cor 15:54).

The "governorship" of a husband over his wife (not all men over all women) is a result of the fall. The husband/wife conflict was part of the curse, not God's original plan, and a Christian man should never "lord over" his wife, especially when she has a longing for his affection and approval.

If naming a person indicates rulership of the person named, the fact that Eve named Seth should be considered (see Gen 4:25). Rachel and Leah named the tribes of Israel. Jacob overrode Rachel in her chosen name for their son Benjamin, but 11 out of 12 is quite a record. Before Joseph learned of Mary's pregnancy, the angel of the Lord told her to name the baby Jesus.

In today's world, men and women continue to suffer the effects of the fall—spiritually and physically. Although in many nations women participate in society and government, men have more often than not ruled and dominated, even in Christian circles. But is this the way the body of Christ should conduct itself? Did the after-the-fall condition of the husband/wife relationship establish male rulership and dominance in society at large and in the church for all time? Should the status of

Christian women in the church be based on the post-fall consequences of sin or on the atoning work of Jesus?

Restored by Christ

For as in Adam all die, even so in Christ shall all be made alive.
1 Corinthians 15:22

God's creation undoubtedly suffered the effects of mankind's fall, but did its failure forever alter his intentions for humanity? Did the disobedience of Adam and Eve intrinsically change the Lord's purpose that men and women, united together, would bear his image in the world? Undoubtedly, the glory of God was stripped away, revealing mankind's nakedness, but consider the words of the wisest man on earth, "Whatsoever God doeth, it shall be for ever: nothing can be put to it, nor any thing taken from it" (Ecc 3:14).

The blood of Jesus did a mighty work at Calvary. Through Christ the world was offered salvation, but not all respond to the opportunity. Whoever accepts the Lord's gracious gift, however, becomes a joint heir of Christ and partaker of the reversal of the fall's spiritual effects.

Born again believers no longer live under the repercussions of disobedience. The righteousness of Jesus makes them new creatures and brings them into a new spiritual realm. Yes, mankind still lives in a fallen world, but within the church redemption reigns. *Logos*, the very plan of God, became redemption and brought redemption. The power of grace is that it brings restoration of what was lost. Mankind's loving Father did not abandon his children to the consequences of sin.

The work of the cross set humanity free from the curse of the law and offers liberty and restoration to those who believe. In Christ all things can be made new. Jesus restores. Jesus renames. Jesus resurrects.

Some glad morning there will be a restoration of "all things" (see Acts 3:21). Meanwhile, for believers, what was wasted spiritually in Eden is now restored. Paul wrote

Romans 8:20–21 to let Christ-followers know that while there is sin, death, and decay in the world, these curses will someday disappear altogether. The world is in a process of yielding to the will of God, and it will one day join in glorious freedom from sin.

But how does this apply to the role of women in ministry in the church today? Did the blood of Jesus provide the opportunity for all to be restored to a pre-fall condition in relationship with God? In relationship with other believers? Did not Christ redeem humanity and set believers free from both the constraining power of sin and their corrupt natures?

For those who are in Christ, sin no longer dominates. Believers are restored. They not only have access to God but have God-given authority to serve as his priests and ambassadors in the community of his reconciled people. Outside the church darkness and sin promenade with the prince of this world, but God's people are part of a new covenant.

Jesus came to earth on a mission—to restore abundant life (see John 10:10). He imparted his righteousness and divine nature into sinful, fallen lives. As the first Adam represented all humanity in the fall; Jesus, the last Adam, represented all humanity on the cross. Through his sacrifice the very life and nature of God were imparted back into the world (see 1 Cor 15:45).

The Lord implanted his redemption plan into the womb of a "daughter of Eve." In his flesh Jesus abolished the hostility between Jews and Gentiles (see Eph 2:16). He brought two opposite peoples together and made them one. This harmonizes with Galatians 3:28 that proclaims in Christ there are no divisions, "There is neither Jew nor Greek, there is neither bond nor free, there is neither male nor female: for ye are all one in Christ Jesus." Through his sacrificial death, Jesus removed the partitions for all, allowing equal access to every believer to the presence of God, the family of God, and the service of God (see Eph 2:14).

The Power of Pentecost

Jesus accepted women as disciples, and this precedent continued with his followers after his death, burial, and resurrection. Before and after his ascension, both men and women were baptized as part of their new birth experiences. This was incredibly significant, because in the old covenant only men could be circumcised, and circumcision was the outward sign of covenant with God. Through baptism women experienced the "circumcision made without hands" (see Col 2:11–12) and the infilling of the Spirit gave them full membership and participation in the church (see Acts 2:38).

In the upper room both men and women received the gift of the Holy Spirit and individually acquired the power of God in their lives (see Acts 2:4). Every person present spoke divine utterances and extolled the wonders of God among the people. It was the dawn of a new age, the church age, and it changed the world forever.

On that day, as men and women from all stations of life and nationalities heard the believers speaking in tongues and the message of salvation in Christ, their hearts were pricked. Joel had prophesied it, and the Lord fulfilled his promise. He poured out his Spirit upon all flesh, and the sons and daughters prophesied (see Joel 2:28).

Not only was the fulfillment of this "all flesh" promise significant to women, it opened the door to Gentiles. With the outpouring of the Holy Spirit every perceived hindrance was stripped away and mankind entered an age in which every person could access God for him or herself regardless of race, gender, or social status. It was what they had been waiting for—what Jesus had promised would empower them to be his witnesses.

The fact that every man and woman received the Holy Spirit evidenced God's intention that all believers should participate in the Great Commission—one of the main reasons the Lord gave for receiving divine empowerment. To further bolster this point, notice how the outpouring happened on the only Jewish feast day women were required to attend (see Deut 16:1–15). Jewish women were not commanded to participate in other feast days (see Deut 16:16). On this day of celebration, however, women followers of Jesus assembled with the men in the upper room, and in the streets of Jerusalem women would have been among those who heard the Spirit-filled believers preach the good news of salvation by Christ Jesus.

Following the outpouring of the spirit of God on the day of Pentecost, ministry roles in the infant church took a dynamic shift from a priestly Judaic hierarchy to a new form of government. Scripture mentions many women by name, including Dorcas and Lydia, as disciples and followers of Christ. Many women (including the mother of Jesus) remained with the eleven of Jesus's disciples after the Lord's ascension, and they devoted themselves to prayer (see Acts 1:14).

Women took part in coed services alongside men. In addition, the Bible mentions the presence of many "chief women" and many honorable Greek women (see Acts 17:4, 17:12). A reading through the book of Acts and the Epistles lets us know churches met predominantly in women's homes and most likely under their leadership.

Further reading in the book of Acts reveals that although Peter received the Holy Spirit and preached the incredible message on the day of Pentecost, he lacked revelation about the magnitude of what God had done. Oddly enough, this man who had no lineage or education—this fisherman turned apostle by the grace of God— held to some prejudices the Lord had to deal with by sending him a special vision (see Acts 10:9-16). As a result of this spiritual encounter, Peter received revelation of God's plan to include the Gentiles in salvation. His concepts and ministry transformed and he became a minister and advocate for receiving Gentiles as fellow members of the New Testament church.

Like Peter, contemporary believers should be willing to evaluate their perception of ministry roles in the church to determine if they are based on God's intentions or accepted cultural norms. God is no respecter of persons. There may be those who, like Peter, have not offered all their preconceptions to the Lord. Our church and ministry paradigms should agree with God's revealed plan and the whole counsel of his Word.

Some confusion may lie in a faulty misapplication of the role of the Old Testament priesthood to the structure of the New Testament ministry, but the old model was never God's plan. It could be that a few intentionally corrupted God's plan for personal gain and power and what they established as norms have been accepted by God-fearing people in the church at large. But the Lord was careful to teach his believers not to lord one over another. In fact, he was very clear when he gave a counter-culture directive to his disciples in regards to their call to leadership: "It shall not be so among you" (see Matt 20:26).

In the early church, preaching was not relegated only to men, but women also preached. As believers everywhere continue to receive the gift of the Spirit, sinners become saints. Individuals are restored spiritually to a pre-fall condition with God. Both men and women have direct access to the throne of God. The curse of sin is broken, and believers become part of one body. In Christ—in the spirit-realm—gender is no longer relevant; and a caste ranking of humanity simply does not apply.

In Christ

The body of Christ is a unique spiritual organism composed of men and women from all ethnicities and social stratum. The Word gives a picture of heaven in which the redeemed includes "every kindred, and tongue, and people, and nation" (see Rev 5:8).

In Christ, Jews and non-Jews had access to the righteousness of God. It sprang from faith and led believers into more faith (see Rom 1:16–8). As faith grows, believers have clearer insights into the righteousness of God. Paul, the writer of Galatians, Romans, Timothy, and Corinthians certainly experienced the transforming power that leads from "faith to faith" (see Acts 9).

As a Pharisee, Paul (when he was known as Saul) would likely have started his morning with the prayer recited daily by devout Jewish men. According to Rabbi Judah bar Ilai (the second-century sage most frequently mentioned in the *Mishna*, ancient rabbinic literature), the following benedictions were recited by Jewish men every day:

Paul (who wrote passages some believe restrict women from ministry) authored a pivotal verse of Scripture: "There is neither Jew nor Greek, there is neither slave nor free, there is neither male nor female; for you are all one in Christ Jesus" (Gal 3:28). Any perceived restrictions written by Paul elsewhere must harmonize with this passage that clearly expresses the basic composition and function of the church. All are one.

1. Blessed be he who did not make me a Gentile.
2. Blessed be he who did not make me a woman.
3. Blessed be he who did not make me an uneducated man (bondman or slave).

Imagine the hopeless state for women. Gentile men could be circumcised and accepted as converts to Judaism. Slaves could earn or be given their freedom. But a woman had no hope of ever "bettering" her station in life.

The good news of the gospel contains the good word that in Christ, racial, gender, and social differences are irrelevant. They are transcended. This concept does not negate the family structure, but affirms that women in the body of Christ have equal access and opportunity to a relationship with God and function in ministry. This overturned hundreds of years of social history in every major culture. What we assume is ordinary is actually ordinary because it was extraordinary.

Could it be that in writing to the Galatians Paul expressly identified the three categories the daily Jewish prayer demeaned as subordinate in rank to the basest male Jew (Gentiles, slaves, and females)? "There is neither Jew nor Greek, bond nor free, male nor female." Was Paul revealing to this new community of believers that discrepancies held in Judaism no longer applied in the church of Jesus Christ?

> The concept of parity in the function of the members of the body reflects back to Eden and forward to heaven. In the Spirit-filled church of God, gender is no criteria to serve the Lord.

This passage in Galatians acknowledges the reality of distinctions in gender, ethnicity, and social standing. In Paul's day, there was also the legal standing of free and slave. Paul reiterated his Galatians 3:28 statement in Colossians when he spoke of the unity within the church. For those who "put on the new man ... there is neither Greek nor Jew, circumcision nor uncircumcision, Barbarian, Scythian, bond nor free: but Christ is all, and in all" (Col 3:10–11).

These passages are important to anyone who might be discriminated against. Imagine these scenarios in the first century church:

- Slaves hear Paul declare spiritual emancipation in Christ.
- Gentiles receive the revelation that God would accept them regardless of their bloodline and without adhering to all the Jewish ceremonial law and rites.
- Women are given a public voice and allowed to function in the congregation of believers.

When evaluating Paul's words, remember the apostle was dealing with relationships within the church that did not align with the customs of his contemporary secular or Jewish society. For instance, slavery was a common practice, but in the assembly of believers a slave was free to be a fully participating member.

In Christ any differences recognized elsewhere should not have impacted a believer's position or practice in the church.

In most churches today, discrimination based on a person's race would not be tolerated. The color of a person's skin could neither elevate nor bar them from ministry. Ideally, this same freedom should be enjoyed by every member of the church. Allowing for differences in giftings and callings, every Christian is of equal value through the blood of Jesus.

In Paul's letters he addressed the churches "as they were," while he held up a standard of "this is what you should be." The early church came with a lot of baggage from strict religious orthodoxy to paganism. Believers were new creatures in Christ, but they were not mature. They were in the process of being discipled and growing in their understanding of the Lord's ways in a culture that was often not on the same page as Christianity.

Paul's declaration "there is neither Jew nor Greek, bond nor free, male nor female" in Galatians is sandwiched between two verses that specify:

1. Who he was referencing (those who had been baptized into Christ), and
2. The result (baptized believers are now in the lineage of Father Abraham and heirs according to God's promise).

As a member of the family of God every believer, male or female, has an inheritance. After all, people simply wear robes of flesh over their eternal souls. Body and soul create one harmonious unit, but one does not define the other. I am not a Caucasion woman. I am a soul, enlivened by the spirit of God, wearing the "garment" of a Caucasion woman. As long as a believer is wearing his or her "wedding garment," they should receive the full benefits of their invitation to be part of the bride of Christ.

First Century Culture and Biblical History

This thing was not done in a corner.
Acts 26:26

To correctly understand the New Testament requires some study of ancient Jewish and Roman history. The following is a brief tour of the land and culture in which Jesus was born.

In 510 BC, ancient Greece emerged from the fall of a tyrannical reign in the fifth and fourth centuries BC. Following the subsequent leadership and death of Alexander the Great, classical Greece entered what is known as the Hellenistic period. The Hellenistic period was a time the Greeks saw great advances in sciences and a transition from Classical Greek philosophies to one that embraced decadence, pleasure-seeking, new gods, and eastern deities. It was at this time Greek influence peaked and spread throughout Europe, Africa, and Asia.

Through a series of wars, Rome emerged as a super power in the second century BC and brought the Hellenistic period to a close when it acquired both Greece and Asia Minor. After a period of instability and unrest, the Roman Empire eventually gained control of the entire Mediterranean basin and several other lands including Germania, Britannia, and Mesopotamia.[58]

A New World

Greek and Roman civilizations interlocked into what became known as the Greco-Roman world. This Mediterranean world was bilingual, with widespread use of Latin and Greek. It was ruled by the Roman Empire with assigned governors and kings to rule on its behalf. Greek philosophies, dress, and entertainments were pervasive in the

Hellenized urban areas of the Empire—the places where Greek ideas and customs were adopted. The Empire, for the most part, was controlled by a small wealthy elite, and there was a huge gap between the "haves" and the "have-nots." The population included a large number of slaves, often taken as the spoils of battle.[59]

At the time of Jesus's birth, the Mediterranean world was in the middle of a long period of relative peacefulness. It was a period called Pax Romana, which is Latin for "Roman Peace." During this 200-year era, the population of the Roman Empire grew to an estimated 70 million people, and the empire experienced unprecedented peace and economic prosperity. Roads were built, commerce was established, and people traveled freely.

Religious philosophies varied greatly and included:
- Dualism (Plato's "two worlds" view)
- Stoicism (Zeno's reason-based philosophy)
- Epicureanism (Epicurus's doctrine of "pleasure is the highest good")
- Gnosticism (ancient heresies that stressed gaining hidden knowledge)
- "Mystery Religions" (secret cults with private initiation ceremonies)
- Judaism (the monotheistic religion of the Jews).[60]

The most influential religion in the first centuries of the Roman Empire involved the "Mystery Religions." In the Greco-Roman world there was no lack of deities. According to their writings, mythological gods and goddesses (the "immortals") were not of human origin. Roman and Greek gods and goddesses were quite similar in nature, but bore different names. For instance, in Roman mythology, Venus was worshipped as the goddess of erotic love, beauty, and fertility; while Greeks venerated Aphrodite for the same reasons.

In a culture that worshiped a goddess who celebrated adultery and prostitution it's no wonder the "goddess of marriage" (Juno for the Romans and Hera for the Greeks) was portrayed as the enemy of the goddess of erotic love. For many, marriage became a duty to carry on the family name, and wives were relegated to lives of obscurity.

Women in the Greco-Roman World

In ancient Rome, freeborn women were considered Roman citizens but they could not vote or hold political office. They held limited public roles, although a few aristocratic women gained some influence.

In Roman culture, it was customary that a woman was not given her own name but was instead called by the feminine form of her father's name.[61] In fact, it was not unusual for sisters to share the same name. When a woman married, she kept her family name but would then become identified in relation to her husband. For instance, a man named Julius might call his daughter Julia. If Julia married Gaius, she would be called, "Julia Gaius," or "Julia [wife] of Gaius."[62]

A woman's religion was a given. In her father's home, she held the faith of her father. When she married, she worshipped according to her husband's beliefs. In a Greek world filled with goddesses, most women found themselves on the opposite side of the "veneration coin." Men generally mistrusted those of the fairer sex. In the Greek account of creation entitled the *Theogony*, Zeus was known as the "allfather." Out of anger, he ordered the creation of the first mortal woman. Her name was Pandora and she was maliciously designed to be both beautiful and evil. When Zeus gave Pandora to Epimetheus (a god formed by the union of heaven and earth, also known as a Titan), Pandora promptly opened and scattered the contents of a jar she brought with her. In so doing she unleashed misery on all mankind. The impetus behind the creation of the first mortal woman according to Greek mythology (revenge) is diametrically opposed to God's loving intention in creating an Eve for his Adam.

In Greek society, women were not to be trusted and had little to say about their destinies. They were on the same legal footing as slaves. They could not receive inheritance or engage in more-than-insignificant domestic business transactions.[63] In fact, women were often not referred to by their own names, but called "the wife of" or "the daughter of.'"

Demosthenes, a Greek orator and statesman in the fourth century BC, said, "Mistresses we keep for the sake of pleasure, concubines for the daily care of our persons, but wives to bear us legitimate children and to be faithful guardians of our households."[64] In the Greek world, respectable women kept to their homes which were segregated into male and female quarters. Their interaction with men was limited, even at mealtimes.

A Side Trip to Corinth

In addition to understanding the world Jesus entered, recognizing the culture of the Corinthians at the time Paul wrote the church there could make the difference between rightly dividing or misapplying Scripture relevant to the subject of women in ministry. Corinth was a New Testament "sin city," and the apostle had his work cut out for him.

Located at a major crossroads, Corinth had grown to become Greece's greatest city. As we also see in our large metropolis' today, the opulence of the rich stood in stark contrast to the deprivation of the poor. The city was the heart and hub of the arts, culture, trade, athletic competitions, and wantonness. It had such a bad reputation, Aristophanes (a fifth century playwright) coined the word *korinthiazethai* in its honor. *Korinthiazethai* is a verb which translates "to act like a Corinthian" and meant "to practice fornication."[65] Plato used the Greek *korinthia kórē*, which translates "Corinthian girl" to mean "prostitute."[66]

The sexual morals of the Corinthians were markedly dissimilar to those observed by Jews and Christians in the first century church. Greek pagans were engrossed in promiscuity and drunkenness. Prostitution was not only a huge factor in their economy, it was a revered practice in pagan worship in many of the city's vast religious cults.

When reading Paul's writings to the Corinthian Christians, consider the challenges he faced planting a church in this pagan environment. In the spiritually young congregation, elements of Corinthian practices would have filtered in through new converts just starting their journey of sanctification. The church was likely made up of members from a broad base of social classes.[67] Racially and culturally, the church was a melting pot—a spiritual nursery to newly converted slaves, Jews, and Gentiles.

In his letters to the Corinthians, Paul stood strong against the prevailing attitudes and ideologies of the Greeks, Romans, and even the Jews in the Mediterranean world. He taught the more excellent way—the better way of love. In the pagan and patriarchal culture that dominated his world and assigned a status of inferiority to women, Paul taught the words and works of Jesus Christ:

- The leveling of all status at the foot of the cross (see Gal 3:26–29)
- The washing away of every barrier by the blood of Jesus Christ (see Eph 1:5–6)
- The regenerating work of the Holy Spirit that made all things new (see 2 Cor 5:17).

Judaism

In the last part of the first century BC, Jewish and Roman cultures began to overlap. The Jews had been dispersed and migrated to Rome, Asia Minor, Babylon, and

Alexandria. In Israel proper, women had a lower role in society, but in other cities of Rome they held more prominent roles. Records have been found from the time of the dispersion that document female elders or rulers of synagogues.[68]

In Israel, women were not provided the opportunity for formal religious education. In fact, they had virtually no legal, social, or economic liberties. They enjoyed little esteem from men and their voices were often restricted and suppressed.

Into This Was Born a Savior

Jesus was born into this segment of the world controlled by the Roman Empire. Born a Jew, he lived in Palestine. And as a man, he was a citizen of the Roman Empire. It was a pluralistic world—an assortment of ethnicities, ranking officials, merchants, slaves, and minorities. In this time of peace, people of diverse religions were allowed to worship in the Empire according to their beliefs but under strict Roman authority and governorship.

Understanding the political, social, cultural, and religious values and beliefs of the people of Jesus's day helps believers today understand the magnitude of the Lord's words and actions. They were in high contrast to the world in which he lived. For women of the day—especially intelligent, gifted, and spiritually motivated women—this Gentile-Jewish world could well have been a disheartening place. Perhaps that is why so many women responded with adoration to the Savior and his gospel that offered them freedom they were forbidden elsewhere.

Biblical History

When Jesus began his earthly ministry the wheels of change creaked and moaned before they rolled out of the ruts of some comfortable old paths. Although not everyone wanted to be steered into new ways of thinking, the Messiah came to bring change. Jesus was revolutionary. He turned many of the standard practices of his day completely upside down. In the gospels, themes replay like Jesus's words, "You have heard it said," followed by, "but I say to you."

Jesus built upon former teachings. He called people to live by higher standards of morality and spirituality than they had previously known. Other times he redirected their ways of living and worshipping back to "in the beginning it was not so." Jesus addressed controversial issues like polygamy, adultery, divorce, revenge, and even giving money to religious causes. His interaction with women was revolutionary, as well.

In his teaching, Jesus used women over and again as examples to reveal spiritual truths. His parables included women kneading bread, searching for a lost coin, petitioning an unjust judge, giving sacrificially, and serving as bridesmaids. Three of these parables were direct comparisons to the kingdom of God.

Jesus was not gender prejudiced, but gender impartial. From the manger to the sermon on the mount, from his crucifixion to that glorious resurrection morning, women were a part of the life and ministry of the Messiah. When Jesus spoke, he purposely used inclusive language. Many places in Scripture where translators chose the word "man" to identify who he was addressing or teaching, the Lord's language could be more accurately rendered "human" or "person." His use of the term "daughter of Abraham" was unprecedented (see Luke 13:16).

Mary and Martha

When Jesus taught in public places like the hillsides and in the villages, he opened his ministry to women in a new way. Teaching was offered to men in the temple and synagogues, but Jesus taught everywhere in both public and private settings. It was in Martha's home Jesus affirmed a woman's right to learn. When Martha spoke to Jesus about her sister Mary's lack of support with food preparation, he said Mary had "chosen that good part, which shall not be taken away from her" (see Luke 10:42). Jesus didn't reprimand Mary for choosing learning over "women's work." He commended her. This scenario provided the perfect opportunity for Jesus to settle the question of women learning once and for all, and he advocated on the side of women learning.

Jesus not only taught Mary, he taught Martha as well as evidenced in their conversation at the time of her brother Lazarus's death. The Lord revealed himself to Martha as the Resurrection. She answered, "Yea, Lord: I believe," testifying that she understood the remarkable mystery wrapped in the deity of the man standing before her (see John 11:27). Jesus knew Martha was capable of learning and receiving spiritual revelation.

Mary Magdalene

Some theologians have characterized Mary Magdalene as a prostitute, but the Bible tells us only that she had been possessed by seven demons. With such a history she likely suffered from serious mental and emotional issues in addition to her spiritual needs. This desperate woman's encounter with Jesus brought her spiritual deliverance, a renewing of her right mind, and a passion to follow the one who delivered her from her terrible bondage. As a result Mary Magdalene became an ardent disciple of Christ.

The Lord chose this woman to be the first witness to the resurrection. He could have appeared to any number of people who held positions of power and authority—the High Priest, Pontius Pilate, or Peter—but instead he chose Mary Magdalene, a woman whose testimony, ironically, would not have been allowed in a court of law.

It's been said Jesus is perfect theology; in other words, he is the perfect study of God. When we see how he treated women, we know how women should be treated by those professing to be Christians. He talked one-on-one with them. He taught them biblical truths. He revealed himself as Messiah and allowed a woman to anoint him for his burial. He approved a woman's right to listen, learn, and be his disciple.

Following Jesus's sacrifice at Calvary, the veil in the holy place split from top to bottom. Where previously only a representative few had access to the Lord's presence, Jesus opened the way for all. Following the death, burial, and resurrection of Christ, every born-again believer becomes a member of the Lord's royal priesthood (see 1 Pet 2:9). The opportunity to enter his presence is no longer restricted to certain Jewish males, but believing Gentiles—and women, too.

The ripping of the veil at his death symbolized the breaking down of barriers and opening access (see Matt 27:50–51; Heb 10:19–20). Gender barricades were broken. Patriarchal authority (a result of the fall) was no longer the code men and women used to define worship protocols or establish governance in the New Testament church.

A Womanly Issue

In Jesus's day, both Hebrew men and women had bodily discharges considered unclean. An "unclean" status restricted anyone from public contact and by implication from ministry also since a woman's monthly cycle placed her in a position of regularly recurring uncleanness.

One woman who had a twelve-year "issue of blood" pushed beyond societal protocols and touched the hem of Jesus's garment. When she did, the Lord felt virtue leave him. He didn't correct this woman for presuming to contact him in her unclean state, which would by Jewish standards have made him unclean. Instead, Jesus addressed her tenderly and commended her faith. "Daughter, thy faith hath made thee whole; go in peace, and be whole of thy plague" (Mark 5:34). Not only was the woman healed, she gained a new status of "clean" which restored her dignity and reopened connectivity to those around her.

This may seem like a sweet story, and it is. The point in bringing it up, however, is to draw attention to the fact that Jesus purposefully stepped beyond a religious boundary line. In fact, in his treatment of women in general, we never read of any instances in which Jesus treated women as lower in rank or importance than men. One incredible example is found in his remarkable interaction with the Samaritan woman recorded in the fourth chapter of John.

Jesus broke through longstanding prejudicial barriers when he spoke to the woman of Samaria. Jews had no dealings with Samaritans (see John 4:9). Cultural norms combined with racial and religious animosity restrained observant Jews from interacting publicly with most women, let alone one of mixed race and "inferior" religious standing.

Many of the rabbis of Jesus's day would only speak to women who were close relatives. But Jesus came to seek and to save the lost. Although he was fatigued, thirsty, and hungry, he saw something worth reaching for in this broken Samaritan woman and breached several stigmas to reveal himself to her. Not only did he speak directly to the woman, Jesus engaged her in a discussion of theology and doctrine in his longest recorded private conversation.

Jesus often spoke in parables and riddles that forced people to come to their own understandings, but he blatantly told this woman he was the Messiah (see John 4:26). When Jesus's disciples returned from the town they marveled that he had talked with her and even questioned his decision to do so. They asked, "What are you looking for?" and "Why are you talking with her?" (see John 4:27).

It seems Jesus had preplanned this meeting. Before setting out with his disciples on a journey from Judea to Galilee, he told those traveling with him he *needed* to go through Samaria (see John 4:4). It's a commonly held belief that due to the hatred between Jews and Samaritans, Jews did not normally walk through Samaria but instead purposely travelled around it even when it added length to their trip. While we don't know for certain, Scripture does clarify that upon the group's arrival in Samaria, Jesus sent all those traveling with him away to get food (see John 4:8). It was while they were away Jesus had his conversation with the woman, and when the disciples returned, she went into the city to tell the people the Messiah had come.

Some have said this woman was the first female evangelist. She didn't hold the "office" of an evangelist as commonly thought of today, but the word translated "evangelist" (from the Greek word *euaggelistēs*) means someone who is a "bringer of good tidings, an evangelist."[69] "Glad tidings" is used in reference to the good news or the Gospel of Jesus Christ. Its second meaning is the name given in the New Testament to "those heralds of salvation through Christ who are not apostles."[70] This Samaritan woman heralded the arrival of the Messiah, and many responded (see John 4:39). She was a true evangelist. Her proclamations of Jesus made an eternal difference for those who responded. The result was a two-day revival meeting in her home town—the very community in which she had been an outcast much of her life.

Jesus's disciples questioned him that day, but the Lord never restrained the woman from going to the townspeople with the good news. Because of her words many came to faith. From the moment Jesus stepped on the path to Samaria, he knew this woman would "go" and "tell." And he is still calling women today to "go ye therefore."

Dr. Herbert Lockyer, a minister and prolific Christian author of the twentieth century, wrote in his book *All the Women of the Bible,* "With the coming of Christ a new era dawned for womanhood, and wherever he is exalted woman comes into her own."[71] He went on to say, "Through the examples of Jesus in his attitude toward women, and as the result of the truth he taught, women were prominent in the activities of the Early Church."[72] He also concluded that women "came to hold official positions of spiritual influence in the church."[73]

Disciples: Both Male and Female

Scripture identifies the Twelve apostles hand selected by Jesus, but also records many other male and female disciples who traveled with him. A disciple is "a learner" and "one who follows one's teaching."[74] The women who traveled with Jesus were more than curious onlookers, friends, or financiers. They were learners and followers of the Lord.

Jesus broke tradition when he accepted women disciples as part of his entourage. In the past, women had supported rabbis, but the Lord's acceptance of women as part of his inner circle broke contemporary barriers and made a strong countercultural affirmation of women.

Among those who traveled with Jesus, Scripture specifically names Mary of Magdala, Joanna, and Susanna (see Luke 8:1–3). These women were identified as those who "followed him, and ministered unto him" along with "many other women which came up with him unto Jerusalem" (see Mark 15:41). In following Jesus, these women made an *avant-garde* commitment to abandon all, including tradition and accepted social behavior.

Women were witnesses to Jesus's miracles and attendants at his crucifixion and burial. Women were eyewitnesses to the resurrection, and they spoke with the Lord at the gravesite. Jesus charged them with the task of sharing the good news of his resurrection with the men.

The fact that none of the original Twelve were women should be no surprise. Jesus came first to the Jews, and they were living in a time when patriarchy was the rule of the day. Jesus was born into a Jewish-Roman-Greek world that considered women inferior. Even so, many of Jesus's disciples were women. And in the centuries that followed, ministers of the gospel came from all walks of life.

It was always in the heart of God to expand salvation to all the world *from* the Jews, but not limited to them (see John 3:16). In the same way ministry was extended to Gentiles, it was to women as well. The Lord's invitation to discipleship continues to be open to all. What he spoke when he walked the earth is still true today for men and women alike, "If ye continue in my word, then are ye my disciples indeed" (John 8:31).

Joachim Jeremias, a German theologian and professor of New Testament studies, offered this perspective: "Only against the background of that time can we fully appreciate Jesus's attitude to women."[75] That Jesus was revolutionary and courageous enough to accept female disciples is no surprise, but the great courage of the women who dared to break the societal mold to learn from him alongside men should be recognized and honored.

Women Ministering in the Old Testament

*Strength and honour are her clothing; and she shall rejoice in time to come.
She openeth her mouth with wisdom; and in her tongue is the law of kindness.*
Proverbs 31:25–26

The Old Testament records individuals and groups of women who served the Lord in a variety of roles. One group of women "assembled at the door of the tabernacle of the congregation" (see Exod 38:8; 1 Sam 2:22). The word "assemble" is defined as: "to mass (an army or servants):—assemble, fight, perform, muster, wait upon, war."[76] Author Edith Deen wrote in *All the Women of the Bible* that these women assisted the Levites in preparations for the service. In so doing, they provided "one of the earliest examples of women's ministry in the house of God."[77]

Heman's daughters served in music ministry alongside his fourteen sons. "All these were under the hands of their father for song in the house of the Lord, with cymbals, psalteries, and harps, for the service of the house of God" (see 1 Chron 25:6).

Among the Jews exiled after Nebuchadnezzar's conquest were "two hundred forty and five singing men and singing women" from the tribe of Judah (see Neh 7:67). These likely referred to those who sang in an official capacity. The same word for singers (male and female) is used for those who participated in a religious procession: "The singers went before, the players on instruments followed after; among them were the damsels playing with timbrels" (Ps 68:25).

The Lord chose to speak first to Manoah's wife before speaking to Manoah with the detailed instructions the couple was to follow in raising their son Samson (see Judg 13:2–7). Women greatly impacted their families and communities—sometimes stepping up in unique circumstances. Shallum's daughters worked beside their father to repair the walls of Jerusalem (see Neh 3:12). Moses's wife Zipporah circumcised their children. This was a unique and desperate situation and certainly not a wife's normal function, but Zipporah did perform a priestly duty her husband should have carried out (Exod 4:24–26).

Sarah honored her husband Abraham by calling him "lord" and obeying him, but there is more to the story of their relationship. Scripture records an equal number of times Abraham complied with his wife's instructions as she followed his. God himself instructed Abraham, "In all that Sarah hath said unto thee, hearken unto her voice" (Gen 21:12).

Five Old Testament women are specifically mentioned in prophetic ministry; Huldah, Miriam, Deborah, Noadiah, and Isaiah's wife (see 2 Chron 34:22; Exod 15:20; Judg 4:4; Neh 6:14; Isa 8:3). Women of old were not rebuked for prophesying in itself, but some were corrected when they prophesied their own words (as all false prophets should be). This indicates that women were recognized as operating in the prophetic gifts by the people of God (see Ezek 13:17). Rev. F. W. J. Schroeder noted in the *Commentary on the Holy Scriptures,* "Prophecy in Israel was a gift of the Spirit, and already, as being so, had no restriction as to sex."[78] Not only did he believe this to be true in Old Testament times, he said, "When it [prophecy in Israel] came to be upheld by the Spirit of Christ, in whom there is neither male nor female, this overlooking of all sexual distinctions of necessity still more characterized it."[79]

Miriam, the Prophetess

Miriam. Her name is said by some to mean "bitterness," but one Greek lexicon listed the meaning of her name as "their contumacy."[80] *Contumacy* means "stubborn perverseness or rebelliousness" or "willful and

> The ministry women performed under the old covenant would not reasonably be restricted by New Testament teaching. No Scripture indicates a cessation of calling and opportunities given to women to prophesy, judge, lead, interpret the Word, lead worship, or announce the good news.

obstinate resistance or disobedience to authority." Poor Miriam. What a name.

Perhaps a look at this woman through the lens of her childhood will give us some appreciation for the person God made her to be—willful and strong by his design. Miriam, along with her family, was a slave. They lived in Egypt when the pharaoh ordered all male Israelite infants executed at birth (see Exod 1:16). But at her mother's prompting, Miriam intervened and Moses's life was saved (see Exod 2:5–10). At the time of Moses's birth, the babe destined to be Israel's deliverer was in need of a delivering of his own. The situation required a bit of willfulness and stubbornness, and God gave Miriam the strength she needed to stand strong.

Decades later, in the time of Miriam's insubordination, God called her to present herself along with her brothers before the tabernacle. The Lord came down in a pillar of cloud. He spoke specifically to Aaron and Miriam, and God held Miriam personally accountable for her actions (see Num 12:4–5).

After the crossing at the Red Sea, Miriam led the delivered nation in a great celebration (see Exod 15:20–21). The first song recorded in Scripture was sung by this woman. Centuries after Israel's exodus from Egypt, the prophet Micah identified Miriam as one of the three leaders sent by God to rescue his people from captivity (see Mic 6:4).

The Daughters of Zelophehad

In ancient Canaan, five unmarried women presented a legal case to Moses on their own behalf and won. Their father's name was Zelophehad, and he had no sons (see Num 26:33). When it was time for the Israelites to be allotted their portions of the promised land, Zelophehad's husbandless daughters were deemed ineligible to receive their father's inheritance.

With hopes of reconciling their predicament, the courageous women stood before the door of the Tabernacle. There they addressed an assembly that included Moses, Eleazar the priest, the princes of the twelve tribes, and all the congregation of Israel (see Num 27:2). It is remarkable these women were given an opportunity to speak before all Israel on their own behalf. The women successfully pleaded their case and received the inheritance due their father's offspring.

The Jewish Talmud highly honors these women. One translator of rabbinical Scripture said:

It stands to reason that if they had not been ... female expounders [of law], they could not have known the correct interpretation of law, which even Moses, the prime legislator himself, as we see from the context, was not aware of: while we have the Divine testimony to justify the conclusion that they were correct in their exposition, and, in the whole case, a warrant for the inference, which is inevitable, that education in the law was not forbidden to females by Moses.[81]

When Moses went to God for judgment in the case, the Lord said, "The daughters of Zelophehad speak right: thou shalt give them a possession of an inheritance among their father's brethren; and thou shalt cause the inheritance of their father to pass unto them" (see Num 27:7). God did not instruct Moses to correct the women for speaking publicly. Neither did he fault their interpretation of the Law.

The daughters' plea was deemed "right" by the Lord. They received their inheritance, and their courage caused a precedent to be established for women in the future. The Lord said, "And thou shalt speak unto the children of Israel, saying, If a man die, and have no son, then ye shall cause his inheritance to pass unto his daughter" (Num 27:8).

Hannah, Woman of Prayer

A barren woman named Hannah longed to have a child. When she went to the house of God to pray, her inaudible request was so impassioned the priest assumed she was drunk. God, however, understood Hannah's desire. He had compassion on her and opened her womb. She conceived and gave birth to a son she named Samuel, and the boy eventually became a great prophet in Israel.

Hannah brought the child to the house of the Lord to fulfill the vow she made in prayer (see 1 Sam 2:24). As she prepared to leave her son with the priest, she offered a joyful exaltation, and her words became a part of the canon of Scripture (see 1 Sam 2:1–10).

Old Testament scholar Walter Brueggemann suggested Hannah's song paved the way for the major theme of the book of Samuel, the "power and willingness of Yahweh to intrude, intervene, and invert."[82] Hannah's hymn of praise is significant—regarded in Judaism as the prime role model for how to pray—and is traditionally chanted by Jews all over the world on the first day of *Rosh Hashanah,* the Jewish New Year.[83]

Esther, Advocate and Queen

Leadership is defined as influence, and although Esther didn't hold a religious office, she certainly held a position of influence. Her story is the basis for the festival of Purim still celebrated today.

Esther was a Jewish girl who lived in exile in Persia with her cousin Mordecai. Although King Cyrus had given permission for the Jews to return to Jerusalem, Mordecai and his family remained in Persia where Esther was elevated from orphaned exile to royalty.

With no army or armory, God used Esther to save his people. An involuntary hero, Esther pushed past her fears and defied the law of the land by presenting herself without summons to the king. At the risk of death, Esther exhibited courage, wisdom, and integrity. In her time of distress, she turned to prayer and found the confidence she needed to step forward.

Often acknowledged for her beauty, discretion, and good judgment, readers may gloss over the full record of her achievements. The king not only listened to her request, he gave her the authority to determine tactical procedures in a military endeavor (see Esth 9:12–14). Esther played a key diplomatic role that affected the lives of people in 127 provinces from India to Ethiopia. She also regulated how the Jewish nation would commemorate their great victory with an annual feast called Purim. "So Queen Esther, daughter of Abihail, along with Mordecai the Jew, wrote with full authority to confirm this second letter concerning Purim" (Esth 9:29). Mordecai sent letters to all the Jews to establish the days of Purim that he and Esther together decreed (see Esth 9:31). Scripture verifies it was Esther's decree that confirmed the regulations concerning the celebration of Purim (see Esth 9:32).

A nation was saved through the intervention of an orphaned girl, and one of the 66 books of the Bible bears her name. This woman's story of valor and leadership continues to influence people around the world.

Deborah, Judge and Leader

During the time following Joshua's death, the twelve tribes of Israel had no central government. It was the time of judges who served as rulers, military leaders, and legal judges.

Women of Deborah's day didn't typically serve as political leaders, but God used this woman as a judge, a prophetess, and as a spiritual and military leader. Deborah was the third of Israel's judges and she mediated the Word of God to those who came to her. She exercised both judicial and political power. She communicated the will of God to the people and judged disputes in an outdoor courtroom.

For that time, Deborah was Israel's head of state. Her courage and boldness inspired the men to rise in battle against their Canaanite oppressors. Deborah gave Barak, the army general, the opportunity and strategies to lead the charge. He was willing to follow her military orders, but only on the condition she went with the men into battle. Israel's victory over the Canaanites was ultimately credited to two women, Deborah and Jael. Following their military achievement, Israel experienced a forty-year period of peace.

God chose to use Deborah in a culture that strongly favored male leadership. As one of Israel's twelve judges, she may not have established a pattern of women in leadership. She did, however, set a precedent for women to serve in the highest level of Israel's government as a military leader, administrator, and judge.

While she was worthy of many titles, Deborah spoke of herself only as a "mother in Israel" (see Judg 5:7). More than just a wise and bold leader, she had a heart of compassion for the people she served. Also to Deborah's credit, she authored a song of praise that became part of the canon of Scripture. Scholars have called the Song of Deborah the most remarkable example of Hebrew poetry in the Bible, "a specimen of poetical representation that cannot be surpassed."[84]

The Lord entrusted Deborah with the spiritual, civic, and military leadership of his people. She functioned in his plan and with his authority. Deborah was never corrected for being out of order when she served in a position primarily filled by men. Instead, this gracious, successful leader was commended. If God called a Deborah then, he can call a Deborah today.

Jael, Courageous Warrior

Jael, the wife of Heber, was a woman placed in a unique and challenging position. Scripture identifies her husband as a Kenite, a descendant of Moses's father-in-law. Although the Kenites were not Israelites, they lived among the tribes in the southern part of the promised land (see Judg 1:16). Heber, however, moved his family from the rest of his people and set up camp in the north.

Israel's enemy, the Canaanite King Jabin, waged war against them. When Israel's troops won a decisive victory over the Canaanite army, Sisera, the captain of Jabin's army, ran from the battlefield. He sought refuge in Heber's camp, and as he neared Jael's tent, she invited him inside. Given the peace alliance between their people and the prevailing codes of hospitality, Sisera accepted Jael's invitation believing he had entered a safe place.

Exhausted from the battle, Sisera accepted a drink of milk (although he asked for water) and a cover from Jael. He then fell fast asleep on the floor. Jael seized the moment. She picked up a tent stake and hammer. Carefully and quietly, she approached the sleeping man and then drove the stake through both of his temples and into the ground (see Judg 4:21).

In Jael's day women were fully in charge of the tents (and tents could be as large as small houses). They spun goat hair, wove it into fabric, and made their portable homes with their own hands. The women were the ones who set up and took down their dwellings. Given Jael's extensive experience with hammer and stakes, she would have approached sleeping Sisera with confidence she could execute the job—and she did.

Deborah called Jael the most blessed women in the tents (see Judg 5:24). In her song commemorating the victory, she

SIDENOTE
from the Author

In the middle of writing *Preach Like a Lady* the Lord gave me a sweet confirmation. It was quiet in the house. Everyone had gone out and I was in the prayer room with my Bible on my lap. My daily reading happened to conclude with Deborah's story in Judges 5.

I closed my Bible, reached for my phone, and checked my email. It's rare that I would only have one new email in my inbox, but that was the case this day. What was the subject line that arrested my attention?

"Deborah has endorsed you."

It took my breath away. I know things at times happen by coincidence, but I don't believe that was one of those times. For close to a year, my life had been consumed with writing this book. Many times in the past decade I faced opposition and criticism to do what God has called me to do as a woman minister. What a beautiful affirmation that little "coincidence" was to me.

Deborah has endorsed me. If God used her, he can use me. He can use you. I felt such a peace sweep over my spirit. God knows just what we need.

According to Dr. Beth Jan Smith, many individuals with a call to minister receive confirmations like this one. She coined these incidents "God markers"—where the Lord places a little "mark" in a person's ministry to confirm he or she is heading in the right direction. These markers aren't coincidences, but they are powerful touches from God to continue in the direction a person is going in their calling. Like dreams, they encourage individuals to continue.[85]

compared Jael with Shamgar, a judge and godly warrior who lived at the same time and who had killed 600 Philistines (see Judg 5:6). The Bible lauds Jael as one among distinguished champions. The *Midrash* (an ancient commentary on Hebrew Scripture) praises Jael among other devout women who converted to faith.

The Kenites had traveled with Israel for generations. Jael would have known the history of the delivering power of God and likely had sympathies for God's people. From her actions it appears she had faith to believe God would deliver his people from their oppressors.

At Jael's hand the captain of Israel's enemy was defeated. It was a bloody, horrific act, but wartime conduct often is. Jael proved herself and her family to be Israel's friends and supporters and secured their future safety.

One Bible commentator said, "This thing was of the Lord, no one can doubt, who considers that Deborah had before pointed out, under the Spirit of prophecy, that the Lord had sold Sisera into the hand of a woman" (Judg 4:9). When Sisera hid in Jael's tent, she used wisdom and the tools she was familiar with to bring him down. She didn't "fight like a man," but she won using her devices, skills, and experiences. Jael stepped outside the bounds of "normal" to perform a courageous act on behalf of the people of God.

Huldah

During the time of King Josiah, a woman named Huldah lived in Jerusalem in "the college" (2 Kgs 22:14). Her husband Shallum was the king's wardrobe keeper and Huldah is presumed by many to have been a scholar who instructed in the college.

Undoubtedly Huldah lived in a place of influence—possibly a religious educational environment. She was renowned as a clear-thinking, godly woman of high social rank, and she enjoyed a good reputation among the priesthood and royal cabinet.

A contemporary of two male prophets, Jeremiah and Zephaniah, Huldah served as a prophetess from 641–609 B.C. During her tenure, King Josiah ascended to the throne at the age of eight. Eighteen years later, a "book of the law of the Lord given by Moses" was discovered during a temple building restoration project (see 2 Chron 34:14). When the book was delivered and read to the king, he instructed Hilkiah the priest and other officials to, "Go ye, enquire of the Lord for me, and for the people, and for all Judah, concerning the words of this book that is found" (2 Kgs 22:13).

Hilkiah and his companions "enquired of the Lord" by consulting Huldah the prophetess. The priest chose this woman over Jeremiah and Zephaniah to interpret the meaning of the Scripture. After hearing the king's inquiry, Huldah delivered a "thus sayeth the Lord"—a prophetic word for the people and their leader. Author William E. Phipps proposed Huldah was the first person ever to declare specific writings were "Holy Scripture."[86]

The priest and officials held Huldah in high regard. Sought out by notable officials, this woman served a significant prophetic role in a pivotal time. By taking the book of the law to Huldah, the fate and future of the nation was placed in a woman's hands.

Huldah delivered the word of the Lord clearly, decisively, and authoritatively. She validated the king's concern that the kingdom was on the precipice of judgment, and the king's response to her words sparked a considerable religious reformation. Immediately after hearing the word of the Lord from this prophetess, Josiah purged the land and reaffirmed Israel's covenant with God. Through Huldah's ministry, revival came to God's people (see 2 Kgs 22:13–20; 2 Chron 34:22–28).

The Old Testament record verifies that many women ministered in various ways in ancient Israel. At times, extenuating circumstances arose and duty called certain women to act in ways that were out of the ordinary. In other examples we see women serving ordinarily in roles such as those who assembled at the door of the congregation or regularly leading in singing. And the record is clear: throughout history, God chose women to serve in specific ministerial roles including prophesying, judging, interpreting Scripture, and leading his people.

Women Ministering in the New Testament

*And on my servants and on my handmaidens I will pour out
in those days of my Spirit; and they shall prophesy.*
Acts 2:18

The roles women served in ministry in the Old Testament were in no way diminished in the New Testament age. In fact, Jesus ushered in a new era for women. From his miraculous birth onward, women played important roles in the life and ministry of Jesus. They were welcomed as his disciples, but some even seem to have risen to the rank of apostle. And after his ascension, they continued their commitment by fulfilling the work of the Great Commission.

Mary, Mother of Jesus and Handmaiden of the Lord

Mary the mother of Jesus has been admired for her devotion and courage. Little is known about her life although some can be deduced from Scripture.

Scripture introduces her as a resident in the city of Nazareth in Galilee (see Luke 1:26–35). Mary was a young virgin—perhaps just twelve or thirteen—betrothed to marry a man named Joseph. The arrival of an angelic visitor frightened her, but her response to his message revealed the depth of her faith. Mary didn't doubt the angel's words. She simply asked, "How could this be?" (see Luke 1:34). Once the angel provided the details her answer was one of a willing, obedient servant. "Behold the handmaid of the Lord; be it unto me according to thy word" (Luke 1:38).

Not long after this encounter, Mary visited her cousin Elizabeth. The song she sang during her visit revealed her knowledge of prophecy. In a time when girls weren't formally trained in the Scriptures, her song affirmed she was well-versed in the Word. In fact, her words became part of the canon of New Testament Scripture (see Luke 1:46-55).

The Lord used Mary as his conduit for salvation (see Genesis 3:16). She had the unique opportunity to be a part of Jesus's life from his conception to his birth, at the times of miracles and teachings, and at his death as well. Scripture identifies her as highly favored and blessed among women.

What did God see when he looked down upon Mary with such favor? She was young, female, and presumably not well-to-do. An unlikely candidate from a human perspective, God saw her heart and a woman of worth. He knew Mary would answer his call no matter the cost. Perhaps it was due to the Word she had hidden in her heart that she so willingly agreed to God's invitation and rejoiced in his plan. She was ready to say yes even to the unexpected.

Mary influenced the life of Jesus. She was the one who urged him to begin his public ministry with the first miracle at the marriage in Cana. Perhaps it was his humanity that led Jesus to respond to her request saying, "Woman, what have I to do with thee? Mine hour is not yet come" (John 2:4). Jesus was in essence saying, "It's not my time yet," but ultimately he deferred to Mary's wishes and turned the water into wine. He submitted to his mother's request and launched his miracle ministry even when it seemingly went against his initial timeframe.

How often Mary traveled with Jesus or heard him speak isn't recorded. She did travel with him and others to Capernaum after the wedding feast (see John 2:12). Scripture bears no record of her personally ministering as a disciple. She did, however, recognize the one she bore was her Lord, God, and Savior (see Luke 1:46–47). She was the first believer in Jesus as the Messiah, and as such perhaps his first disciple. How she must have listened intently to his words.

Mary was the human vessel God used to fulfill Messianic prophecy, and she willingly suffered ridicule to fulfill the purpose of God in her life. Her devotion continued after Jesus's death, and she is specifically named among those in the upper room who received the gift of the Holy Spirit on the day of Pentecost.

Anna, the Prophetess

Anna was a prophetess from the tribe of Asher who loved the things of God. Following the passing of her husband after just seven years of marriage, she spent upwards of sixty years in dedicated service to the Lord. A woman with an incredible passion, dedication, and spiritual hunger, Anna was continually in the temple. She never left. She "worshiped night and day, fasting and praying" (see Luke 2:37).

The Lord honored Anna's singular devotion and sacrifice by allowing her to see the Messiah. She recognized and proclaimed Jesus as Israel's redemption when he was just forty days old.

Anna first saw the infant Jesus in Herod's temple. The massive complex was constructed with four courts built successively. Courts were arranged one behind the other, and a person had to pass through one court to enter the next. Each court was more exclusive than the one before. The first court was the Court of the Gentiles. Next was a divided inner court that had two sections: the Court of Women, where Anna was allowed to worship, and the Court of Israel. The fourth court, the Court of Priests, surrounded the temple building and was only accessible to members of the Levitical priesthood.

It's significant that Anna's declaration of Jesus as the Messiah took place on the temple grounds. This was the Israelite's central place of worship. Anna's public proclamation was made in the hearing of both males and females on the temple grounds, and she continued to speak of Jesus "to all them that looked for redemption in Jerusalem" (see Luke 2:38). This verse indicates that Anna spoke beyond the singular moment she saw the baby Jesus and continued to proclaim the arrival of the Messiah to all who looked for his coming.

When Anna entered the scene that day, Simeon, a priest, was still holding the baby Jesus. Moments before her arrival he made the declaration that he had seen the Lord's salvation and could now die in peace (see Luke 2:28–32). In the Jewish tradition of the day, truths were considered established by the words of two or three righteous witnesses, and the Lord chose Anna to be a witness to Jesus's true identity at his presentation in the temple.

Anna's worship and devotion gained the attention and favor of God and the Lord used her voice to proclaim the arrival of the Savior. She was an eyewitness about whom little is known but so much can be discerned. Her name means "grace" and she was gifted by God to be his prophet and his voice among his people.

Tabitha, the Disciple

In writing the book of Acts, Luke distinguished Tabitha with a unique title of a "certain disciple" (see Acts 9:36). She was a member of the church in Joppa, a seaport town on the Mediterranean coast outside Jerusalem. Her Greek name was Dorcas, but the meaning of both names is "gazelle." The word translated "disciple" in this verse is the Greek word *mathētria,* which is used just once in Scripture. It means "female pupil:—disciple"[87] and is identified as the feminine form of the masculine noun *mathētēs,* which means "a learner, i.e. pupil:—disciple."[88] This language infers that Tabitha was a student and follower of Jesus in the same way men were students and followers.

We don't know if Tabitha served the same functions as other disciples who served in varying roles. It is evident, however, Tabitha was indeed a disciple known and loved for her practical acts of charity. This woman was "full of good works." She continually and diligently worked to serve the poor and widowed in the Joppa community.

Acts of service did not earn a believer a designation of disciple. Works are an outflow of person's faith and followership. Although Scripture is silent about anything beyond Tabitha's acts of kindness, it would be hard to imagine this faithful pupil didn't share the Lord's words with her works—his compassion with her coats and his gospel with her garments.

Told in seven short verses, the record of Tabitha's story began with her death, but ended in a triumphant resurrection. She was so highly regarded that when she died, her church family sent men to fetch Peter from a nearby town. Upon Peter's arrival, he heard the testimonies of the city's widows mourning the loss of their beloved benefactress. He saw the coats the widows held before him while tears streamed down their faces. He sent the mourners away and with godly power and authority said, "Tabitha, arise." The woman sat up and was presented alive to the saints and widows.

When word of Tabitha's resurrection became known, great rejoicing and revival broke out in Joppa. Yes, it was the result of a miracle—a miracle that happened because this anointed disciple made a difference in the lives she touched in Jesus's name.

Philip's Daughters, the Prophesying Ones

In Acts 21:9 Luke established record of Philip's four daughters. Since no wife is mentioned, scholars assume Philip was a widower and that his daughters lived at home with him. The daughters were unmarried virgins, and Scripture says they prophesied. Most scholars believe these were mature women who chose to remain celibate in their devotion to the Lord.

The four women fulfilled important roles in the church. The language of Scripture implies they didn't just prophesy when Paul came to visit, but they were known for being women who prophesied. The Greek literally interprets this way: "But, to this one [Philip], there were four virgin daughters, prophesying-ones."[89] Luke didn't use a noun or a verb to describe the girls, but a present-tense participle that indicated they were prophesying girls. The implication is that the daughters engaged in ongoing prophesying activities.

From the simple phrasing used, it seems these daughters were allowed to freely exercise their gifts of prophecy. Neither Philip nor Paul nor Luke mentioned any objection to the daughters exercising their spiritual gifts.

Although Philip's daughters were unnamed in Scripture, they were well known in their generation and beyond. An annual Greek calendar claims two of the daughters were named Hermione and Eutychis, and that after Philip's death, they went to live with the apostle John in Ephesus. Eusebius, an early Christian writer who lived in the third century, highly regarded Philip's daughters and their ministry. He referred to them as "great lights" in Asia.[90]

The Elect Lady, Local Church Leader

It was a predominant Greek practice to name the recipient of a letter at its beginning. The openings of 2 John and 3 John are identical in structure. The only difference is that in the second epistle, the recipient may have been given a title; and in the third the recipient is clearly identified by name. The latter, Gaius, was John's convert, his "child" in the faith (see 3 John 1:4). Although he was not specifically identified as a pastor, he was clearly a church leader. And it's likely he was the head of a house church overseen by John. The apostle, after all, wrote him concerning the church—in particular, the correct way to handle an issue with a man named Diotrephes. John opened his letter, "The elder unto the wellbeloved Gaius, whom I love in the truth" (3 John 1:1).

In his second epistle, the apostle John opened his letter with a greeting he specifically addressed to a lady and her children. He opened with a greeting to the "elect lady." The fact John was writing to warn her not to allow false teachers into her home indicates she was a prominent woman who likely held authority in the church. The term "house" may well refer to the local church, not simply this woman's familial residence.

Some purport the "elect lady" was another name John used for a local church. However, if the church is the lady, who would her children be? To accept this proposition would mean John was writing his letter to the church (the elect lady) and to the church (her children). This position is weakened also by the lack of any New Testament reference to a local church as a woman or lady elsewhere. The apostle's approach was straightforward. He didn't use metaphors or flowery language in the remainder of his correspondence. There is no reason to believe he deviated from that pattern when he addressed the letter to this particular woman.

Applying normal grammatical usage to *eklektos kyri* (unto the elect lady), the phrase could be translated one of three ways:
- "to an elect lady" (an undetermined person)
- "to Eklekte Kuria" (two proper names)
- "to the lady Eklekte" (a descriptive word and one proper name)[91]

John's elect lady was obviously known and loved by the apostle and the local church assembly he was writing from. "Lady" is the feminine form of the Greek word rendered "Lord," "lord," "master" and "sir." It's a title of honor and refers to "he to whom a person or thing belongs, about which he has power of deciding; master, lord."[92] This is a word associated with royalty, and it is also a proper name. Some translators have rendered *kyria* as the proper name, "Kyria" or "Cyria," a woman's name used in John's day.

Dr. Rendel Harris proposed the identity question of the elect lady was settled "by the discovery in the papyri of numerous instances which prove that kurios and kuria were used by ancient letter-writers as terms of familiar endearment, applicable to brother, sister, son, wife, or intimate friend of either sex."[93] The *International Standard Bible Encyclopedia* concluded, "In the light of this suggestion we should naturally translate, 'to my (dear) lady Eklekte.'"[94]

Whoever she was, the elect lady was a chosen woman of God—one who had authority over at least an estate and who functioned without being under guardianship. Her children belonged to her the same way John's children belonged to him (see 1 John 1:2). The content of John's letter to her makes the most sense when it is read as if he was writing a particular person who served in church leadership.

The tone and pastoral directives John gave indicate his instructions were meant to be applied in the local church not just one woman's family or household.

The last verse of this short epistle is a greeting to the elect lady from her elect sister's children. Taken literally, John was saying the chosen lady had a chosen sister. This sister was also a church leader who had children in the same church John was writing from.

An interesting possibility about the identity of these two ladies comes through the writings of an early church historian named Eusebius. He recorded that in Philip's later years, he and two of his four daughters (the ones identified as prophetesses) lived at Hierapolis in Phrygia. A third daughter lived in Ephesus where John preached. John was the only apostle who lived a long life. Given his close ties to Philip and his daughters, it has been suggested John's letter was written to one of Philip's daughters while she still ministered in Hierapolis. This could be the elect lady, and John may have been extending greetings to her from her sister's church in Ephesus.

In the last part of the second century, Polycrates, the Bishop of Ephesus, wrote, "For in Asia, also, mighty luminaries have fallen asleep, which shall rise again at the last day, at the appearance of our Lord, when he shall come with glory from heaven, and shall gather again all the saints. Philip, one of the twelve apostles who sleeps in Hierapolis, and his two aged virgin daughters. Another of his daughters who lived in the Holy Spirit, rests at Ephesus. Moreover, John, that rested on the bosom of our Lord … also rests at Ephesus."[95] The elect lady and the elect sister could well be two of the "mighty luminaries" Polycrates mentioned or the "great lights" mentioned by Eusebius.

The elect lady of John's affection is one more New Testament example of a woman who served in leadership in the early church and very likely in the position of pastor.

Lydia, Patron and Local Church Leader

The city of Philippi was a prosperous Roman colony, but it didn't have the requisite ten male Jews to form a synagogue. Paul customarily preached first in the synagogue, but in Philippi he found only a group of God-fearing women who met at the river for prayer (see Acts 16:13).

One of the worshippers was Lydia, a successful businesswoman who dealt in the commercial trade of rare purple dye or fabric. She had previously lived in the hub of the purple dye industry in Thyatira and was a woman of means. Purple dye was expensive and highly sought after.

What did it mean that Lydia was a worshipper (also translated "God-fearer")? First, although there were Jewish colonies in Asia Minor, Lydia's ethnic descent is unknown. Her name was not Jewish, but one of foreign origin that literally means "from Lydia," and her home town was located in the ancient Lydian Empire. Lydia may not have been her personal name but instead meant she was "Lydian."

Thyatirans primarily worshipped Apollo, along with Sibyl, Tyrimos, and Artemis. Given the foreign origins of her name and the environment in which she was raised, it's unlikely she was Jewish. However, she could have converted to Judaism. Perhaps through her neighbors, commerce, or staff of servants, Lydia was introduced to the Lord and began to fear him, to seek him. She was a devout woman of faith. Presumably, she went often to the river for prayer. It's evident by her immediate response to Paul how tender her heart was to the things of God.

Since Lydia was the head of her household she was either a wealthy widow or heiress. The lack of mention of either husband or father in a society where women were almost always under legal male guardianship signals her social prominence and presumed singleness.

When Lydia heard Paul speak she believed and heeded his words, and she and the members of her household were baptized. As head of the household she not only led her servants, staff, and possibly family members to the Lord, she took seriously her responsibility to establish them in the faith. This responsibility—along with her personal desire to know more of God—may have been what motivated her to invite Paul to her home.

Immediately after her baptism Lydia extended hospitality to Paul and his traveling companions. She said, "If ye have judged me to be faithful to the Lord, come into my house, and abide there" (see Acts 16:15). This woman had strong communication skills, especially when considering Paul didn't generally accept assistance from new converts. Her offer to "abide" was more than just a proposal that he stay for a night or two. *Abide* means "to remain," "tarry," "not to depart."[96]

Luke, the writer of the passage, said she "constrained" them—a strong word meaning she compelled and obliged them with her earnest, challenging offer. She was insistent and confident, and Paul heeded her request. Her fervor is perhaps better understood when we realize God may well have been answering her prayers when the Spirit led Paul to redirect his travel plans and minister in Macedonia instead of Bithynia (Philippi was a city in Macedonia, see Acts 16:7-12).

Lydia's home became the first meeting place for the church in Philippi, and she became a patron for the evangelists who brought the gospel to her city. There is no record of Paul and his company staying in any other home in Philippi during his first trip or others. Lydia's home could well have become their headquarters in the region. As evidenced by Paul's letter written to the Philippian church years later, her house church grew into a large congregation.

Lydia was Paul's first European convert, and as such the first member of the Philippian church in which she ultimately assumed a position of leadership. Her home could be considered Europe's first church plant. The Bible makes no mention of any person designated by Paul to minister in the fledgling Philippian church. It's likely Lydia continued to oversee this work.

Not only did Lydia and her household host Paul and his ministry team when they first arrived in Philippi, she welcomed them in her home after they had been beaten and imprisoned for preaching the gospel (see Acts 16:40). This was quite a brave move on her part which could have caused damage to her reputation and business. Lydia's leadership may have been more readily accepted in Philippi than in other places in the Roman Empire. The Philippian culture was more favorable to women. Philippi was in Macedonia, and Macedonian women had the benefit of greater autonomy in political, social, and religious affairs.[97] They held significant positions in public life and "built temples, founded cities, engaged mercenaries, commanded armies, held fortresses, and acted on occasion as regents or even co rulers."[98]

In his later writing to the Philippian church, Paul mentioned the women who labored with him "in the gospel" (see Phil 4:3). The record of Lydia's ministry should be particularly uplifting to single and widowed women. Her story provides a strong message that a woman's marital status should not impede her ministry, nor should a woman feel she has to wait until marriage to fulfill her call.

It's interesting that Scripture doesn't document any specific missionary endeavors to Thyatira, but John mentioned a church in that city in Revelation 2:18. Lydia may have been instrumental in establishing a church in her native community. As mentioned earlier, Thyatira, famous for its dyeing facilities, was a hub in the purple cloth market in which she was engaged. Ancient inscriptions have been found in Thyatiran ruins that confirm the many guilds of cloth dyers in the city, greater than any other city of its day in Asia Minor.[99] With Lydia's commerce and connection to Thyatira via this industry, it is quite possible she played a part or was the direct means in the establishment of a church in Thyatira. Under her godly leadership, Lydia's household of faith grew to become a dynamic and vital constituent of the first century church.

Chloe, Influential Leader

Scripture mentions Chloe just once. Her singular acknowledgement, however, brings several questions to the fore: Who was she? What was her role in Corinth? Just who were the members of "the house of Chloe?"

Chloe is mentioned in Paul's letter to the Corinthian church. The Bible doesn't specify where she lived, but there is no reason to assume she lived outside Corinth. Paul's use of her first name indicates she was well known in the community and that she needed no introduction to those receiving his letter.

It's notable the Greek text doesn't contain any word that would be translated "house" as is rendered "the house of Chloe" in the King James Version. Instead, the language used is *tōn chloēs* which translates literally "those of Chloe." Other translations render this "Chloe's people," "the ones of Chloe," "them that be of Chloe," and "those of Chloe."

From Paul's letter we learn that he was aware of some serious issues in Corinth. He had received a report from *all* of Chloe's people. This would indicate an official correspondence on behalf of the church, not just a report from a disgruntled person or two. Although Scripture doesn't disclose the identity of those who brought forth the report, when Paul responded in writing noting that he had received the information from Chloe's people, he acknowledged the authority behind the report he had received. His writing the letter in itself emphasized the point that the issues at hand were not merely idle tales or complaints. They obviously bore enough weight to receive a lengthy letter of explanation.

Commentators have identified Chloe as:
- A respected member of the church"[100]
- A woman of character and good standing"[101]
- A godly matron and a "good office herein she did her neighbours"[102]
- An "eminent Corinthian lady, known to the Church, who, like Lydia at Philippi, kept an establishment, and her people."[103]

In his *Exposition of the Whole Bible*, John Gill wrote Chloe seemed to be the name of a woman who "very probably lived at Corinth, and was a member of the church there, and at the head of a family of great worth and credit; who being grieved at the growing animosities, and disturbances there raised, wrote to the apostle ... desiring him to use his interest to put a stop to them."[104]

Chloe may well have been the leader of a house church, especially given that no other person is indicated in Scripture as the leader of the Corinthian church. In Corinth, as in Rome and Ephesus, several house churches comprised "the church" of the city. Paul's letter indicates that Chloe contacted Paul because he was the one who had established the work in her area. She had questions on governmental and doctrinal issues and she most likely sent representatives with her written concerns to Paul to get his advice.

Some of the lack of detail about Chloe can be pieced together from issues transmitted in Paul's letter to the Corinthians. Much of the content of 1 Corinthians is Paul's response to the letter he received. He said, "Now concerning the things whereof ye wrote unto me" (1 Cor 7:1). The primary reasons Paul wrote the Corinthians was to address the divisive spirit and correct errors and abuses that had sprung up among them.

Whoever Chloe was, she was well known to Paul and the church and was obviously a person of influence. In Paul's day, a letter written to a woman would have mentioned her name alongside her husband or father, but that wasn't the case with Chloe. If a husband or other male had been present (especially one in leadership), he would have been mentioned. Chloe's "people" most likely were the members of a Corinthian house church. If they were simply those of her household, they would still have represented a large number of people. Households in ancient Rome included family, slaves, freedmen, and women, aunts, uncles, cousins and even ex-in-laws,[105] all of whom would have been under Chloe's leadership and care. The bulk of the evidence conveys the idea that Chloe was the head of her house and also the leader of a local church that assembled therein to worship.

Priscilla, the Teacher

Political strife uprooted Priscilla and Aquila (a Jewish married couple) from their home when Claudius expelled the Jews from Rome in 49 A.D. Mentioned six times in four books by two different authors, Priscilla and Aquila are always referenced together. In three places Aquila's name is mentioned first, and in the other three, Priscilla is mentioned first. This may not seem relevant in our day, but in Greco-Roman society the man was always named first unless the woman was one of high standing and influence. By mentioning Priscilla's name first on three occasions, at the very least she is considered on equal footing ministry-wise with her husband. They were both valued disciples and Priscilla may have been the prominent partner in ministry.

When Aquila and Priscilla moved from Rome they worked as tent makers in Corinth with Paul. The apostle lived with them for eighteen months before the three left together on a missionary journey. During the considerable amount of time the three lived, worked, and ministered together, there is no indication Paul advised Priscilla to refrain from teaching or speaking in public. If that was his position for all women in all churches, it seems he would have shared it with this prominent ministry couple.

After arriving in Ephesus, Aquila and Priscilla remained in the city while Paul traveled on to Syria. According to Paul both husband and wife were his helpers. They risked their lives for his sake. Paul commended and thanked Aquila and Priscilla and noted their work and sacrifice had such impact it had reached all the Gentile churches.

Priscilla is considered by many scholars to be the first example in Scripture of a Christian woman serving as a preacher or teacher. The couple's ministry to a prominent man named Apollos was significant. Apollos was zealous for the things of the Lord and known for being an eloquent speaker. In 1 Corinthians 4, Apollos was one of the "us" Paul referenced as an apostle in the context of his letter. Paul extensively addressed factions that had arisen in the church in 1 Corinthians. Some people had been divisively contending over which leader they were "from." Some said they were from Paul, others said Apollos, and still others claimed to be from Peter (Cephas).

Why would church members boast about following Apollos instead of a known apostle? The most probable answer is that the Corinthians believed Apollos *was* an apostle, and Paul held this position as well. If he had not, he would have corrected them. Apollo's apostleship is important in the discussion of Priscilla and Aquila's ministry because the two became his teachers in an era when women were forbidden to touch the Torah scrolls or participate in the discussion of Scripture in the synagogue.

> "And a certain Jew named Apollos, born at Alexandria, an eloquent man, and mighty in the scriptures, came to Ephesus. This man was instructed in the way of the Lord; and being fervent in the spirit, he spake and taught diligently the things of the Lord, knowing only the baptism of John. And he began to speak boldly in the synagogue: whom when Aquila and Priscilla had heard, they took him unto them, and expounded unto him the way of God more perfectly" (Acts 18:24-26).

Scripture notes both Priscilla and Aquila invited Apollos, an educated, eloquent man strong in his knowledge of the Word into their home. He was not a child, but a capable teacher and powerful orator of their shared Jewish heritage. Priscilla's teaching of this highly educated man seems to set a precedent. A woman skilled in the Word may teach men—a concept that when applied in our day would include Bible colleges and seminaries.

Priscilla and Aquila's teaching was so effective Apollos was eventually sent by the Ephesian church to Corinth. There he furthered the work in the church Paul, Aquila, and Priscilla had established. Ironically, some of the verses used to restrict women from teaching or preaching were written by Paul to churches where Priscilla was directly involved in ministry. Paul was not shy to call people out who needed correcting; but instead of rectifying a "problem," he praised Priscilla for her ministry and leadership.

Paul called Priscilla and Aquila his *synergos* in Christ. The King James Version renders this Greek word into the English word "helpers," but additional renderings include "a companion in work," "a fellow worker," and a "joint promoter." The word *synergy* is derived from this word which means "working together." The Merriam-Webster dictionary defines *synergy* as "the increased effectiveness that results when two or more people or businesses work together."

Paul was making the point that by his joint labor with Priscilla and Aquila, the work of the kingdom was dynamically impacted with increased effectiveness. He used the word again in reference to Apollos when he wrote that he had planted and Apollos watered, but God had given the increase. These early church leaders were *synergos*—laborers together with Christ (see 1 Cor 8:9).

Priscilla and Aquila hosted a church in their home and likely co-pastored this work (see 1 Cor 16:19). When Paul recognized

> "We can't limit pastoral ministry to a stereotypical gender role; God uses both males and females in spiritual leadership."
> —David K. Bernard, Dth, JD
> General Superintendent,
> United Pentecostal
> Church International

Priscilla as a woman laborer in the gospel, he used the same term he used to describe Clement and Timothy (see Phil 4:3; 1 Thess 3:2). The vocabulary Paul used when noting his co-laborers and colleagues referred to more than hospitality. He considered them his partners in the work of God.

Junia, the Apostle

In his letter to the Romans, Paul praised two particular believers, Andronicus and Junia. These leaders were Paul's blood relatives. They shared his imprisonment for their faith and were identified as "of note among the apostles." In fact, Andronicus and Junia were believers prior to Paul's conversion to Christianity.

In the passages before and after Romans 16:7, Paul listed his greetings to and appreciation of many who served alongside him. What makes this commendation unique and consequential is Junia's gender and connection to apostleship. Of course, Paul recognized the service of many women, but Junia being noted "among the apostles" is compelling—if not pivotal—in understanding the role of women in ministry in the early church.

The first thing to establish before discussing apostleship is the question of Junia's femininity. Most contemporary New Testament scholars agree Junia was a woman. In fact, the majority of Greek New Testament manuscripts refer to her as female. Junia was a popular name for nobility, and throughout early church history Junia's feminine gender was widely accepted.[106] While some have proposed Junia is a Greek variant or nickname for a man, Junia was not Greek, but Latin.[107] Others have suggested Junias (as some later translators rendered the name) is a contraction of a masculine name, but Eldon Epp, author of *Junia: The First Woman Apostle,* found no use of the masculine name Junias in the first century in non-biblical Greek literature and only rare usage in the eras following.[108]

Jerome, a fourth century scholar best known for his translation of the Bible into Latin, referred to Junia as a woman. John Chrysostom, the Archbishop of Constantinople (c. 349 – 407), did as well, which is significant due to his generally negative thoughts towards women. Of Junia, however, he wrote, "Oh! how great is the devotion of this woman, that she should be even counted worthy of the appellation of apostle!"[109] An appellation is a name, title, or designation; and Chrysostom, who was no fan of women in ministry, concurred that the woman Junia was indeed an apostle.

The first to propose Junia may have been a man did so in the early third century. It was suggested by Origen, a philosopher whose views on women in general (like Chrysostom's) were quite negative. Ironically, in his earlier works, Origin spoke of Junia as a female.[110]

According to the *Anchor Bible Dictionary,* "Without exception, the Church Fathers in late antiquity identified Andronicus's partner in Romans 16:7 as a woman, as did minuscule 33 in the 9th century."[111] (Miniscule 33 is an ancient manuscript that included all but one of the books of the New Testament.) The fact there was so little questioning of Junia's gender in her era and in medieval times is remarkable.

Junia's gender has been fiercely debated primarily due to Paul's reference to apostleship. The title "apostle" indicates the highest level of leadership and authority in the first century church. If in fact Junia was a female apostle, her position established a weighty precedent for women in ministry.

The language Paul used—specifically in the English translations of his words—made room for confusion. What exactly does "of note among the apostles" mean? Was the couple just "known to" or "well regarded" by the apostles?

While some have come to the latter conclusion, the Greek indicates Adronicus and Junia were *not* simply "known by" or even "known as" apostles, but were considered exceptional in their calling.[112] Consider the vocabulary and grammar used specifically by Paul, "Salute Andronicus and Junia, my kinsmen, and my fellow-prisoners, who are of note among the apostles, who also were in Christ before me" (Romans 16:7). The word translated "among" is the Greek word *en*. It denotes position and by implication a relation to the rest.[113] This would mean Adronicus and Junia were noted to be "in" the group of people called apostles—"in the interior of some whole."[114]

Looking at the clause "who are of note among the apostles," the two prepositional phrases "of note" and "among the apostles" both modify (are subordinate to and describe) the pronoun "who." The "who" were the "two" (Adronicus and Junia). The two were "of note" and "among the apostles." It would be highly unlikely for the prepositional phrase "among the apostles" to modify the adjective phrase "of note." For example, in the sentence, "The cat is asleep on her bed," both "asleep" and "on her bed" refer back to the cat.

The Greek word *en* is used twice in Romans 16:7. Rev. Kevin M. Shaw explained the language this way, "Just as surely as they were 'in' *[en]* Christ, they were also 'in' *[en]* the apostles." The language indicates that Paul commended Adronicus and Junia as notable fellow laborers and as members of a special group of people called apostles which included the original Twelve, Matthias, Paul, Silvanus, Timotheus, and even Jesus (see Acts 1:25–26, 1 Thes 1:1, 2:6; Heb 3:1).

Paul's usage elsewhere of the word "among" indicates his intended meaning in this passage was their significance within the group of people called apostles. Paul declared Jesus the firstborn "among" the brethren (see Rom 8:29). Jesus was firstborn, and he was one of the brethren. Paul mentioned that he wanted to bear fruit "among" the other believers (see Rom 1:13). He wanted to bear his own fruit, and he wanted the believers to bear their fruit. They were all to be fruit bearers. The angel who spoke to Mary said she was blessed "among women" (see Luke 1:28). Being "among" meant being one of them. These phrases, similar to the one used by Paul regarding Adronicus and Junia, reveal the magnitude of the prestige the ones identified held within the group they were among. In the case of Adronicus and Junia, the apostles.

An apostle is one who is "set apart" and "sent out" as God's messenger to bring the gospel to a place it was not previously known and establish a church. That is what Adronicus and Junia did. They weren't self-appointed, but a God-given gift to the church (see Eph 4:11).

Beyond the debate over her correct title, there is no doubt Junia was a venerated leader in the early church and was honored by Paul as a fellow laborer in the gospel. Whatever "laboring" meant to Paul, he applied also to her as he used the same language when he wrote to the church in Philippi: "And I intreat thee also, true yokefellow, help those women which laboured with me in the gospel, with Clement also, and with other my fellowlabourers, whose names are in the book of life" (Phil 4:3). Paul's fellowlaborerers were engaged in the same type of apostolic work he did—preaching, teaching, and evangelizing. On a side note, tradition identifies Clement (mentioned in the above verse) as the bishop of Rome. Sadly, much of the history of the early believers in Rome was destroyed due to the persecution of Nero and burning of the capitol, but the Bible indicates Adronicus and Junia may have been the ones who laid the foundation for the first century church in the Roman Empire's capitol.

Paul honored this dynamic duo as his relatives, prisoner companions, fellow apostles, and predecessors in the faith. His declaration that they were "before" him may indicate that the two were some of Jesus's earliest disciples.[115] In Paul's acknowledgment of their precedence, he gave respectful and courteous regard to their positions and leadership.

Scot McKnight, biblical scholar and author of *Junia is not Alone*, wrote, "Junia was an apostle. Which means … she was in essence a Christ-experiencing, Christ-representing, church-establishing, probably miracle-working, missionizing woman who preached the gospel and taught the church."[116] Junia was a person any Christian could look up to as an example of a church leader and an inspiring role model for the called women of God in every generation.

Joanna, Follower of Jesus

Joanna was an upper-class woman in Herod Antipas's court. Married to Herod's household manager, Chuza, Joanna was a woman of high rank and means. Her wealth and position, however, could not buy her health.

At the hand of Jesus, Joanna experienced divine healing from an unknown sickness. Luke mentioned healings that occurred among the women from both "evil spirits" and "infirmities." Whatever Joanna's condition, Jesus cured it.

Joanna became a dedicated disciple and follower of Jesus. She supported the Lord and his disciples in their travels and provided for them financially from her substance. She is mentioned along with Mary Magdalene and Susanna (see Luke 8:1–3). These women traveled with Jesus and his disciples throughout the cities and villages where he preached and shared the glad tidings of the kingdom of God. It was in large part due to the backing of influential women like Joanna that Jesus and his followers were able to travel and minister as they did.

With wholehearted devotion Joanna immersed herself in Jesus's ministry. This woman (who had previously lived a life of opulent comfort) chose to lower herself socially and wander with people of lesser positions as a disciple of Jesus.

Although Scripture doesn't specifically name Joanna as one of the women at the crucifixion, it's likely she was among the unnamed women mentioned who had followed Jesus from Galilee and watched the crucifixion from the distance (see Luke 23:49). These same women went with the men who carried the body of Jesus to the sepulcher (see Luke 23:55).

Scripture documents Joanna's presence at the gravesite on resurrection morning (see Luke 24:10). She held the distinct honor of being one of the first witnesses to the resurrection and even saw the angels present at the tomb. Joanna was privileged to be one of the first to proclaim the magnificent news of the resurrection of Jesus to the world.

Joanna's identity has received speculation in recent years. Some scholars have proposed she is the same woman identified as Junia in Romans 16:7. In Richard

Bauckham's book *Gospel Women: Studies of the Named Women in the Gospels,* he concluded the Roman name Junia (*Iounias*) is a form of the Hebrew name Joanna (*Iōan(n)a*).[117] It's not unusual in Scripture to find people identified by more than one name and in relation to the people being addressed. For instance, the man attributed to writing the book of Mark is called John, Mark, and Marcus. Paul stopped using his Hebrew name Saul when he began his mission to the Gentiles. When multiple languages are used in the same region, multiple names makes more sense.

Dispersed Jews were known to adopt names that fit in with the communities in which they lived. Joanna may have adopted a Latin name close to her Hebrew name. The names Junia and Joanna were both used for aristocracy and were similar in sound. Many indicators could point to the conclusion that Joanna and Junia were two names for the same person. Junia was connected with Rome. Paul stated that she was in Christ before his conversion in 34 A.D. The title "apostle" used for Junia would apply even more confidently if she had been a direct witness of the teachings, miracles, and resurrection of Jesus. Joanna, according to a traditional understanding of apostolic prerequisites (which included being with Jesus from the beginning and a witness to the resurrection), would have qualified as an apostle.

Joanna was part of Jesus's inner circle and is presumed to have continued on with the disciples. Acts 1 notes women in the crowd on the day of Pentecost. Joanna was likely among them, and if so, she would have received the infilling of the spirit of God in the upper room and continued to serve the Lord in his Great Commission (see Acts 1:12–14; Matt 28:19).

Few details are known of Joanna's life but much can be discerned about her character. It is conceivable this woman knew Jesus as well as any—if not most—of his followers. She was faithful to the man and his mission. Scripture records her service to the Lord using the same word for "ministered" (*diakoneō*) as is translated elsewhere in the New Testament for the "office of a deacon" (see Luke 8:3; 1 Tim 3:10). This woman may well have been both missionary and apostle. She was certainly a disciple of Jesus and a blessing to the early church.

Phebe, Deacon and Leader

Who was Phebe? What was her role in the church? Paul's commendation of her in his letter to the Roman church begs these questions and more.

Phebe is perhaps the most controversial woman in Paul's epistles. She received an important letter from him and delivered it at his request to the church in Rome. The apostle documented his approval of Phebe and her standing with him personally and in the church. By calling her "sister" he connected the two of them with the family of God in Rome.

The most interesting word in Romans 16:1 is the one translated "servant." In Greek, Phebe's title is *diakonos*. This word is translated "deacon" and "minister" elsewhere in the New Testament. Given that Paul introduced Phebe as a *diakonos* of a specific church, it's reasonable to believe she held the position of "minister" or "deacon." After all, he was sending her on an official church mission.

Paul commonly made introductions with titles, including his own. He began several letters, "Paul, an apostle" (see 2 Cor 1:1; Gal 1:1; Eph 1:1; Col 1:1). When he introduced himself as a "servant," he used the Greek word, *doulos*, which means a bondservant or slave (see Phil 1:1; Rom 1:1).

Throughout Scripture, when *diakonos* referred to a man, translators rendered the word "deacon" or "minister" (see 1 Cor 3:5; Eph 3:7, 6:21; Col 1:7, 23, 25) but for some reason chose a different word (servant) for Phebe. When Archipus and Onesimus were active or doing *diakonia* and *diakonea* respectively, the Greek words were rendered "ministry" (see Col 4:7, Phlm 13). In fact, the only place Paul used the word with a personal name and it was not translated "minister" was in the case of Phebe (see Rom 16:1). Inconsistent translations, such as in this case, may have influenced the modern understanding of some in regards to the role of women in ministry.

Diakonos in general means "attending to another's interest." In addition to menial duties, *Strong's* outlines its use in reference to "a Christian teacher and pastor (technically, a deacon or deaconess):—deacon, minister, servant."[118] The term is gender inclusive; it's a masculine/feminine noun. Contemporary understanding of the role of deacon often relates it to a specific church office; however, in Scripture it doesn't have a clearly delineated job description. What should be apparent, however, is its gender application.

The same Greek word used to identify Phebe's role in the church appears in different forms throughout the New Testament:

- Jesus said he was a minister (*diaconon*) of the circumcision (see Rom 15:8)
- Paul and Apollos are identified as ministers (*diaconoi*) who caused others to believe (see 1 Cor 3:5)

- Paul and Timothy were able ministers (*diaconous*) of the New Testament (see 2 Cor 3:6)
- Paul said he and Timothy, in everything they did, tried to show they were true ministers (*diaconoi*) of God (see 2 Cor 6:4).

In Edith Deen's comprehensive work on more than 300 women in Scripture, she concluded Phebe "was a Deaconess of the Church at Cenchrea."[119] For those who give little weight to the title "deacon" due to the lack of organizational structure in the early church of an official body of deacons, one important fact should be understood— whatever it meant for men, it meant for women.

In the verse following Phebe's introduction, Paul instructed the church to receive her "in the Lord, as becometh saints, and that ye assist her in whatsoever business she hath need of you: for she hath been a succourer of many, and of myself also" (Rom 16:2). Paul was telling the members of the Roman church that Phebe had been a leader over many and they should make themselves available at Phebe's disposal.

The Greek word *prostatis* is a noun rendered "succourer" in the King James Version. It means "a woman set over others" and "a female guardian, protectress, patroness, caring for the affairs of others and aiding them with her resources."[120] No doubt Phebe held a prominent role in the church community.

First century historian Josephus used the masculine form *prostates* when referring to important leaders and always with positive connotations. Author Aída Besançon Spencer conducted extensive research on the word as used by Josephus in his historical writings. She discovered:

"Moses and Joseph are called *prostates* of the people ... Solomon was made *prostates* of the temple ... Josephus as 'governor' is a *prostates* ... Antipater calls Caesar the *prostates* of the world. God is *prostates* over all ... Clement calls Jesus Christ the *prostates*, the leader who champions his followers."[121]

It seems clear *prostatis* (translated "succourer" in the KJV and "helper" and "sponsor" in other versions) means much more than assisting or providing financial aid. In verb form, it means:

1. to set or place before
   A. to set over
   B. to be over, to superintend, preside over

C. to be a protector or guardian

    i. to give aid

D. to care for, give attention to

    i. profess honest occupations[122]

Phebe obviously held a leadership position in the church in Cenchrea, a port in Corinth. Paul's choice of words lets us know Phebe was a *diakonos*. She served as minister or deacon and *prostatis*, one set in a position of official leadership. The literal meaning of *prostatis*, "one standing before," emphasizes Phebe's position was one of authority, not inferiority.

Paul entrusted Phebe with more than the practical elements of service like those deacons chosen to wait on tables in Acts 6. Surely this godly woman served, but Phebe was also someone who acted with authority. Paul authorized her to deliver his missive to a church he had not yet visited. In it, he spoke of her as a minister worthy to be assisted with anything she required while she acted as his ambassador.

It's highly probable she read the letter to the congregation and answered any questions about its contents. Paul's letter included considerable doctrinal elements that could have been questioned by the people. It would have been Phebe's responsibility to expand on what Paul wrote and clarify any issues.

When Paul identified a person as his co-laborer or fellow servant, he in essence indicated they were in positions of authority similar to his. Some theologians believe women may teach, speak, or preach, but they

> If Paul believed all women were to be silent in all churches, it would have been inconsistent with his position for him to delegate Phebe as his representative and voice to the congregation in Rome.

don't believe any woman should have authority over any man in the church. Phebe gives an explicit example of a woman placed in a position of authority over both men and women.

In the Greek *prostatis* is the noun form of the verb used in relation to deacons. In his letter to the Romans, Paul said Phebe had been *prostatis* over many (see Rom 16:2), and elsewhere he said a deacon was to *proïstēmi* (rule) his own house well (see 1 Tim

3:12). As this pertains to the discussion of women in ministry, we have two possible applications: 1) Phebe ruled over the church, providing for them, making decisions, and maintaining in the same way a deacon should rule over his or her house; or 2) The rule of a deacon was limited to a position of financial support, which seems unlikely and divergent in the translation and Paul's appointment of her as his chosen emissary to the church in Rome.

Phebe was a devout Christian of excellent character, a giver and servant. Theodoret, an influential theologian in the fifth century, noted, "The fame of Phebe was spoken of throughout the world. She was known not only to the Greeks and Romans, but also to the Barbarians."[123]

The women mentioned in this chapter provide ample documentation to the active ministerial and leadership functions women served in the New Testament church. Women were disciples, prophets, and teachers. There is no doubt they held positions of great influence in the early church. The roles and duties women served under the direct supervision of the apostles, they should be allowed to serve in the church today.

Paul and "The Big Three"

Nevertheless neither is the man without the woman,
neither the woman without the man, in the Lord.
1 Corinthians 11:11

For a doctrinal position to be valid it must be based on a true premise that leads to an unalterable conclusion. With that thought in mind, let us make a careful examination of Paul's letters to his son in the faith, Timothy, and the church he founded in Corinth. Much rides on a correct interpretation of a few verses in two letters that have been interpreted by some as restraining women from ministry. I call these passages in 1 Corinthians 11, 1 Corinthians 14, and 1 Timothy 2 "the big three."

1 Corinthians 11

In 1 Corinthians 11 Paul instructed both men and women in the appropriate ways to conduct themselves when speaking in church meetings. He specifically addressed the way Christian women were to present themselves when praying and prophesying. Much attention has been given to defining Paul's teaching on head coverings in this chapter. It's critical, however, when studying, that we don't overlook the key issue at hand. Paul's words affirmed women were indeed permitted to pray and prophesy in public (see 1 Cor 11:5–6). In his letter to the Corinthians he gave women the "how tos" of functioning in these ministry capacities with reverence and propriety. If Paul's intention had been to forbid women from praying and prophesying, it seems he would have crafted this portion of his letter as a correction rather than a teaching on the proper manner in which women were to present and conduct themselves in public ministry.

In Paul's letter to the Corinthians he addressed congregational deeds and functions. Chapter 11 is the beginning of a four-chapter segment in which he specifically wrote on the subjects of prayer and prophecy. In verses four and five, when we read Paul's parallel statements that begin "every man praying or prophesying" and "but every woman that prayeth or prophesieth" respectively, we see Paul was addressing both men and women. Clearly both genders participated in co-ed public prayer and prophecy.[124]

Throughout Scripture women prophesied. Some women believers functioned regularly enough in the prophetic to gain notoriety as women "who did prophesy" (see Acts 21:9). To clarify, the act of prophesying, according to Paul in this letter, includes:

- Comfort (see v 14:3)
- Edification (see v 14:3)
- Evangelistic witness (see vv 14:22, 24)
- Exhortation (see v 14:3)
- Instruction (see v 14:31).

According to the authors of *Why Not Women?*, "'Every woman who prays or prophesies' summarized the full scope of the Jewish concept of priestly ministry. To pray is to speak to God on behalf of God's people or oneself. To prophesy is to speak to God's people on behalf of God."[125] Together, prayer and prophecy demonstrate the essence of congregational worship. Through prayer, those who gather to worship access the presence of God. In response to their prayers, the Lord speaks back through his people by giving prophetic words to those who function in this gift.

In the New Testament the role of priest is no longer designated or functioning in the same manner as it did in Old Testament days. With the death, burial, and resurrection of Jesus accomplished, the role of priest previously assigned exclusively to Levite men was granted to every believer (see 1 Pet 2:9). Men and women speak to God for themselves, receive direct words from him, and intercede for others, as well.

> In a church comprised of converts from many faiths, the principles Paul taught in 1 Corinthians 11 accommodated the public ministry of women in a society that had previously silenced them.

While all the specifics Paul was dealing with in Corinth are unknown to us today, we do know the church was a melting pot of people from a wide variety of ethnic groups, social classes, and religions. In each of the cultures present in the church, the hairstyles and veils of men and women held different meanings—from mourning to prostitution.

Gender Distinction ≠ Limited Function

Paul's teaching on head coverings in the first part of 1 Corinthians 11 affirms gender distinction without placing limitations on the exercise of spiritual gifts in the body. In fact, Paul taught that every believer, male and female, should desire spiritual gifts (see 1 Cor 14:1).

Paul clearly recognized a differentiation between women and men, but at the same time stressed their interdependence (see 1 Cor 11:8). He noted:

- Woman came from man
- All men and women enter the world through the womb (mutual dependence)
- Every human is the creation of God made in his image.

In the Creation timeline, Adam was made before Eve; chronology, however doesn't in itself imply superiority or competency. Every man and every woman is the handiwork of God—fearfully and wonderfully made—uniquely gifted and called.

Paul taught men and women how to conduct themselves as they served and participated in the church. His teaching lets us know that a woman's ministry function doesn't override her obligation to appropriately conduct herself in all her life roles. A woman's femininity isn't removed by the infilling of God's Spirit, and neither does a new birth experience disestablish gender distinctions.

Paul explicitly taught that wherever men and women found themselves and in whatever role they functioned, women were women and men were men. When it comes to public worship, gender distinctions should be honored while allowing opportunities for all to serve in the manner established by God for his church, which is a casteless, genderless, spiritual organism.

Headship

"But I would have you know, that the head of every man is Christ; and the head of the woman is the man; and the head of Christ is God" (1 Cor 11:3).

The context surrounding the above verse indicates Paul's audience was a public assembly of believers. His mention of heads in this verse prepares the way for the next two verses in which he spoke directly to both men and women about appropriate conduct in public prayer and worship. The context lets us know the verse is about personal behavior, and not exclusively about "male headship."

The apostle began his teaching in this chapter with the concept of godly order. After praising the church for keeping the ordinances he had taught them (see v 2), he began verse 3, "But I would have you know...." The teachings Paul outlined following these words pertain to what he wanted God's people to know, and that is how men and women should conduct themselves in worship.

A concept of "male headship" or "male authority" as some have interpreted from 1 Corinthians 11:3 has at times been used to limit women in ministry. Let us look to the original texts and see if we can comprehend the true intention of the author.

First, we must recognize the vast horizon of interpretations on the subject of headship. Educated, scholarly, godly men and women strongly support polarizing views. If experts cannot agree, individuals and/or religious organizations may be wise to refrain from using a disputed passage to establish a universal church doctrine—especially when elsewhere in Scripture the same author supports a position differing from a personal interpretation. Since scholars have not reached consensus on the meaning of "head" (the Greek word *kephale*) in 1 Corinthians 11:3, I will not make a dogmatic presentation one way or the other. It's simply not necessary to support the position that women may indeed serve in ministry roles in the church. For your information, however, following is a simplified overview:

Some scholars argue that *kephale* refers to rulership and implies submission. It does in some cases. Other scholars believe *kephale* means "source" or "origin." It does in some cases. In seven places in the New Testament, the word *kephale* was used in reference to Jesus. Christ is the head of all. He is the ruler of all. He is the source of all (see John 1:3–4).

While I do not have enough training in the Greek language to make a case that proves one meaning over the other, Daniel Segraves, Professor of Biblical Theology at Urshan Graduate School of Theology, said, "It seems most consistent to understand the meaning of [head] *kephale* in I Corinthians 11:3 in the same way we understand it in all three uses [in the verse]. If it means something other than source or origin, difficult questions arise: Is Christ not the head of woman as well as man? Must women come to Christ through men? In what sense is God the head of Christ? What are the theological and Christological implications of this?"[126] For now I will leave the debate to the scholars, but consistency and universal applicability do seem to be legitimate factors in making a determination of a word's meaning. And even if a person believes "head" exclusively means "ruler," submission is not mentioned or implied in Paul's teaching in 1 Corinthians 11. In fact, the only authority mentioned is the authority the woman has over her own head.

Context determines how a particular term is being used in a given passage, and the context in 1 Corinthians 11 does not indicate all males have authority over all females. In fact, when Paul said "the head of the woman is the man," the singular use of "the woman" and "the man" indicates he was referring particularly to a husband-wife relationship. With that in mind, it seems Paul was not presenting a creation-based hierarchy in 1 Corinthians 11, but a chronology. "Who came first" does not always indicate "who is in charge." In fact, when we read the Bible, we see many times the Lord chose a younger-born to lead. Moses was Aaron's younger brother (see Exod 7:7), Joseph was Jacob's eleventh-born son (see Gen 37:5–11), and God chose David over his seven older brothers (see 1 Sam 16:1–13).

What lesson then, could Paul have been conveying with his talk of heads? One of the points he made in this chapter is that women, by the grace of God, have their own authority to stand in God's presence (see 1 Cor 11:10). Perhaps the apostle was attempting to teach newly converted patriarchs and pagans the Lord's original paradigm for men and women—one based in Creation itself. Because the first woman came from the first man, she not only reflects the glory of man, she also reflects the glory of God.

> ## SIDENOTE
> ### *from Daniel Segraves*
>
> The statement "man ... is the image and glory of God; but woman is the glory of man" (1 Corinthians 11:7, NKJV) must not be taken to mean that men are somehow superior to women, for women are also the image of God (Genesis 1:26–27). In this case, the idea is that in addition to being the image and glory of God by virtue of creation, woman is also the glory of man.[127]
>
> —Daniel Segraves, PhD
> Author and Professor, Urshan
> Graduate School of Theology

This is not a place of lesser capability or worth. The woman was created for man's glory, completion, and companionship. Their union blessed both the husband and the wife.

When it comes to the concept of *kephale,* theologians may never come to a consensus of opinion; however, everyone should agree that Paul's message in 1 Corinthians 11 came in the form of a metaphor. He wasn't talking about literal heads, but giving an analogy. This form of speech is especially sensitive to context, and context is critical when making evaluations of Scripture.

Even in the strongest case made for a male, authoritarian, ruling headship, the greatest head of all became servant of all. Jesus served both men and women—unto the point of death. He never attempted to dominate people, and he specifically instructed his followers not to be lords one over another, but to serve one another as he served them. He gave his disciples authority and charged them to minister. Jesus never taught or exhibited male dominance. And in regards to authority in the church, Paul's teachings may well promote quite the opposite of the restrictive interpretations some have taken them to mean.

1 Corinthians 14

It's interesting that while the concept of male authority is often at the fore of the debate on women in ministry, Scripture uses the word authority only once in the New Testament in reference to the relationship between husband and wife. In 1 Corinthians 7:4, before Paul addressed the "keep silence in church" issue later in his letter, he first dealt with the subject of authority in marriage. And he did it in a surprising way. Paul said that a wife doesn't have authority over her own body; but in marriage, she gives that "power" to her husband. He went on to say that in the same way, the husband doesn't have authority over his own body, but yields that authority to his wife. This was a radical statement in a culture where most men considered women to be possessions.

Mutual submission is the very essence of Christ. It's the model and prototype for Jesus's dealing with people and how people, in turn, should submit one to another in the love of God. Serving God is a sweet surrender to him, and it includes giving yourself in service to others as well. This is the polar opposite to harsh authoritarian demands for obedience and submission. The authority exercised by Jesus was firm, but infused with gentleness.

Elsewhere in Paul's letter to the Corinthians, he brought forth another thought-provoking concept. An unbelieving husband can be sanctified through his wife. A Christian wife brings holiness into her marriage even when the spouse is not a believer (see 1 Cor 7:14). Paul asked believing wives to lay down their rights to leave unbelieving husbands (see 1 Cor 7:12–13). These words may be among some of Paul's most unexpected as they indicated a wife had the authority to make such a decision (even if it was not the best decision for her, her family, or the church).

While the message of salvation hasn't changed over the years, methods of worship and church organizations have. Comparing today's structured church services with New Testament house church gatherings must be done carefully and with integrity. We cannot superimpose our modern-day formats upon our perception of early church gatherings in a way that both are seen as a perfect fit. Neither can we assume similarities that aren't supported in Scripture.

For example, in contemporary church services, believers most often sit in seats facing a pulpit on a raised platform, but Paul's writing paints a different picture. In the early church believers predominantly met at homes. People from all walks of life and social classes assembled in environments where everyone was welcomed and encouraged to bring a song or a word similar to Amish and Mennonite practices today (see Col 3:16). In this environment women were free to minister as long as things were done decently and in order.

The problem addressed in Paul's first recorded letter to the Corinthians pertained to disruptions that occurred during public assembly. Apparently some women believers (who should have been listening) had created disorder by asking questions during teaching. A solution was offered to correct this practice that included women holding their questions until they could ask their husbands at home.

It has been proposed that men and women may have sat apart from one another in worship—the women on one side, the men on the other. If this was the case—and women were calling out questions—it would certainly have caused a noisome confusion. Regardless of a congregation's seating arrangement, disrupting an assembly with questions would be out of order and seems to be the issue at hand. Let's look at a passage in Paul's letter that has been the source of much confusion and discussion:

"Let your women keep silence in the churches: for it is not permitted unto them to speak; but they are commanded to be under obedience as also saith the law. And if they will learn any thing, let them ask their husbands at home: for it is a shame for women to speak in the church" (1 Cor 14:34–35).

To correctly apply these verses, we must first understand as much as possible the writer's intention. What message was Paul trying to get across? Who was he writing and why? And then, how should his teachings apply in today's church? What did Paul mean?

Learning in quiet submission was the customary position assumed by novice students. In Paul's day, dialogue was allowed in some forms of education, but not in situations when there were vastly varying degrees of general knowledge. Learning in silence did not degrade an uneducated person. It meant students accepted a position and demeanor in which they learned without challenging their instructor.

Keeping silent and being submitted could have referred to a student-teacher relationship in which disruptive speaking, and not all verbal utterances, should be restrained. For instance, the words "rest in the Lord" reference a silencing of self, submitting to the Lord with an attentive demeanor (see Ps 37:7). Solomon wrote, "The words of wise men are heard in quiet" (Ecc 9:17).

The words in verses 34 and 35 exclusively addressed wives (not all women), which could well indicate the instruction was meant to silence specific women who were questioning and disrupting the flow of service. Verse 35 speaks to the unlearned asking questions in a disruptive manner and doesn't imply barring educated, skilled women from public teaching or speaking.

The case that specific married women were being addressed is strengthened when we consider the remedy put forth to deal with the situation. Asking your husband your questions at home wouldn't have provided a solution for the comprehensive needs of the church body. Not all women were married. How would asking a husband at home apply to single women or widows? And what about those who had unbelieving husbands, as was obviously the case (see 1 Cor 7:14–15)? Where would women with unsaved husbands receive answers to their questions?

A universal application of silencing all women doesn't seem to be intended. Would a married woman who received a prophetic word first talk privately with her husband at home before sharing what she received from God for the edification of the body? Even if her husband validated her message, when could she share it if she wasn't allowed to speak in the assembly? How would this scenario allow for a woman to be properly used by God to exercise her spiritual gifts? And what opportunity would a single or widowed woman have to share any oral gift of the Spirit?

Paul purposely chose inclusive language when it came to instructing the church on the exercise of spiritual gifts. The word translated "any man" in reference to the one who spoke in a tongue in the church refers to a "certain one" and would apply to males and females (see 1 Cor 14:27). In the verse following the word translated "himself" also means "herself" and "themselves" (see 1 Cor 14:28). Paul's next words were, "Let the prophets speak" (see 1 Cor 14:29). This command had no reference to gender at all, and two verses later he wrote, "Ye may all prophesy one by one" (1 Cor 14:31).

If Paul was truly teaching the silence of all women, he would have been advocating a position that opposed the prophetic word of God that said, "I will pour out my spirit upon all flesh; and your sons and your daughters shall prophesy" (Joel 2:28). Not only that, but a literal interpretation and application of silencing married women would mean they would not be permitted to utter a sound in church. The root of the word silence indicates a verbal hushing—to "command silence by making the sound *st* or *sch*."[128]

Imagine a congregation where women weren't allowed to sing in the choir, pray out loud, teach Sunday school, recite a Bible verse, testify, make an announcement, or even greet a fellow believer. Few churches would literally apply this passage.

It was Paul's desire that every person in the church would prophesy and speak in tongues (see 1 Cor 4:1, 5). He said that everyone in the church seemed to have something to say—some psalm, doctrine, tongue, revelation or interpretation (see 1 Cor 14:26). And while he encouraged orderly conduct, he never denied the ability of every believer to connect with God and receive something from the Lord to share with the church.

> Perhaps one of the best ways to understand the concepts in this chapter is to determine what they must *not* mean based on other more easily understood passages. Scripture, after all, should interpret Scripture.

The gifts of the Spirit are available to everyone regardless of gender. Of the nine gifts listed in this same letter many are necessarily oral in nature. Others, to be properly applied, would involve speaking (see 1 Cor 12:8–10), such as:

- A word of wisdom
- A word of knowledge
- Prophecy
- Divers kinds of tongues
- Interpretation of tongues.

In Paul's letter to the Corinthians, the same Greek word is translated "silence" five times (see 1 Cor 14:28, 30, 34). Both men and women were addressed and instructed to keep mute when appropriate for the proper exercise of spiritual gifts. No person or group of people were meant to be silenced for all time. Paul used the word "if" in two of these verses, confirming those silencings were contingent upon certain conditions, not universally applicable to specific church members (see 1 Cor 14:28, 30).

In verse 34, keeping silence has the straight-forward meaning of withholding sound. There is more discussion, however, to be made on the word rendered "speak" in the same verse and verse 35. In Catherine Booth's work, *Female Ministry,* she cited several scholarly comments on this word. She first offered Rev. J. H. Robinson's remark: "The silence imposed here must be explained by the verb to speak (*lalein*) used afterwards."[129]

Booth cited other lexicon listings for *lalein* including Johann Friedrich Schleusner's: "I answer, I return a reason, I give rule or precept, I order, decree;" William Greenfield's: "to prattle—be loquacious as a child; to speak in answer—to answer;" and Liddel and Scott's: "to chatter, babble; of birds, to twitter, chirp; strictly, to make an inarticulate sound, opposed to articulate speech; but also, generally, to talk, say."[130]

Looking at these entries, we can conclude that *lalein* certainly could mean something other than speaking words out loud. If Paul did in fact make a prohibition on speaking for women, it wasn't necessarily a regulation against all speaking, but could apply to improper speaking, questioning, demanding, or babbling. Each of these scenarios would bring chaos into the orderly church service Paul was seeking to promote.

The phrase being "under obedience," according to Robinson, means "to refrain from such questionings, dogmatical assertions, and disputations, as would bring them (the women) into collision with the men." He went on to say, "This kind of speaking, and this alone, as it appears to me, was forbidden."[131]

Considering the ample scholarly definitions of *lalein* and the history of the church before, during, and after these words were written in which women did speak, pray, and prophesy, it seems fitting that godly, educated women be given the opportunity to minister. It's certainly evident it was never the Lord's intention to silence his daughters. They are invited to sing, clap their hands, give words of praise, share their testimonies, and be witnesses for him.

There has been a case made by some scholars that Paul was actually quoting Judaizers in verses 34 and 35 and then refuting their words in verse 36. While I believe this could be a possibility, I don't want to cause unnecessary confusion. The words as written are enough on their own. In reading the apostle's letter with deeper understanding of the culture, grammar, and context, it seems evident Paul wasn't universally silencing women, but was conversely attempting to promote universal, orderly participation in the church body by all. After all, he concluded his discourse with these words (in which "brethren" includes all believers, male and female), "Wherefore, brethren, covet to prophesy, and forbid not to speak with tongues. Let all things be done decently and in order" (1 Cor 14:39–40).

In the same way healthy families include the voices of both father and mother, God's church will thrive when both women and men speak—in the congregation and in the conference rooms. That said, a woman called to speak should always do so in an orderly, non-disruptive manner—in a way that edifies the body, and doesn't draw

> Any understanding of Paul's writings in 1 Corinthians 14 must be kept in context with those in the same chapter in which he used inclusive language when he addressed the whole church coming together and exercising spiritual gifts. Elsewhere in the Word, the apostle spoke positively of women in ministry. Some believe Paul restrained women, but it is more likely he swung doors open for women to minister in their God-given callings.

attention to herself. One principle should be clear from Paul's teachings. Neither men, nor women, should be disruptive in the assembly of believers.

1 Timothy 2

So much regarding the role of women in ministry rides on the proper understanding of some of the least understood and most contested words in the Bible. Written by Paul to his protégé around 64 AD, 29 words of Scripture's 783,137 words comprise the only passage in the Word of God that explicitly restricts any woman from teaching. "Let the woman learn in silence with all subjection. But I suffer not a woman to teach, nor to usurp authority over the man, but to be in silence" (1 Tim 2:11–12).

A straightforward reading of these verses may seem to present a sound argument against women teaching; however, their same author wrote to, "Study to shew thyself approved unto God, a workman that needeth not to be ashamed, rightly dividing the word of truth" (see 1 Tim 2:15). So let's look beyond the English translation of this passage, beyond twenty-first century linguistics and culture, and to the historical record to see if we can discover what the author was saying, to whom he was saying it, and why.

Verse 11: Learning in Silence with Subjection

"Let the woman learn in silence with all subjection" (1 Tim 2:11).

The word translated "let" is a connecting word. Yes, it begins a new sentence, but it certainly joins the above verse to the verses preceding it: "In like manner also, that women adorn themselves in modest apparel, with shamefacedness and sobriety; not with broided hair, or gold, or pearls, or costly array; But (which becometh women professing godliness) with good works" (1 Tim 2:9–10).

According to these words of Paul, women professing godliness should be modest, given to good works, and must be allowed to learn. He specified, however, they learn in silence. It's important to determine if the apostle was presenting a timeless principle for all Christians in every culture, or if he was addressing a particular situation. To answer the question requires an examination of the historical, cultural, and literary context.

Paul wrote to Timothy with the purpose of giving him instructions on how to lead the church in Ephesus. First Timothy is one of three books considered Pastoral

Epistles. The Ephesian community where Timothy ministered was steeped in religious cults, particularly those who worshipped the goddess Artemis. Ephesus was home to the largest pagan temple in Asia Minor. Timothy grew up in this community and undoubtedly understood the pervasive influence Artemis worship exerted in the region. Ephesus was saturated in paganism and close in proximity to Corinth. That is why Paul's writings to the Corinthian and Ephesian churches bear strong similarities.

The church in Ephesus was a composite of converted Jews and pagans. The fledgling congregation was home to some who attempted to blend practices in the worship of Artemis, Judaism, and Christianity. Given the writings of Paul and what is known of Greek society, chastity and modesty were issues among the new converts. Some even promoted heresy. Uneducated, assertive women went from house to house causing problems. There were gossips, and some went so far as to stray from the truth to follow Satan (see 1 Tim 5:15).

The content of 1 Timothy, along with a look ahead into the book of 2 Timothy, reveals a serious problem in the church. People were teaching false doctrine. The Ephesian church had its share of liars who wrongly and brazenly called themselves apostles (see Rev 2:2). Paul also noted there were those who desired to be teachers of the law but didn't understand it (see 1 Tim 1:7).

As touched on in the previous section, in the era Paul penned his words, learning in silence was not an insult but an uplifting to women who had previously been banned from the opportunity for religious education. Aida Besançon Spencer, in her book *Beyond the Curse,* concluded that silence was a "positive attribute for rabbinic students. Paul's words declared to his Jewish friends that women should be learning the same way rabbinic students learned."[132]

Simeon, the son of Rabbi Gamaliel (Paul's famous teacher who was a leading authority in the ancient Jewish court in the early first century) said, "All my days have I grown up among the Sages and I have found naught better for a man than silence."[133] Not only were learners to be silent, but silence was venerated and practiced by both learners and the wise. From this viewpoint, it could be considered that Paul was treating women as having the potential and opportunity to be wise students.

The word Paul used for "learn" is the Greek word *manthanō*, which means:

    to learn, be appraised

    1a) to increase one's knowledge, to be increased in knowledge

    1b) to hear, be informed

1c) to learn by use and practice

1c1) to be in the habit of, accustomed to[134]

Manthanō was written in present tense, which means it was a statement of fact or reality at the time it was written. The mood of the word is imperative, which means it "expresses a command to the hearer to perform a certain action by the order and authority of the one commanding."[135] Paul was in essence saying, "Learn now, ma'am. Get into the habit of increasing your knowledge and being informed." His use of the word *manthanō* was significant because it implied formal religious training. It was the word used by the Jews who were astonished at Jesus's teaching. They asked, "How is it this Man has learning [is so versed in the sacred Scriptures and in theology] when He has never studied?" (John 7:15, AMPC).

Paul was expressing a positive opportunity for women to learn. Learning in silence and submission, according to author David Hamilton, "was a frequent formula in the Near East for a model student."[136] It indicated having a teachable attitude—the attitude expressed in James 1:19, "Let every man be swift to hear, slow to speak, slow to wrath." Paul was saying to these women who had never been allowed scholarly education in the synagogue—if they approached learning with an attitude of humble submission, they could have access to the same education male disciples enjoyed. Spencer's research agreed with Hamilton's: "Ancient Jews esteemed silence as a state of calm, restraint at the proper time, respect and affirmation of a speaker."[137]

The word translated "silence" in this passage is not the same as the shushing in 1 Corinthians.[138] It doesn't mean silence as in muzzling, being speechless, being still, or even holding your peace. It has to do with quietness. In fact, the same word was used when Paul addressed the Jews, "And when they heard that he spake in the Hebrew tongue to them, they kept the more silence" (Acts 22:2). In this situation, the people who had been in an uproar chose to still themselves to give Paul their full attention. Quietness connotes deference; it's a respectful submission as opposed to resisting, striving, or arguing.

The root of the word translated *quietness* was used earlier in this same chapter when Paul spoke of living a "peaceable life in all godliness and honesty" (see 1 Tim 2:2). Certainly Paul didn't mean people should live without speaking. Peter also spoke of having a "meek and quiet spirit, which is in the sight of God of great price" (see 1 Pet 3:4).

Learning with a still spirit is the right way for a serious student to learn the ways of the Lord and should be a desire of all believers, male and female. Paul's words, rather than being a derogatory regulation, offered respect to a woman's ability to learn. The true import of his statement was that the woman should no longer be restricted from learning. He quite adamantly told the church she *should* learn—she *must* learn. What some consider harsh words went a step beyond a gracious invitation and made a strong statement to the men, "Let her learn." In the patriarchal culture of Paul's day, the apostle believed and taught women should be granted an education where it had been previously withheld. In fact, educating the uneducated would be his remedy for false teaching in the church.

Verse 11 of 1 Timothy 2 specified that women were to learn "with all subjection." The word translated "subjection" is the same Greek word Paul used when he spoke to both men and women who were obediently subjecting themselves to give to the church (see 2 Cor 9:12–13). All believers, male and female, are to be in subjection to the Word of God.

The Woman in Ephesus

It's important to note how Paul transitioned from speaking from the manner in which men and women should conduct themselves (verses 8–9) to address "the woman" (verse 12). He switched from plural to singular, and then back to plural. This could certainly indicate his restriction was meant for one specific Ephesian woman. In that case, "the woman" who had caused damage in the church (likely by teaching false doctrine) was to be silenced and instructed in the truth. Regardless of gender, any person displaying this conduct should be corrected. If this was Paul's motive, his words demonstrated a pastoral heart that exercised patience and loving discipline.

If Paul had indeed restricted a singular woman from teaching in answer to a specific issue in the Ephesian church, it is simply reading too much into the text to suggest he was establishing a universal church policy for all time and all people. If that was his intention, there should be evidence in Paul's other writings or other places in the Word of God. Remember, for a doctrinal position to be valid it must be based on a true premise that leads to an unalterable conclusion. Since the information on Paul's writings in 1 Timothy is incomplete (a one-sided conversation), probability comes into play. In other words, given what is known, what is the most likely scenario?

In 1 Timothy it's evident there was a serious situation with false teaching in the church. Paul opened his letter with a request that Timothy stay in Ephesus because false doctrine was being taught (see 1 Tim 1:1–3). Within the chapter are further references (see 1 Tim 1:10, 19, 4:1–3), and the letter concluded with Paul's charge to Timothy to keep what had been entrusted to him and not get entangled with some who professed faith but erred concerning it (see 1 Tim 6:20–21).

Paul's concern for the false teaching in Ephesus is part of a theme that runs throughout his letter. In his correspondence he also mentioned some women who were wandering from house to house, "tattlers also and busybodies, speaking things which they ought not" (see 1 Tim 5:13). Not all women were doing this, but some were, and the specific situation needed to be addressed.

It stands to reason that in 1 Timothy Paul instructed the young minister to silence false teachers. This doesn't of necessity apply to godly, educated women. In fact, later Paul reminded Timothy of the spiritual heritage he had received from his mother and grandmother (see 2 Tim 1:15). Paul didn't correct Timothy for listening to women. Instead, he commended the women who had passed on a true, pure faith in God. That was a beautiful heritage.

Verse 12: Teaching and/or Usurping

In verse 12 Paul continued his instructions with these words: "But I suffer not a woman to teach, nor to usurp authority over the man, but to be in silence." In contemporary vocabulary, the word *suffer* has a negative meaning, but Jesus used it to express his positive desire to allow children to come to him. He said, "Suffer little children, and forbid them not, to come unto me" (Matt 19:14).

The verb in this sentence (suffer) is present tense. In other words, the verse could accurately be translated, "I am presently not permitting or allowing a woman to teach." The use of this tense implies a temporary policy. Why would Paul state these words about teaching right after instructing the woman to learn? A logical answer would be that in order to teach, one must first learn, and the woman was just beginning to receive instruction.

When a person meets necessary moral and educational qualifications, any previous prohibition to teach could be lifted. This harmonizes with the whole of Scripture, for if Paul truly restricted women from speaking everywhere, how could he reconcile that position with biblical precedents? Women like Miriam, Deborah, Priscilla, and Huldah spoke, prophesied, judged, and taught. It would have been a notable contradiction, and the Word of God does not contradict itself.

Paul was a master wordsmith who chose his words carefully. His temporary injunction "not allowing a woman to teach" was in stark contrast to the strong command that came directly before it, "Let her learn." One of Paul's contemporaries was Philo of Alexander. He was a Hellenistic Jew thoroughly educated in Greek philosophy and culture. Philo said, "Ignorance is an involuntary state, a light matter, and its treatment through teaching is not hopeless."[139] There is a cure for lack of education: education.

Teaching, however, must be done by one who is competent. The Greek word *didaskō* translated "teach" in this passage means "to hold discourse with others in order to instruct them" and "deliver didactic discourses." Didactic teaching is formal, lecture-style teaching usually intended to give moral instruction. If the woman in Ephesus was not learned, she was not ready to teach.

Teaching conducted in the first century church was different from what we see in today's pulpit ministry. The teaching taking place in the early church was primarily transmitting the gospel: the death, burial, and resurrection of Jesus. It included teaching on spiritual growth and how to live as a church body, but it was not likely exegetical biblical instruction of Old Testament Scripture (exegetical meaning critically explained or interpreted). It was certainly not expository teaching that detailed the meaning of New Testament writings because at that point, what is now New Testament canon was in the form of letters circulating from church to church. The Bible had not yet been assembled.

It seems reasonable Paul's goal was to ensure qualified teachers instructed those who came together for worship. He wrote elsewhere, "And the things that thou hast heard of me among many witnesses, the same commit thou to faithful men, who shall be able to teach others also" (2 Tim 2:22). The word translated "men" in this verse is the Greek word *anthrōpos,* which means "a human being, whether male or female." If it had been Paul's intention to restrict all women from teaching, he could have chosen a gender-specific word. Instead he deliberately, under the inspiration of God, chose a word that represented all humanity.

In the Greek, verses 11 and 12 are one sentence. The transition word of verse 12 translated "but" is *de* in the Greek. It is an adversative particle which means it expresses opposition. It is "used to connect one clause with another when it is felt that there is some contrast between them, though the contrast is often scarcely discernible."[140] Paul was in effect saying, "Let the woman learn, but (in contrast, however) I am not allowing her to teach. The *de* was placed between the two thoughts because there is some contradiction, some tension between them. Why would a woman learn and not be able to share what she has learned with others?

Some would cite 1 Timothy 2:11–12 as a proof text that women should not hold teaching positions or otherwise minister in the church. These two verses, however, should not be isolated from their biblical context. Paul sandwiched his "not teaching" instruction between two "learn" statements. In a church full of new converts—some coming from a very different world than an ordered, respectful church environment— Paul required the young Christians to be restrained learners, not to assert themselves, but to receive instruction. In other words, a learner must earn their credentials before attempting to teach.

It should also be considered in this personal letter written by Paul to Timothy that although the apostle conveyed his advice and the reasoning behind his words, he didn't say, "thus saith the Lord." He didn't use strong words like "ought" and "duty" and "must needs" and "bound" as he did in other portions of Scripture (see Rom 15:1, 27; 1 Cor 11:7, 10; Eph 5:28). Paul's advice to Timothy to handle this particular church situation should not be treated as a mandate for all churches at all times.

Authority

"But I suffer not a woman to teach, nor to usurp authority over the man, but to be in silence" (1 Tim 2:12). I've often wondered why Paul, who was such a wordsmith and scholar, chose to use the word *authenteō* (translated "authority" in verse 12) only once in all his correspondence and teaching. Think about it. Able to communicate in Greek, Hebrew, Aramaic, and likely Latin, he dropped this word in the middle of what would become one of the most controversial passages in the Word of God. *Authenteō* was not the word he used dozens of other times for exercising authority. If Paul had meant the conventional operation of authority, he had several other words to choose from. Many problems could have been avoided if he had simply selected another word that had a more widely understood definition. But he chose it on purpose. Paul used uncommon vocabulary for an uncommon situation.

Authenteō is a rarely used word that has a violent association. "In the earlier usage of the word it signified one who with his own hand killed either others or himself. Later it came to denote one who acts on his own 'authority;' hence, 'to exercise authority, dominion.'"[141] This word was associated with extreme abuse of power and exercising absolute mastery over others. Josephus (a first century Roman-Jewish historian) used the noun form of the word to render the word "assassins."[142]

Since the word *authenteō* is used only once in Scripture, any meaning found for it must be limited to fit within the constraints of the subject at hand. In extra-biblical writings, the word is infrequently used, which makes it difficult even for experts to come to a consensus as to its meaning at the time of Paul's writing. In the case of 1 Timothy, the word is in the middle of Paul's teaching on the outward behavior of church members especially relating to appropriate dress, manner, and conduct.

Authentein is joined to the word translated "teach" by the word *oude*. *Oude* is a conjunction that requires the person writing to keep the same perspective on what comes before and after. If either the "teaching" or "authority" can be proven to be positive or negative, the other connected word will have the same meaning.[143] The implication is that since Paul used *authenteō* in the context of Christian conduct and keeping uneducated or misinformed women from teaching, the word relates to the women's deportment. This would refer to conduct, behavior, attitude, and even facial appearance. Noel Bullock, who wrote on the subject for a theological journal, said, "Literary context suggests that something about their demeanor seemed forceful or heavy-handed."[144] It seems a domineering demeanor is the issue, not having authority, which in itself can be neutral, positive, or abused. Additionally on the subject of *oude*, some scholars believe the word would be more appropriately translated "in a manner of," which would render Paul's prohibition "teaching in a manner of usurping." Usurping means to seize and hold a position by force or without legal right.

It is possible *didaskō* (teaching) and *authenteō* (usurping authority) were purposely paired together to make a singular point. Paul utilized this writing technique elsewhere in the same letter. For example, he paired words like prayers and petitions, peaceful and quiet, godliness and holiness, good and acceptable. Coupling *authenteō* and *didaskō* could indicate that both words apply to the same activity: forbidding women to teach heresy to men with a domineering approach and bearing.

Philip Barton Payne, a specialist in New Testament studies agreed. He said, "In the Pauline corpus, *oude* is usually employed to bring together two closely related ideas."[145] He further clarified the words teaching and authority connected by *oude* indicate "*authentein* explains what sort, or what manner, of teaching is prohibited to women."[146] He offered this example: "If we should say, I forbid a woman to teach to discuss differential calculus with man, it becomes clear that the subject in which she could not give instruction is high mathematics."[147] In this case, Paul would have not allowed a woman to teach men in an overbearing, tyrannical manner.

Regardless of gender, it's never right for a teacher to domineer. That was not Paul's approach, nor was it the manner Jesus used to convey his message. The bottom line is this: no one is to assume authority for their own purposes—to wrest it for themselves instead of receiving it from God with confirmation from their spiritual leadership. Peter concurred with this concept when he told the elders to refrain from dictatorially leading the flock (see 1 Pet 5:3). Nadab and Abihu provide a sobering example of what happens to those who operate under their own authority (see Lev 10:1–2).

With so much uncertainty surrounding 1 Timothy, two things are evident: it is unclear and uncertain. To appeal to this passage as the cornerstone for doctrines and practices for women in ministry is problematic at best. A vaguely understood passage should be held against the light of those more easily comprehended. In context, it appears Paul was explaining to Timothy that women were not to usurp, hijack, or commandeer authority God did not give them. It's not hard to imagine some of the women who had been raised in the pagan culture or converted from restrictive Judaism were anxious to be involved. Perhaps even with good intentions, some overstepped; and perhaps that is why Paul's response, when properly understood, was so gracious.

Paul wanted to make sure Timothy knew his duty to ensure teachers were doctrinally sound. Any person teaching false doctrine should not be given a forum in the church. Any ministry must be conducted under proper spiritual authority, and any teacher who would pervert the Word of God should not be given a position of influence.

While some (who truly believe they have sound biblical backing) would silence all women from teaching or even speaking, the issue at hand applies equally to both genders. In the same way a man could err by teaching while usurping authority, conversely a woman could teach and *not* usurp authority. A woman can teach without an arrogant, bossy manner of presentation—and without presuming absolute mastery over others.

The concept in question is a person seizing what does not belong to him or her—of acting for oneself. If a woman is under her spiritual authority, especially if she has received a license from her church organization, she is not usurping, she is serving. She is not domineering; she is doing the work of the Lord according to his call on her life.

A proper application of Paul's intention in this verse puts to rest the misunderstanding that he was forbidding all women from holding positions of authority.

One thing is certain: *authenteō* is not *exousia*, the word used for exercising authority. Paul used a far different word that represented vulgar abuse of authority. He didn't forbid women from possessing and utilizing *exousia*. Perhaps Paul did, after all, do what was best when he penned that little-known word to make a strong differentiation between the type of authority he was addressing.

> Note that in the King James Version the translators specifically rendered *authenteō* in a way that doesn't bar a woman from having authority, but forbids her usurping authority.

The apostle Paul didn't close doors for women. He invited them to participate in a new era. Now they may learn. They must learn. But as beginners, they must conduct themselves calmly and exercise restraint in the educational process as they receive and assimilate sound doctrine. Paul's teaching in the first century church is applicable to the church today. The uneducated must first be trained before they speak. If they are engaged in false teaching, they must be silenced and instructed. If their motive is for self or domination, they must be restrained and lovingly disciplined.

Oftentimes the controversy involving women in ministry is rooted in the subject of who holds authority. Sadly, there are those who misunderstand the Word and consider any position of authority to automatically belong to men. At the time Paul authored his letter to Timothy, the New Testament was neither complete nor considered sacred. Authority was God-given then, as it is today. Since the completion of the full canon of Scripture, believers turn to the Word of God as the source and validation for all authority.

Should a woman have authority over a man? In truth, every believer is a volunteer in the kingdom of God, and every individual chooses to submit him or herself to God and his Word. True authority rests on the Word. No preacher or teacher can force anyone to do anything he or she doesn't choose to do. Any teacher, preacher, or person in a position of authority who operates outside the parameters of the Word wields power but no true authority. But when a woman ministers under the covering and blessing of her spiritual authority and in agreement with the call of God on her life, any authority she exercises is based on the Word, not the woman. The proper motive for ministry is working to fulfill the Great Commission, not to gain authority or position.

The call to pulpit ministry may never be proportional between men and women, and it may not always be as comfortable for women in certain settings, but it's okay to be in the minority when you are in the will of God. What is comfortable or familiar for you is not necessarily what is right and best. That applies to organizational leadership and members of the congregation as well. Being in God's will is more important than staying in the comfort of the familiar.

When we look to the Bible we see the church is not the originator of authority, but is the recipient of authority delegated from the Lord for the oversight and care of his people. Spiritual authority isn't something you and I gain by self-promotion or demanding "rights" to minister. Samuel Brengle, an early commissioner in the Salvation Army, expressed it this way, "It (spiritual authority and leadership) is attained by confession of sin, and much heart-searching and humbling before God; by self-surrender, a courageous sacrifice of every idol, a bold uncomplaining embrace of the cross, and by an eternal, unfaltering looking unto Jesus crucified."[148]

Authority in the New Testament Church

New Testament writings affirm a collective authority in the church. There is not one chief, absolute position of authority among God's people. In Bible days, spiritual and doctrinal authority rested not with a local pastor, but collectively. The biblical precedent was one of interchurch accountability, control, and management. When a question arose about what should be required of Gentile converts, a council met, came to a consensus, and then issued a protocol they expected to be implemented in all the local churches (see Acts 15:2–35). When Peter stepped outside the conventional parameters of Judaism to preach to the Gentiles, he was held accountable by the church (see Acts 11:2, 18). Paul, who taught and trained others, submitted to the directive of the church when he and his traveling companions arrived in Jerusalem (see Acts 21:17–26).

When the apostles died, one by one, the established councils of God-called and commissioned believers continued the work that endures today through apostolic succession. We never see biblical record of dictatorial power or controlling leadership in the early church. Dominating and controlling others with any type of compulsion or intimidation is rebellious and dangerous for all those involved.

Biblical authority flows from God's chosen vessels. In the Garden, God gave rulership to both Adam and Eve. He created them excellent in every way and gave them dominion over all the earth to bless it and protect it. Authority can flow from a man or a woman, but its origin is God, and it is meant to be used to influence others for good. Any authority given to God's people is given to serve under one supreme ruler, and that is the Lord Jesus Christ (see Matt 28:18). He is the one who chooses and commissions disciples to preach the gospel message.

For those who profess a literal application of the English translation of 1 Timothy 2:11–12, a faithful interpretation of Scripture would mean all Paul's instructions should be followed in the same way they were written in the epistles. In 1 Timothy 5, for instance, Paul gave lengthy regulations about the care of widows. In chapter 6 he gave instructions to slaves and masters. According to Paul's other writings (four times in the New Testament), all Christians should greet one another with a holy kiss.

To be consistent, if 1 Timothy 2:11–12 teaches a universal truth, no Christian female with integrity should teach males in Sunday school, public school, or homeschool. On the other hand, however, if it is biblical and appropriate for a woman to teach in Sunday school or on a mission field, it's only logical she should be allowed to speak elsewhere, including a church pulpit.

If in his letter Paul was reemphasizing an established tenant of the faith to Timothy—that women should be silent—of the thirteen to fourteen letters Paul authored, we would expect to find reiterations of this "truth." Given the huge implications these instructions would have on every church, it stands to reason Paul would have mentioned them to the churches he wrote in nine other locations, especially in the epistles in which he dealt with the roles and function of ministers in the churches. Would he not have at least advised Timothy to circulate this letter to other churches? And why did other key apostles like Peter and James neglect to support or transmit this concept in their writings?

Paul commended Priscilla, a teacher and founding leader in the Ephesian church Timothy oversaw. The present tense of Paul's prohibition in verse 12 indicates he would not apply a teaching restriction to women like Priscilla who taught truth (see Acts 18:26). If women-led ministry was contrary to Paul's understanding of God's will, it seems he would not have praised Priscilla as his helper in Christ, but corrected her erroneous ways.

In two other books considered Pastoral Epistles, Paul directly addressed false teaching problems and how they were to be handled (see 2 Tim 2:16, 25–26; 3:5; Titus 1:10–11; 3:10–11). Linda Belleville wrote in *Women Leaders and the Church* that 35 percent of the content of Paul's first letter to Timothy dealt with correcting false teaching.[149] Among the false teachers were women and men, including two men named Hymenaeus and Alexander (1 Tim 1:20). That Paul was dealing with a specific situation in Ephesus is reemphasized by his warning that wolves had entered the church to hurt and hinder (see Acts 20:29). This is what happens when people teach doctrine contrary to the established teachings of the church.

The backdrop for 1 Timothy 2:8–15 is false teaching. It is against this backdrop Paul's words unfold, progress, and build. This unit of Scripture should not be interpreted apart from its context in this chapter or in the whole of the Word. Its language is tied to the rest of Paul's letter. Understanding his intent is the key to unlocking this passage that is a portion of Paul's appeal for appropriate behavior of both men and women in their homes, in the church, and in their community.

The context is public prayer, specifically prayer everywhere, not just in an assembly of believers. In verse 8 Paul expressed his desire that men should pray everywhere with uplifted, holy hands, without wrath and doubting. The next verse begins "in like manner also." Paul linked the instruction on prayer given to men with instruction on prayer to women. He said women should present themselves modestly when they pray. Paul made a presupposition (similar to what he stated in 1 Corinthians 11) that women would pray in public. Women were not silenced, but instructed in the correct conduct as they spoke.

Sir William Ramsay, a Scottish archaeologist, New Testament scholar, and professor, believed the use of "likewise" connected verse 9 with the subject in the previous verses, which is prayer. Ramsay wrote, "The necessary and inevitable sense of the word ["likewise"] is that the whole body of women is to be understood as affected by what has been said about men."[150] He believed the sentence was wrongly punctuated and that Paul wanted women to pray everywhere—just as he had expressed this desire to the men. With the current punctuation, a literal interpretation of the Scripture would render a non-biblical position: that women should dress in the same manner as men who were to be praying with uplifted hands.

The Husband and the Wife

What exactly does it mean that "a woman" is not allowed to teach or usurp authority over "the man?" The Greek word interpreted "woman" most often means "wife." The Greek word translated "man" refers to either a husband or a betrothed or future husband. Note that *woman* and *man* are both singular in this verse. If these words referenced a husband and wife, Paul's instruction meant that a wife should not take authority over her husband. In this case, the issue had nothing to do with every woman being subject to every man.

Today, wives who would never dream of stepping into a pulpit but regularly boss their husbands around are the ones who are most likely disobeying Paul's teaching. A wife was to learn, but not instruct (tell what to do) or dominate (have authority over) her husband. In conversation, Rev. Kevin M. Shaw offered this thought, "The apostle Paul was pretty 'dead-set' against bossy wives. Sadly, people who think 1 Timothy 2:11–12 is about preaching or pastoring actually miss the full impact of what Paul is teaching."

We would be hard pressed to find evidence 1 Timothy 2:11–12 refers to the public function or ministry of women in the church as it is often applied. Many scholars believe these verses were written about the relationship between a husband and wife in their home. Rev. J. H. Robinson wrote in regards to this passage, "It is primarily an injunction respecting her personal behavior at home. It stands in connection with precepts respecting her apparel and her domestic position; especially her relation to her husband."[151]

Robinson went on to say in this same work, "The 'teaching,' therefore which is forbidden by the apostle, is not every kind of teaching ... but it is such teaching as is domineering, and as involves the usurpation of authority over the man. This is the only teaching forbidden by St. Paul in the passage under consideration."[152]

The type of teaching being forbidden in the passage is dictatorial and domineering—a taking "absolute mastery" over another. Given this information, an alternate (paraphrased) version could be rendered, "I do not allow a wife to teach absolute mastery or commandeer God's authority over her husband. Instead, she should learn in agreement with Scripture, giving deference and respectful submission to its authority and the authority God has placed in her life."

A strong case can be made that Paul's words addressed the conduct and character of a wife with her husband. In this case, the instruction would not apply to women in right biblical relationship with their spouses and would lead to the conclusion the passage does not effect a woman's call to preach or teach.

Apostle Paul, Friend and Advocate

Paul understood deep things in God, but many have misunderstood him. Paul insisted true worshippers were not saved by following the jots and tittles of the old rabbinical law. Ironically, over time church leaders developed "Pauline theology" that suggests this champion of grace became the New Testament church's primary lawgiver.

Lack of understanding by people in contemporary Western culture has been due in part to inadequate translation. Polarizing conclusions have resulted in different branches of Christianity that developed over time. It's important to remember when reading Paul's writings that he was addressing the first century church in the first century culture in the first century context. His writings must be understood in the framework of the era in which he lived and the audience he addressed in each of his epistles.

As Paul worked to evangelize and establish churches in the Gentile world, he faithfully interpreted and applied what he had learned from Jesus—the one

SIDENOTE
from Kevin M. Shaw

In my opinion, the argument over whether women may "teach" in a church setting is not solved by discourse analysis. That issue goes to Paul's intended meaning of the words for woman/wife, man/husband, teach, exercise authority, and learn, and quietness.

I can and must obey the first portion of the chapter in real life by praying with all four of the types of prayer Paul mentions. I must obey by praying for persons who are in authority so that the society may be peaceful—and by praying everywhere, lifting up clean hands and heart.

I can live in comportment with the doctrine ... like a true believer. Women can live in obedience to the Word by not bossing their husbands, telling them what to do, "instructing" them, but rather live in quiet submissiveness, and profess and live in godliness ... to continue living in faith and love and holiness, with sensibleness.

> Those wives who refuse to speak the Word publicly but who nonetheless are always telling their husbands what to do are not in alignment with this important passage.
>
> —Kevin M. Shaw
>   Pastor; Denver, Colorado

who came to fulfill the Scripture he had been trained to know from his youth. On the subject of a woman's place in the church, Paul didn't back away from the revolutionary stance Jesus exampled. He had received a transformational revelation from the Lord himself. Jesus capsized the established patriarchal practices of the Jews as surely as he overturned the moneychanger's tables in the temple. Paul and Jesus were both radical, but what Jesus initiated, Paul had the responsibility to organize and apply to the fledgling church.

Some consider Paul a chauvinist, but I believe readers have at times improperly understood his words. While some of his writings are easily misinterpreted by the translations and limitations of our Western understanding, they must be examined for what they truly say and in the light of the larger context of his teachings and example. Twenty-three percent of the New Testament is attributed to Paul's writing—possibly more—and he has been mischaracterized because Christians have misunderstood the deep spiritual concepts he was conveying.

Jesus primarily ministered in Palestine, a drastically different setting and social environment than the Mediterranean culture Paul missionized. This is the culture in which Paul endeavored to introduce the liberty of the gospel. In the Greco-Roman world, Paul was wise enough to respect the cultural differences and attempt to be "all things to all people" (see 1 Cor 9:22). The Mediterranean world was home to both Greeks and Romans. Women in Roman society often had more freedom than Greek women, but in the eyes of the law, all women were considered inferior to men. History records a few Grecian women who attained some acclaim and influence, but they had no legal status of their own. In pagan worship women weren't allowed to teach, but they could hold a position of priestess or prophetess. Also included in the group were Jewish Christians called Judaizers. These converts wanted Gentile believers to conform to the law of Moses—in essence to make Messianic Jews out of Gentile Christians. But Paul believed Jesus had instituted a new covenant. He knew that because Jesus had come, the world was different. In Christ, men and women of every ethnicity and social class could unite in true worship of the one Lord who gave his life to redeem them all.

As Paul attempted to unite the factions of the young church, he faced a plethora of circumstances including pagan practices, unconventional home environments, and controlling marital relationships. As he navigated the issues discussed at large in other chapters of this book, it's clear he continually viewed women with high regard and offered them the opportunity to not only be a part of the church, but to minister in it.

It's doubtful Paul had the slightest inkling his letters would become part of the canon of Scripture. Undeniable inconsistencies exist between what some scholars interpret Paul's letters to mean and what a close study of the original languages and Paul's practices disclose. What he wrote to validate and liberate has been taken by some to mean the exact opposite of what he most likely intended. This champion of women would surely lament any skewing of his words.

In the letters attributed to Paul, he wrote to nine different people or church locations. Of those nine, two cities were deeply entrenched in goddess worship: Corinth, where Aphrodite was worshiped; and Ephesus, where Artemis (also called Diana) was worshiped. These two cities received the letters that contained what some perceive to be Paul's strongest restrictions on women in ministry. This specific pagan element is our key to understanding these verses.

It's important to remember Paul's main goals were to evangelize, make disciples, and establish churches. In doing so, he was careful not to offend when possible. For instance, he told the Galatians that circumcision was unnecessary. He forbade Titus (a leader in the Galatian church) to be circumcised (see Galatians 2:3). But when Paul took Timothy to minister with him, he had the young man circumcised (see Gal 5:2; Acts 16:1–3).

Was Paul talking out of both sides of his mouth? Or was he doing what he felt would create the best conditions for the gospel message to be received? Considering Paul's words and his examples—on the matter of circumcision, for instance—how should a believer today determine his authoritative position on the matter? And whichever position a person may side with, should any individual's personal conclusion be applied to the church universally when it's clear circumcision and uncircumcision were both endorsed in word and deed by the same man?

Paul's words taken in context with his practices reveal he was a man on a mission. He was not duplicitous or double-dealing. Without compromising biblical principles, the apostle was willing to go beyond requirements and tailor his conduct to meet a need in a specific situation. Circumcising Timothy was not a practice that was endorsed by the church for New Testament believers, but Paul circumcised Timothy to reach the Jews. Silencing women was not a practice Paul endorsed unilaterally, but he silenced the woman teaching in Ephesus to protect the church from false teaching.

Although people have misunderstood and mischaracterized Paul, an examination of his interaction with women reveals his true position. He followed Jesus's example and gave women the opportunity to respond to the gospel and be included in ministry. In fact, his first convert was a woman named Lydia who had gathered with women to pray by a river. The record of Scripture bears out that Paul valued women as his strong, capable co-laborers. He was a friend and advocate of women in the New Testament church.

Early Church History

But ye are a chosen generation, a royal priesthood.
1 Peter 2:9

In contrast to the contemporary culture in which they lived, women in the first century church could participate in both membership and leadership. Some served in prominent roles and ministered side by side with the apostle Paul. As we examined elsewhere in this book, women served as deacons and in the five-fold ministry as apostles, prophets, evangelists, pastors, and teachers. They served under the direct supervision of the apostles and early church leaders who had walked and talked with Jesus Christ. Women of means used their wealth and homes to support the apostles and local congregations. They facilitated and led house churches where both sons and daughters prophesied.

The Bible contains a few isolated verses that appear to conflict with the pattern of female ministerial leadership revealed in the New Testament. However, it's obvious from the record of Scripture, women were allowed to serve in many different capacities, and the church at large accepted these women without question. Scripture offers some clarity and instruction on how women were to learn and minister, but there is no record of a single woman who was forbidden or "sat down" from ministering simply because of her gender.

In addition to the early church history recorded in Acts, Jesus broke the cultural norm in his day. He ministered directly to women, and he allowed them to minister directly to him. Each of the four gospel writers recorded multiple female followers of Jesus, some of whom were specifically noted as having great faith and discernment.

Scripture indicates that both women and men ministered during the apostolic era. History records a trajectory of the diminished influence of women in the church after the New Testament age. What happened in the centuries that followed and the subsequent suppression of the role of women in ministry? Likely, the influence of surrounding cultures pressed into the church. Also to consider are terms like "clergy" and "laity" that were adopted by the church as it grew in organizational structure. While the early church rightly recognized those called to ministerial elder-ship and oversight, the heightened difference between ministry professionals and regular church members may have curbed the participation of believers in ministry.

Spirit-filled women ministered in the early church, but after Emperor Constantine declared Christianity the state religion of the Roman Empire in the early part of the fourth century, the organism of the church was organized into ecclesiastical rulers with governmental positions and rankings. Although this administration may have been created with good intentions, women's roles changed and they didn't fare well in the new organizational structure.

Some women were notable leaders, and history records their authority in the church. During the Middle Ages (between the fall of Rome in 476 A.D. and the onset of the Reformation in the early sixteenth century) the roles of women varied. Two eleventh century women, Queen Emma of Normandy, and Edith, wife of Edward the Confessor, were appointed bishops in the English church.[153]

Boniface, who was considered the "apostle to the Germans," requested women assist him in his work converting the pagan Saxons to Christianity. In the early seventh century, a woman named Fara founded a community of both men and women, where she served as abbess with priestly authority.[154]

Following the Middle Ages, the Reformation splintered the dominant Catholic church in Europe. With its promotion of a "priesthood of all believers," the Reformation made strides in the right direction, but for the most part people held to the inherited philosophy that restricted women from leadership.

Women Martyrs

The early persecution of Christians, specifically Christian women, testifies to the roles they played in ministry. Before his conversion, Saul sought letters approving his mission to capture those found in the way "whether they were men or women, [that] he might bring them bound unto Jerusalem" (see Acts 9:2). Paul arrested both men and women. In his own words, he said, "And I persecuted this way unto the death, binding and delivering into prisons both men and women" (Acts 22:4).

The record of persecution testifies to the fact women were speaking on behalf of the Lord Jesus Christ. And the persecution continued. Pliny the Younger, a lawyer and magistrate of Ancient Rome, used torture to interrogate two female slaves who were called deacons in the church.[155]

Vibia Perpetua, a second century Christian martyr, journaled her trial and imprisonment for her faith. Before her death in the arena she wrote *The Passion of Saints Perpetua and Felicity,* one of the rare surviving texts authored by a woman in the ancient world.[156]

Two third century martyrs lived in Alexandria during a local uprising against Christians. The stories of the women were recorded by Dionysius, the bishop of Alexandria, in his letters to Fabius, the bishop of Antioch. The first, a woman named Quinta, was seized by a pagan mob and carried to their temple. They attempted to force her to worship their idol, but "as she turned away in detestation, they bound her feet and dragged her through the entire city ... and at the same time scourged her; then, taking her to the same place, stoned her to death."[157]

The second woman, Appollonia, was considered to be at least a deaconess. She was seized and beaten and ultimately plunged herself into the same fire her persecutors threatened to burn her alive in if she did not repeat their blasphemous words or invoke their heathen gods.[158] Dionysius identified Appollonia as "the *parthénos presbûtis."* This term is rendered in Latin *virgo presbytera,* or virgin presbytery.[159] *Presbytera* is derived from the Greek word for "priest" which is translated "elder" in the New Testament. Although we do not know this woman's precise role in the church, Appollonia was certainly an esteemed leader who was persecuted and subsequently died for her faith.

In the fourth century, Catherine of Alexandria, a princess and noted scholar, converted to Christianity at the age of 14. She converted hundreds of people to Christianity before being executed for her faith at the age of 18.[160]

Another woman of renown in the early church was Marcella. She was a woman of substance educated in both Greek and Hebrew. Jerome, a fourth century Italian priest and theologian, spent three years in what he called her "domestic church." It was in Marcella's home he translated the Bible into Latin. Marcella not only facilitated and financed the work, but critiqued Jerome's translation and even settled disputes on the interpretation of Scripture.[161] When Marcella was in her late seventies, soldiers stormed her residence. She went to the church in St. Paul for refuge where she died the next day.[162]

This sampling of women who suffered and died for their faith represents only a fraction of women whose stories were not recorded in the annals of history or in Scripture. Silent women would have remained untouched by would-be persecutors. Those who were actively witnessing, teaching, preaching, and leading were identified and persecuted. Their persecution and deaths authenticate the historicity of their ministerial and leadership roles in the early church and throughout the Middle Ages.

Elders, Pastors, Bishops, Shepherds, and Teachers

The roles and responsibilities of elders have varied throughout time and cultures. While history does not record specific duties elders performed in civic realms or faith traditions, archeology has uncovered some vital information. Tombs document the historicity of female Jewish elders.[163] Ancient writings and artifacts also bear witness to women who served as synagogue rulers in several locations. The list includes Rufina of Smyrna, Peristeria of Thebes in Thessaly, Theopempte of Myndos, and Sophia of Gortyn on Crete.[164]

In the New Testament, gospel writers used the Greek word *presbyteros,* translated "elder," in reference to a rank or office among the Jews. These *presbyteros* included the members of the Sanhedrin (the great council) who were selected from among the elderly men. The term was also used for those who managed public affairs and administered justice as well as those who were simply advanced in years.[165]

As the church became established, it adopted titles used by both Jewish and Gentile believers. While qualifications are given for varying roles, the functions and responsibilities of elders are not clearly defined by Scripture. In attempting to structure contemporary church leadership to the biblical model we must first correctly understand what those titles meant to the first century church. This is especially true given that in today's multi-denominational church world ministry roles and job descriptions differ even though they often use the same titles.

The first reference of "elder" in the early church was used to identify men sent on a relief mission to people suffering in another community (see Acts 11:28–30). Prior to this reference, no official position of elder is documented in the church structure. The first reference to a formal elder appointment is found late in the book of Acts. "And when they had ordained them elders in every church, and had prayed with fasting, they commended them to the Lord, on whom they believed" (Acts 14:23). Note the elders were ordained.

The Greek word *presbyteros* translates as both "elder men" and "elder women." In Luke's chronicling of the above verse, he could have employed the word *presbytēs,* a gender-specific term indicating men, but he did not. Considering the text, the ordained *them* should not be exclusively referred to men. The *presbyteros* could have been both "elder men" and "elder women."

Paul specifically mentioned elder women elsewhere in Scripture: "The aged women likewise, that they be in behaviour as becometh holiness, not false accusers, not given to much wine, teachers of good things" (Titus 2:3). In this passage "aged women" is rendered from *presbytis,* the feminine form of the word *presbytēs.* These female elders were called to holy conduct and to be "teachers of good things" in the same way bishops were qualified and instructed in 1 Timothy 3 and elders in Titus 1.

According to Scripture, the primary role of an elder in the church is to provide leadership and oversight—to superintend. In his book *Biblical Eldership,* Alexander Strauch summarized the functions and role of an elder:

> Elders lead the church, teach and preach the Word, protect the church from false teachers, exhort and admonish the saints in sound doctrine, visit the sick and pray, and judge doctrinal issues. In biblical terminology, elders shepherd, oversee, lead, and care for the local church.[166]

There has been confusion concerning the office of elder, bishop, and pastor in biblical times. In the early church these titles were different names for the same office. In Paul's letter to Timothy, the qualifications to hold the office of bishop parallel those he issued to Titus for the office of elder (see 1 Tim 3:1–7; Titus 1:6–9). In fact, Paul wrote Titus instructing him to ordain elders in the same way he had appointed him an elder (see Titus 1:4–5). Paul continued his discussion of elders using the title "bishop" (v. 7). The apostle referred to Titus as both elder and bishop.

The word "pastor" is used only once in the New Testament (see Eph 4:11). It is the Greek word *poimēn* that is translated "shepherd" 17 times elsewhere. In Acts, Paul specifically addressed elders and admonished them to take heed to the flock "over which the Holy Ghost hath made you overseers" (see Acts 20:17, 28). Overseeing and shepherding are considered pastoral duties. Peter called himself an elder and directed other elders to "feed the flock of God" and take "the oversight thereof" (see 1 Pet 5:1–2).

Again, these are pastoral duties assigned to elders. The main responsibilities of a shepherd are to feed, direct, and protect the flock under his or her care. Paul said an elder was to feed the flock "the faithful word as he hath been taught, that he may be able by sound doctrine both to exhort and to convince the gainsayers" (see Titus 1:9.)

The Greek word *episcopē* translates "bishop" and means "overseership." This word is not included in the five-fold ministry (see Eph 4:11). Since "overseeing" the flock is certainly the responsibility of an elder, it seems bishop is also used interchangeably for pastor and elder. Some denominations differentiate between the offices of pastors, bishops, and elders; however, this application does not seem to be reflected in the early church.

A pastor is a shepherd who feeds the church. A pastor is an elder (not necessarily aged, but mature in the faith), and a pastor provides the function of overseeing and leading local congregations. J. B. Lightfoot, a nineteenth century English theologian and author said, "It is a fact now generally recognized by theologians of all shades of opinion, that in the language of the New Testament the same officer in the Church is called indifferently 'bishop [overseer]' (episkopos) and 'elder' or 'presbyter' (presbyteros)."[167]

In some church cultures the office of pastor has been open exclusively to men. It seems, however, after examining this topic, the biblical position of the contemporary church should acknowledge women called to nurture, oversee, and lead the people of God as pastors. Women called and gifted by God to serve in pastoral roles should be eligible for the same ordination, titles, and positions open to men.

God's Chosen Pastor

The responsibility to appoint men and women as pastors and overseers of the church belongs to the Lord who purchased the church with his blood (see Acts 20:28). Paul specified it was by the will of God and appointment of God that he was a preacher, apostle, and teacher (see 2 Tim 1:1; 1:11).

While God is the one who makes a call and appointment, he also puts the desire in the hearts of his chosen. "This is a true saying, if a man desire the office of a bishop, he desireth a good work" (see 1 Tim 3:1).

The word rendered "man" in the King James Version of this verse is the Greek *ei tis,* which is also rendered "if any" elsewhere in Scripture and implies no gender. If *ei tis* referred exclusively to men, a consistent masculine rendering would mean only men are required to pick up their crosses and follow the Lord (see Matt 16:24) and only men are eligible to have the Spirit of God dwell in them (see Rom 8:9). Context must be considered to correctly interpret the meaning in this passage which will be discussed in more detail in the pages ahead.

Some confuse the new covenant office of pastor with the Old Testament role of priest, but Scripture is clear. The Old Testament priestly function of offering sacrifices was replaced with the sacrifice of Jesus (see Heb 10:12–14). A new covenant was made, and there are no more offerings made for sin (see Heb 10:16–19). Each individual believer goes to the Lord for forgiveness of his or her trespasses. Comparing the New Testament role of pastor to the Old Testament Jewish role of priest is simply an apples-to-oranges comparison.

Pastoring includes an element of "ruling," but never for self. In fact a pastor's authority is limited by the Word to the role of shepherding the people of God. A shepherd guides and leads his or her congregation in the will of God with love and patience and with the goal of helping others grow in spiritual health and maturity.

Men and women bring different gifts to the ministry table. In *Men Are Like Waffles— Women Are Like Spaghetti,* authors Bill and Pam Farrel offer a vivid illustration of how the natures of men and women differ. They propose men are like waffles (each element of their lives has its own separate box) while women are more like spaghetti (everything in their lives touches everything else). Men and women may approach pastoral ministry with similar goals and equal abilities but with manners and methods that differ. Men and women input, process, and deliver information differently.

> ## SIDENOTE
> ### *from Mark Jordan*
>
> People grant enormous influence over their lives to trusted leaders. Each minister needs to guard against any temptation to wrongly use this power. The minister's authority is not absolute.... Nowhere does the Bible give broad, sweeping authority to any minister over the souls in his care.[168]
>
> —J. Mark Jordan
> Former Superintendent, Ohio District United Pentecostal Church

While there are exceptions, for the most part women tend to be more personal than men and more intent on building relationships. This is where the gentler side of shepherding often gets pushed into a corner. When the male perspective dominates a local church body or organization, church leadership can get off-balance. A woman's potential insights and gifts may remain untapped and/or underutilized. Her approach to administration and problem solving could greatly bless the church. What God has given to benefit the body of Christ at large should be broadly shared in the work of the Lord. Men and women serving side by side bring the fullness of God's nature in the church.

Deacons

Organization and offices have evolved since the New Testament was written. From the first century on, the church developed structure as it went along. As with the terms "elder" and "pastor," to correctly apply the meaning of the word "deacon" requires looking beyond modern-day usage to the word's meaning in the early church.

The apostles who walked with Jesus were the church's first leaders. Jesus taught them. He discipled them in "the way." After his ascension, these leaders received on-the-job training when it came to developing the structure and organization of the rapidly growing church. The church is a living organism, and as it grew new issues came up that resulted in new procedures being implemented. Dealing with these issues not only affirmed the leadership of the original disciples, it expanded leadership to others. If not, the work of the church would have died out with the Twelve Apostles.

The Greek word *diakoneō* is translated five times in the New Testament with specific reference to the office of "deacon." The same Greek word is elsewhere rendered "minister" or "servant" twenty-eight times. As discussed previously, Paul used the word *diakoneō* when he commended Phebe's ministry.

The Greek word translated "deacon" is also rendered "serve" in Acts 6. The incident recorded in this chapter is commonly accepted as the first record of deacons in the church. While some have limited the function of deacons to attending to physical needs like those of the widows, the word also means the following:

"wait upon (menially or as a host, friend, or (figuratively) teacher);

technically, to act as a Christian deacon:

—(ad-)minister (unto), serve, use the office of a deacon."[169]

The first deacons served tables, but their ministry included more than passing out food. They would have managed all the resources for the widows provided by the church. These first deacons alleviated the busy work of the apostles by tending to the widows' physical needs. They were also mightily used in other areas. Stephen's message recorded in the chapter following his appointment as a deacon is one of the most dynamic presentations of the overall plan of God in the written Word.

The church was growing, and Peter realized that to continue the spread of the gospel and the ongoing expansion of the church, responsibility and power must be delegated to others. When selecting the first deacons, Peter chose from those who were already being used and had a good reputation.

> Serving is a verb. Deacon is a verb. The office of deacon implies active service in the body of Christ in whatever capacity is needed.

Meeting a person's physical needs (when done in Jesus's name) is a spiritual activity. Jesus set the example. He met physical needs while ministering to souls. The ministry of serving tables in no way hampered the first deacons' ministries. In fact, as a result of Peter empowering the seven to serve, the men appointed were lifted to positions of prominence. Their acts of service may well have launched them into new ministry opportunities. As mentioned, Stephen gained eternal renown as a remarkable preacher. Philip later became an incredible, Holy-Spirit-teleported evangelist (see Acts 8:26–40). What a precedent they set!

Qualifications

First Timothy 3:8–12 is the only passage that specifically outlines the qualifications for the office of deacon. This may not be an exhaustive list, but notice its focus is not on duties, but on spiritual maturity and reputation. According to a straight-forward reading in English of Paul's letter, below are the qualifications for deacons:

1. Grave: of honorable character and deeds, respectable
2. *Not* double-tongued: saying one thing with one person, and then something else to another with the intent to deceive; two-faced, insincere, lacking credibility

3. *Not* given to much wine: addicted to intoxicating substances; lacking self-control

4. *Not* greedy of filthy lucre: eager for gain, a lover of money

5. Holding the mystery of the faith in a pure conscience: continuing in the gospel—the truths of God—in both beliefs and conduct

6. Proved: tested and found to be genuine

7. Blameless: of irreproachable character, unaccused, having a clean track record of service

8. Grave wives: a spouse of honorable character and deeds, respectable, who live out the same morality and faith as their husbands

9. Husband of one wife: faithful, a "one-woman man" who is not connected emotionally or physically with another woman

10. Ruling their children and their own houses well: maintaining and caring for their families.

Points eight and nine above lead to a logical question, "Why discuss the role of deacons in a book about ladies in ministry when these points indicate a deacon must be a man?"

The points come from these verses:

"Even so must their wives be grave, not slanderers, sober, faithful in all things. Let the deacons be the husbands of one wife, ruling their children and their own houses well" (1 Tim 3:11–12).

The first verse begins with the Greek word translated "even so." This word is also translated "likewise" in this unit of teaching addressed to deacons and is translated "in like manner" earlier in the same chapter (see 1 Tim 2:9, 3:8). Paul was outlining responsibilities of leadership and the use of this specific word bridged the discussion of one group of leaders with another.

What was the topic of Paul's conversation before he used the word that means "likewise" or "in like manner?" It was men serving as deacons. As Paul outlined the qualifications, he shifted his focus from men to women. He stated that in the same way the men deacons are to conduct themselves, the *gynē* should also conduct themselves.

Gynē, depending on context, can be rendered either "wife" or "woman." The word "their" is simply not in the original text. The writing was not about women in "their" relationship to men. This phrase should more accurately be translated, "Even so, women...."

In Linda Belleville's examination of 1 Timothy in the *Cornerstone Biblical Commentary*, she recorded the words of Clement of Alexandria who "understood this to be to women ministers and not ministers wives: 'We know what the honorable Paul in one of his letters to Timothy prescribed regarding women deacons.'"[170]

Bible scholar Dr. Charles J. Ellicott said, "The position of this solitary charge, respecting deacons' wives, in the midst of regulations concerning 'deacons,' is, of itself almost decisive against the translation of the English version, adopted also by Luther and many other."[171] Ellicott believed the English rendering of "wives" simply did not make sense in this list of regulations for ministers. He made the point that in this same chapter there was no reference made to the character of a bishop (overseer) who holds higher position in the church. If a man's wife had no bearing on the selection of a bishop, why would this matter concern Timothy when selecting deacons?

Ellicott's commentary further stated, "The literal translation of the Greek words would be, *Women in like manner must,* &c. these *women,* St. Chrystostom and most of the ancient expositors affirm, were *deaconesses.*"[172]

The biblical record affirms women did hold official positions in the early church (see Rom 16:1, Phil 4:2). Ellicott cited a Professor Reynolds regarding deaconesses in the Western church who said, "the order did not cease to exist until the fifth century, and was continued in the Greek Church till the twelfth. The deaconess vanished into the cloister until partially revived in comparatively modern times."[173]

From this perspective Paul's instructions in verse 11 were not meant to prevent women from serving as deacons because they were female. He was specifying qualifications similar to those the men must meet.

Women deacons are to be:

1. Grave: of honorable character and deeds, respectable, who live out the same morality and faith as their spouses
2. Not slanderers: spreading malicious, false reports
3. Sober: temperate, abstaining from wine (from a root word that means watchful)
4. Faithful in all things: trustworthy in everything

The structure of Paul's writing indicates that he was empowering Timothy to select women to serve in the leadership of the church where he served as bishop. Considering that Paul lay the foundations for the Ephesian church with Priscilla and Aquila, this seems reasonable and logical.

The next verse in the chapter deals specifically with spouses:

"Let the deacons be the husbands of one wife, ruling their children and their own houses well" (1 Tim 3:12). At first reading, this verse could complicate the discussion, but does it indicate that only married men with children are eligible to serve as deacons? Could not widowers? Single men? Men who before coming to Christ had been divorced or had more than one marriage partner?

Certainly the meaning of this passage is important to believers today. More important was its meaning to Paul when he wrote it and what his readers understood it to mean. Taken on its own merit this verse would disqualify the very person who wrote it (who served at an even higher level of apostolic leadership) as well as the single man he was writing to. Neither Paul nor Timothy would have been eligible to serve in the lesser office of deacon.

In a society where polygamy was practiced, it's likely Paul included this statement to emphasize marital fidelity. A male deacon should have one wife, and conversely a woman in leadership should have only one husband. Paul discussed this issue elsewhere when he spoke to the fidelity of women (see 1 Tim 5:9). Marital faithfulness was expected from both men and women.

The final qualification was "ruling well" whatever size "house" a deacon might have. Whether a person is married, single, widowed, or childless, a deacon should manage his or her home and provide well for the household.

Jesus elevated serving to the highest place of honor (see Mark 10:43–45). Serving others over self was a fundamental teaching of Jesus and an essential part of a disciple's character (see Luke 22:26). Each of the four gospels gives accounts of women serving alongside Jesus. In reference to these women, three of the gospel writers specifically used the word *diakonia* which is translated elsewhere as "deacon" (see Matt 27:55–57; Mark 15:40; Luke 23:49).

In *The Role of Women in Ecclesial Ministry*, Agnes Cunningham recorded historical sources and church documents from the third century that evidence females serving in the office of deaconess.[174] Among them were the *Apostolic Constitutions* and the *Didascalia Apostolorum*, considered to be the earliest reliable evidence to the office of female deacons. It is notable, however, the term "deaconess" is never used in Scripture, only "deacon" which is a masculine/feminine noun.

Cunningham wrote, "In the *Apostolic Constitutions* we learn that a deaconess was 'a pure virgin or at least a widow who had been but once married, faithful and well esteemed.'"[175] She went on to say, "The compiler locates deaconesses properly within all the categories of membership and functions within the church."[176] According to these ancient church documents, some women were appointed and ordained. Even in a patriarchal church culture, women were officially recognized and authorized to serve in leadership.

The Bible does not outline the specific functions of deacons. These have evolved since the first appointment of those who served the widows (see Acts 6). Early deacons may or may not have had official teaching roles. While qualifications for elders included being "apt to teach," deacons were instructed only to continue "holding" to the faith (see 1 Tim 3:2, 9).

Times have changed and church practices along with them. Independent churches and church organizations have the liberty to define the function of deacons in their frameworks. The primary role of a deacon from a biblical perspective should be to free spiritual leadership to shepherd and teach the people. This will look different in different church environments.

SIDENOTE *from Doug Klinedinst*

Spiritual authority goes far beyond positional authority or a hierarchal structure in the body of Christ. Each and every believer has the opportunity to receive and function in spiritual authority. This dimension of spiritual authority does not negate or supersede positional authority, but rather operates in harmony with established spiritual government.

To understand this kind of spiritual authority, a different definition is helpful. Authority in this context is best described as expertise, knowledge, skill, or capability. These attributes are provided to the individual believer through the anointing of the Holy Ghost, disciplined study, and years of experience.

The Word and the Spirit of God give believers divine authorization. The great commission recorded in Mark 16:15–18 includes preaching the gospel, laying hands on the sick for healing, and casting out demons.

There are times when gifting must submit to positional authority. There are times when positional authority will yield to gifting. Skillful, experienced pillars in the church will provide direction and release to those who are receiving gifting and anointing through prayer, fasting, and study of the Word.[177]

—Douglas C. Klinedinst
International Evangelist, Mentor, and Author; Ocala, Florida

A Nineteenth and Twentieth Century Historical Overview

*But ye are a chosen generation, a royal priesthood, an holy nation,
a peculiar people; that ye should shew forth the praises of him who hath
called you out of darkness into his marvellous light.*
1 Peter 2:9

In Chapter 21 we looked at the duties and functions of men and women in ministry in the early church and how they changed over the years following. In this chapter we will examine the roles women played in key revivals that took place in the nineteenth and twentieth centuries.

The Holiness Movement

Women played key roles in the Holiness Movement, a religious movement that arose among Protestant churches in the nineteenth century that emphasized a doctrine of sanctification. Phoebe Palmer is considered one of the movement's founders. She began missions (including the first inner-city mission in New York City) and evangelized at camp meetings. Through her personal ministry in North America and Europe, 25,000 people turned their hearts to the Lord.[178] In 1859, she published *The Promise of the Father*, a book in favor of women in ministry.

Frances Willard, one of the founders of the Women's Christian Temperance Union, evangelized alongside Dwight L. Moody to audiences numbering in the thousands.[179] Her work in obtaining the vote for women was based on her interpretation of Scripture.[180] She said, "God sets male and female side by side throughout his realm of law."[181]

Hannah Whitehall-Smith was an evangelist and influential woman in the Holiness Movement. She "was known as 'the angel of the churches' both for her eloquence and for her appearance in her evangelistic addresses to huge gatherings."[182] The publication of her best-selling book, *The Christian's Secret of a Happy Life,* coincided with the impact of her preaching in Britain and Continental Europe. In Oxford she preached to 7,000, and her congregation was larger than Charles Spurgeon's.[183]

Catherine Booth co-founded the Salvation Army with her husband, General William Booth. An integral leader and dynamic speaker, she championed the cause of women in ministry, even persuading her husband who was initially not a supporter. In 1859, she wrote a brief but powerful book, *Female Ministry: Women's Right to Preach the Gospel.* Catherine had her own evangelistic itinerary. She was the breadwinner of the family and her preaching earned more money than her husband's.[184] General William Booth, who was one of the most powerful Christian leaders of the nineteenth century, summed up his views on women in ministry when he said, "Some of my best men are women!"[185]

While women were hindered from serving in some churches, they were commonly allowed to minister in many of the denominations of the Holiness movement. Edith Blumhofer, PhD in American Religious History, noted that in the early days of Pentecostalism "having the 'anointing' was far more important than one's sex ... women who were recognized as having the anointing of the Holy Spirit shared with men in preaching ministry."[186] She went on to say, "A person's call—and how other believers viewed it—was far more important than [ministerial credentials]."[187]

Azusa Street Revival

The Pentecostal renewal at the turn of the twentieth century began on January 1, 1901, when Agnes Ozman first received the infilling of the Holy Spirit with the evidence of speaking in tongues. It happened at Bethel Bible College in Topeka, Kansas, run by Charles Parham and his wife Sarah. According to James L. Tyson, author of *The Early Pentecostal Revival,* Brother and Sister Parham were "both doing the work of saving souls, curing the sick, and turning out crops of new evangelists from their Bible school."[188]

It was just after midnight on the first day of the twentieth century when Agnes Ozman made a request to Charles Parham. According to Parham, Ozman "asked that hands might be laid upon her to receive the Holy Spirit as she hoped to go to foreign fields. Glory fell upon her."[189]

The release of the Spirit of God in that Bible college prayer meeting proved to be a harbinger of the Azusa Street Revival that would follow in 1906. Parham was one of two central figures in the early Pentecostal revival. William Seymour was the second. Seymour became involved through a woman who connected him with a work in Los Angeles. He was invited to pastor a small mission church, but after he preached his first sermon from the book of Acts, he was informed that his services would not be needed. The reason given was that he had not received the infilling of the Holy Spirit he had preached about (see Acts chapter 2).

Seymour was padlocked out of the church by its leadership, but then invited to stay in the home of one of its members, Edward S. Lee. Some of the members of the mission church attended Bible studies and prayer meetings at Lee's house on Bonnie Brae Street. People began receiving the Holy Spirit, including Seymour and the woman he would eventually marry. The gatherings were so well attended the worshippers moved to a new location on the same street, and not long after to a much larger building on Azusa Street.

Men, women, and children from all walks of life experienced the infilling of the Spirit of God. People from varying denominations came together including blacks, whites, Hispanics, and Asians. The rich worshipped alongside the poor. The educated knelt beside the illiterate in humble devotion united as brothers and sisters in Christ.

The revival broke out during the peak of the "Jim Crow" racial segregation and fourteen years before women obtained the right to vote on a national scale.[190] The amalgamation of these diverse people was indeed a remarkable work of God. The Azusa Street Mission was a place people laid down their pride and their prejudices. American Pentecostal writer Frank Bartleman said that at the mission, "The religious ego preached its own funeral sermon quickly."[191]

The emphasis in the meetings was not speaking in tongues, but experiencing God. Spiritually hungry people came from around the world seeking to know Jesus in a deeper and higher way. They received the gift of the spirit of God, and then returned to their homes and mission fields to share their experiences with others.

There is something that happens during a revival. As hearts ignite with the fire of God, prejudices burn away. In the early days at the Azusa Street mission, ministry was accepted by all and from all. After times of prayer, in an atmosphere thick with the presence of God, either a man or woman would stand and deliver an anointed word. Even children were allowed to speak. In the early days of the revival both men and women served in its leadership. In fact, when William Seymour passed away in 1922, his wife Jennie became the pastor of their church.

Following are some highlights of women who served in the ministry and leadership of the Pentecostal revival.

- In 1903, Charles Parham prayed with a woman named Mary Arthur who received a physical healing and the gift of the Holy Spirit. She subsequently opened her home in Galena, Kansas, and invited Parham there to preach. The meeting grew to be a three-month revival that was so well attended it moved to a large tent. Hundreds of lives were touched and 250 people received the Holy Spirit. As a result of the revival, Mary Arthur and her friend, Francene Dobson, founded a permanent Apostolic Faith mission. It was the first organized Pentecostal church in North America and became the spiritual home of Howard Goss. Goss was saved in the Galena revival and later became the first Superintendent of the United Pentecostal Church International.

- In 1906, Marie Burgess met Charles Parham and converted to Pentecostalism. She preached in the Midwest and then in New York City, where she founded a mission called Glad Tidings Hall. After her marriage to Robert Brown, she and her husband established Glad Tidings Tabernacle. Their church became a hub in spreading revival in the Eastern United States, and after her husband's passing, Marie continued to pastor on her own for 23 years.

- In 1906, several ladies began traveling ministries. Florence Crawford, Mabel Smith, Ivey Campbell, Millicent McClendon, and Rachel Sizelove were among many who traveled and preached. These women spread Pentecostal revival wherever they ministered.

- In 1906, Ellen Hebden became the first known person in Canada to receive the gift of the Holy Spirit. Following the experience, the Hebden Mission she and her husband founded became a center for the early Pentecostal revival in Canada.

- In 1907, Emma Ladd transformed a local rescue mission into a powerhouse of Pentecostalism. She was the wife of a popular Iowan Supreme Court Justice, and her ministry made such an impact a warrant was issued for her arrest.

- In Rochester, New York, Hattie Duncan and her sisters operated the Elim Faith Home. Originally founded in 1895, this work published a journal, established a church, and founded the Rochester Training School for

Missions. The sisters heard about the Pentecostal outpouring and received it for themselves in 1907. In the wake of that experience, the school became a training ground for Pentecostal leaders including over 400 missionaries. The school promoted the Pentecostal message and became famous for the healings that occurred there.[192]

• Florence L. Crawford established the Apostolic Faith Mission in Portland, Oregon. Over time this work became the hub from which other Northwest missions works turned for leadership. It was from this mission "the first Pentecostal missionaries were dispatched to the foreign fields, as early as 1907 or 1908."[193]

• In 1908, the Duncan sisters and Mary Leanore Barnes, along with Mary's son-in-law, B. F. Lawrence, conducted tent meetings in southern Illinois. Mary became known as "Mother Barnes" and taught at a Bible school in Eureka Springs, Arkansas.

• In 1908, the Pentecostal Assemblies of the World met and elected a woman identified as Sister Hopkins as temporary chairman.[194]

• In 1913, at the worldwide camp meeting in Arroyo Secco, California, Maria Woodworth-Etter was the featured evening speaker. Woodworth-Etter's ministry and involvement with the Holiness Movement earned her the title "grandmother of the Pentecostal movement." She established twelve churches and was responsible for licensing ministers. This prominent Pentecostal leader founded the Woodworth-Etter Tabernacle in 1918 which she pastored until her passing in 1924. An active evangelist, Maria spoke to crowds of over twenty-five thousand "while hundreds fell to the ground under the power of God."[195]

• In 1923, Evangelist Aimee Semple McPherson founded a Christian radio station in the United States as well as the International Church of the Foursquare Gospel denomination.[196]

• From 1924 to 1951, Sister Hilda Reeder led in early foreign missions work that she launched under the ministry of G.T. Haywood, Bishop of the Pentecostal Assemblies of the World (PAW). At the time of her appointment, Reeder served as the only female member of the PAW's Executive Board.[197]

• In the late 1920s, groundwork was laid for what would eventually become the PAW's Sunday School Association. Included in their leadership were Sister Willa B. Howard and Mary Johnson.[198]

Women played significant roles in the rise and spread of the Pentecostal movement. The free move of the spirit of God upon both males and females nullified societal norms. Men and women, sons and daughters, heard God's voice and spoke forth the words he gave them with boldness and authority. The historical record of this movement clearly details women called of God who served in the forefront as leaders, preachers, evangelists, and missionaries, as well as Bible school founders and instructors.

After Azusa

Following the great revival that spread from Azusa Street and the formation of a more formal church structure, the roles of women in ministry began to change. The shift took place over time and after several decades of notable ministry by powerful women of God.

In 1914, one third of the Assemblies of God ministers were women and two thirds of their missionaries. In the earliest oneness Pentecostal minister's directory published in 1919, of the 704 names listed, 29 percent of the credentialed ministers were women.

What happened to these great moves of God that changed the status of women who were once welcomed to participate in ministry and leadership? One factor could be that once a move of God was launched and began to organize, women were often displaced by men or deliberately became less active and accepted lesser positions. When church structures became formalized, the roles women previously served in active leadership and ministry were either designated to men or abdicated by well-intentioned women.

In 1980, Charles H. Barfoot and Gerald T. Sheppard wrote a paper on the changing role of women in clergy. In it they said, "As routinization and regimentation of community relationships set in, reactions did occur against the [Pentecostal] movement's prophesying daughters."[199] It seems the primary factor for the change had to do with the subject of authority.

As Pentecostal churches developed, something shifted. Previously women had been free to function according to their calls, character, and giftings, but with structure came restriction. People began to take issue with women as authority figures—a concept that was not seen in the early days of the Pentecostal revival, as recorded by eye-witness Frank Bartleman. He said, "All obeyed God in meekness and humility. In honor we 'preferred one another.' The Lord was liable to burst through any one ... It might be a child, a woman, or a man."[200]

In 2007, Eric Patterson and Edmund Rybarczyk wrote in "The Future of Pentecostalism in the United States" their shared belief that the roles of women were affected by a variety of influences. "Over the years, the proportion of women ministers and pastors [in Oneness Pentecostalism] has diminished greatly." They report their findings based primarily on three factors:

1. An increase in the number of men who entered the movement and the ministry
2. The influence of Fundamentalism and evangelicalism
3. A backlash against the women's liberation movement of the 1960s and 1970s.[201]

Patterson and Rybarczyk also said, "Pentecostal women did not want to be seen as rebellious or radical.... Sometimes a woman maintained the primary role of preaching while her husband sought ministerial license as well. In many cases, women ... married ministers and worked alongside their husbands without seeking credentials."[202]

The authors noted a recent resurgence in Pentecostal churches of encouragement and affirmation for women in ministry. They wrote that in United Pentecostal Church International, although top positions of leadership continue to be reserved for men, the organization "has always allowed the ordination of women" and "there have been calls for greater affirmation of women in ministry."[203]

The History of
Women in Ministry

Contributed by David K. Bernard, General Superintendent
of the United Pentecostal Church International

I n the earliest directory of Apostolic Pentecostal ministers, from 1919, 29 percent
of the ministers were women. At the formation of the United Pentecostal Church
in 1945, 21 percent of the credentialed ministers were women, including our first
general superintendent's wife.

There has been a decline since then. One reason was that Apostolic women
did not want to identify with the unbiblical values of the secular women's
liberation movement. Another reason was the influence of Fundamentalism, a
conservative reaction to liberal Protestants who denied the infallibility of Scripture.
Fundamentalists emphasized the Bible as the Word of God but did not believe in
miracles for today. The early Pentecostals also reacted against Protestant liberalism,
but they emphasized a revival of the Spirit in addition to the Word.

Early Pentecostals did not have written theology, so they often looked to other
conservative groups such as the Fundamentalists for study materials and training
tools. The Fundamentalists opposed women preachers based on a limited analysis
of two biblical texts in 1 Corinthians 14 and 1 Timothy 2, without considering the
complete literary and historical context, the other writings of Paul, examples in the
rest of Scripture, and the history of the Holiness-Pentecostal movement. Instead of
borrowing theology from others, if we go back to our roots in the New Testament
church and in the early Pentecostal movement we find an active role for women
in ministry.

In church history, when revival movements emphasized the anointing and gifts
of the Spirit, then women's roles were recognized. When churches focused mostly on
institutional ministry, then women's roles declined. During the third century, churches
became more formal with less emphasis on the Spirit, and the institutional church did
not give full recognition to the ministry of women.

In the Pentecostal movement, we appreciate structure but recognize the dangers
of institutionalism. The hallmark of our movement is that every generation must go
back to the first century and be renewed. In other words, we are restorationists. One

thing that every generation should restore is the role of women in ministry. In the last decade, we have seen a significant increase in the number of credentialed women ministers in the United Pentecostal Church International. While the percentage is not as great, we now have more women ministers in the UPCI than ever before.

For further discussion, see David K. Bernard, *The Apostolic Church in the Twenty-first Century.*

Licensing, Ordination and Offices in the Church

And the things you have heard me say in the presence of many witnesses entrust to reliable people who will also be qualified to teach others.
2 Timothy 2:2

The church of Jesus Christ is an organism made of equally valuable people. In it, the Lord established leadership to provide structure and oversight. Jesus painted his ideal for the church as one in which all members loved, served, and mutually submitted to one another—preferring one another in love. This was a "new wine" concept that could not be poured into the "old wineskin" of the Jewish religious establishment (see Mark 2:21–22). The church was birthed to function as a body.

In the early days of the church people met at different locations, primarily in homes. All the believers in a city, however, were regarded as members of one, city-wide church. This is evidenced by the instructions in some of Paul's letters. He wrote one letter "to all that be in Rome," and within the body of the letter he addressed more than one company of believers (see Rom 1:7, 16:5, 15–16). These churches led their own local affairs while maintaining a cooperation and accountability to one another. When the issue of circumcision, for example, was raised in Antioch and in Galatia, elders and apostles met in Jerusalem. Among the leaders gathered, Peter, James, Paul, Barnabas, Judas, and Silas were specifically named. The council discussed the issue, came to agreement on how to handle it, and then issued an official decree (see Acts 15).

The scriptural term "elders" often used for local church leaders is a plural word that indicates shared governmental oversight. In Peter's instructions to church elders, he told those serving they should not act as "lords over God's heritage." Instead, he charged them to be examples to the flock" (see 1 Pet 5:3).

In the first century church, apostles gave direction to the works they established, but no one person held an authoritarian position over all believers or churches. Leaders were expected to work in harmony and council in their local assemblies. In fact, Jesus taught his disciples that when a disagreement arose, the people involved should attempt to handle it themselves. If that didn't work, then the church was to evaluate the situation and determine the course of action needed (see Matt 18:15–20). Jesus, who was our perfect example, spoke and taught with authority, but he also wrapped a towel around his waist and washed his disciples' feet. The Lord exemplified humility and servant leadership.

Church leadership was designed by God to provide oversight to believers who were called to surrender themselves one to another under the authority of the Word of God. Implementing organizational structure brought order and accountability while it offered respect to the diverse roles and giftings in the body. In the framework established, believers were allowed to function in their gifts and callings for the building up of the church.

This concept contrasts the dominance hierarchy exhibited in nature. The chicken pen in my back yard is a living example of dominance hierarchy. Three hens from the first batch rule the roost, and of those, a feather-footed brahma named Cherie is clearly the sovereign fowl. Each spring new chicks are added to the little community, and the new ones quickly learn their places in the pecking order.

In human organizations, hierarchy is established and maintained by a few members who hold rank over other members who submit to the ones in charge. This may work in the corporate world, in politics, and law enforcement (among the "Gentiles"), but it's not God's desire for his church and goes beyond the biblical guidelines of church leadership. Unlike hierarchies that promote individuals to leadership based on lineage, race, gender, social status, or prominence, Jesus wanted his church to function on the basis of God-given calls, gifts, and the authority of the Word.

Jesus went to the cross to restore relationships horizontally and vertically. He is the head of his church, and all infrastructure should come under his leadership. The Lord's ministry was punctuated with teachings that repealed old ways of doing things. He lay a new foundation for the church to build its structure upon (see 1 Cor 3:11). He sat his disciples together and said, "If any man desire to be first, the same shall be last of all, and servant of all" (Mark 9:35).

While certainly anointing and authority flow down from God, a leader is a lifter of others. A leader sees him or herself as servant of all—not from a superior position, but one of humility. Leadership in God's church is not as much about rank or office as it is position. Those who would lead in the Lord's church are positioned in places of service.

Jesus said, "Be not ye called Rabbi: for one is Your Master, even Christ; and all ye are brethren" (Matt 23:8). In this statement, the Lord affirmed the point that there was only one Master—and that was him. He was not advocating that all are equally educated or mature or that new converts should be allowed to teach doctrine to elders. He was speaking of seeking title or prominence.

Every disciple of Christ is equally a brother or sister under the Lord's directorship. This concept contrasted the Jewish culture that venerated patriarchs as fathers and put "learners" in subordinate positions to teachers. In reference to church leadership, Jesus said to call no man "father" (see Matt 23:9). In the same context, neither should one call another "master" (see Matt 23:10).

From the list of *don'ts* in Matthew 23 comes the instruction to *do*. Jesus said, "He that is greatest among you shall be your servant. And whosoever shall exalt himself shall be abased; and he that shall humble himself shall be exalted" (see Matt 23:11–12). Jesus implied that those who think they should be esteemed with titles and position (such as Rabbi, Father, or Master) would be demeaned. Those, however, who humble themselves would become great.

The greatest in God's kingdom are not those who promote themselves, but those who teach and preach the words of "The Teacher." They surrender themselves to the person, the timing, and the purposes of God.

Christ-followers are to honor those chosen by God who serve and invest their lives in ministry. One person, however, should not be revered or have absolute authority in the church. This is not the template designed by Jesus and implemented in the New Testament church. Keep in mind a position doesn't automatically produce spiritual authority. An election or appointment to office doesn't of itself impart anointing. Rather, it's the anointing already active in a believer's life that opens the door for greater ministry opportunities.

As the early church grew, the need for organizational structure expanded. People qualified to lead, teach, counsel, and problem-solve were recognized and utilized in their areas of giftedness and calling. Those who labored to plant churches saw the seedling works grounded as they submitted themselves "one to another in the fear of God" (see Eph 5:21).

After the passing of the apostles, over time and with the establishment of a more formalized governmental structure, the sense of community leadership diminished and authority slipped back into a patriarchal and hierarchal order. Specific ceremonies and rituals were implemented that delegated those who were approved to teach, preach, and lead. The formal rituals and new regulations created an environment in some cases in which women were bypassed as possible ministerial candidates. The more formal the church structure, often the less opportunity women were given.

Church Government

Ephesians 4:11 outlines the primary governmental ministries in the New Testament church: "And he gave some, apostles; and some, prophets; and some, evangelists; and some, pastors and teachers." This statement is not a stand-alone verse. It is part of Paul's run-on sentence that doesn't end until verse 16. Together these verses state the purpose of the ministry is to prepare other believers for ministry and to build the church. In this unit of Scripture Paul outlined the basics of church government and then specified that what he had worked to establish according to the Lord's instructions should continue until everyone in the church was fully Christ-like, mature, and stable—grown up in all things and working together.

In another of Paul's letters he further outlined the functions of leadership in the church. "And God hath set some in the church, first apostles, secondarily prophets, thirdly teachers, after that miracles, then gifts of healings, helps, governments, diversities of tongues" (1 Cor 12:28). In Romans, he listed gifts of prophecy, ministry, teaching, exhorting, giving, ruling, and mercy (see Rom 6:8). God supplied his church with the ministry and gifts necessary for it to thrive and grow.

Government of every kind includes directing, managing, and ruling. Every organization has some form of government. In her book *A Woman's Place in God's Government,* Rev. Sharon Walston explained how government functions differently in civic, home, and church environments. The structure of each is unique.[205]

In our civic government women serve as mayors, senators, representatives, and presidential cabinet members. They work to write laws and set national policies. Female police officers issue citations and make arrests. Female judges impose fines, community service, and prison sentences. Female governors can stay execution orders, and women are eligible for the highest office in the land.

In families the Lord established a governmental order in which a husband serves as head. This ideal does not work in every situation, however, such as with single women, widows, or in single-parent families. God's family structure was designed to be implemented in a loving environment of mutual respect that exemplifies the relationship Christ would have with his church.

The church is comprised of both men and women who "in Christ" are neither male nor female. The nature of a human is found in the union of a body, soul, and spirit. The human soul and spirit are housed in gendered bodies, but Scripture indicates the eternal souls of the children of God are "equal unto" the angels (see Luke 20:34–36), and angelic beings are genderless (see Heb 2:16). The point is this: in the spiritual realm, there is no gender. That is why human men can become part of the bride of Christ.

While believers look forward to the transformational moment they will become like Jesus, the "kingdom of heaven" is more than a future happening. For those who are in Christ, it is also here and now. The kingdom of heaven was in the midst of the people when Jesus walked the earth, and it is currently within believers who are filled with his Spirit. Christianity goes beyond an experience that simply brings sinners into the kingdom. It establishes them as members of the priesthood of all believers.

The New Testament references priests and priesthoods in three areas:

1. The Levitical Jewish priesthood (see Matt 2:4)
2. Jesus as the great High Priest (see Heb 3:1)
3. The priesthood of all believers (see 1 Pet 2:9, Rev 5:10).

The only priesthood Jesus established was a priesthood in which all could participate. In this priesthood, Jesus is the only mediator (see 1 Tim 2:5), and every believer offers his or her own gifts and sacrifices to the Lord.

In the structure of the New Testament church, apostles took a leading organizational role. Prophets gave guidance and vision. Evangelists gathered in the harvest. Pastors/elders guarded, protected, and fed the local assemblies, and teachers grounded the church in the truths of the Word. Each of these ministry roles or offices is important and was designed by God to work in cooperation with the other ministry gifts for the church to operate in the full dynamic of its power. Together these ministry roles create the framework the Spirit of God flows through. And this framework is not restricted by gender. Biblical and historical records testify that women have successfully served in many church leadership roles throughout the ages.

David K. Bernard wrote on the subject of women in ministry, "Currently [in the UPCI], several key offices are restricted to males.... Other key offices are open to women.... The reason for these distinctions appears to be more cultural and historical than theological."[206]

In the United Pentecostal Church International, (which I reference frequently as I am a licensed minister of this organization) women are making advances. Carla Gray Weiser conducted an in-depth study of female ministers in the UPCI in 2015. Her research revealed women are finding their voices to answer God's call on their lives. As she put it, "Tiptoeing through an open door [of ministry]."[207] The way seems to be widening, with the 2016 establishment of the Women in Ministry Network launched to facilitate communication, coordination, visibility, mentoring, and training tools for credentialed women involved in ministry in the organization.

Licensing and Ordination

Many women who faithfully perform the work of God never seek ministry credentials. Licensing and ordination are not for everyone—men or women. Individual believers must prayerfully determine if ministry credentials would help them serve the church in accordance with their gifts and unique call of God.

A ministry license is a license to serve and can at times be beneficial. Credentials do more than validate a person's ministry within a church. They open doors outside as well. One godly woman who serves as a pastor's wife and ministers internationally was recently denied access to visit a church member in the hospital due to her lack of ministerial credentials. A license would have literally opened the door for her to minister in the restricted area of the hospital. Within most church organizations, credentials allow a minister to voice and vote in local, district, and national elections.

Ordination is an official recognition by a church of a member's call of God to ministry. The church must exercise caution before ordination. In his pastoral letter to Timothy, Paul said, "Lay hands suddenly on no man" (see 1 Tim 5:22). Note the word translated "man" in this verse refers to man, woman, or anyone. What Paul was saying to Timothy was, "Don't be in a hurry to give the sanction of the church." Ordination should not be offered suddenly or considered lightly. An ordained

SIDENOTE
from the Author

When I began speaking at youth events and ladies' conferences, obtaining a minister's license never crossed my mind. The path unfolded before me as I walked with God. Holding credentials is not a ticket *to* ministry; it is an evidence *of* the ministry already being performed.

minister acts as a representative of the church investing the credentials in the ministerial candidate. With ordination, comes an identification—a public connection between the church and the person being ordained. It acknowledges the minister holds to the same doctrinal convictions and commitment to the Lord as the church making the investiture.

Debate over the role of women in the church often focuses on whether women should be eligible for ordination. This issue is important because ordination brings with it the opportunity to hold positions of authority. Ordination substantiates the qualification of the ordained indicating he or she is able and authorized to preach, perform religious rites and ceremonies, and/or oversee the administration of a church.

Some have argued that ordination is strictly an Old Testament practice for Jewish priests (see Lev 8). However, in the New Testament, church leaders jointly and publicly acknowledged those called to minister. They anointed them, prayed for them, laid hands on them, and sent them off with their blessings. A modern-day ordination service may not look precisely the same as in the early church, but the intention is equivalent. It validates the ministry already begun by the empowering gift of the spirit of God. The church recognizes those being ordained as qualified to perform certain duties and roles of ministry, activates them, and in so doing protects the church from charlatans, false teachers, or those who might seek to prematurely rise to a position they are not yet ready to fill.

Ordination is precluded by a call of God to separate a certain believer for the work of the gospel. The Holy Spirit spoke and called Paul and Barnabas (see Acts 13:1–4). After the believers in the Antioch church fasted, prayed, and laid hands on them, they sent the men away to minister. The Bible reinforces the concept that God selects his chosen ministers, and this selection is then confirmed by the church (see Acts 13:4). Ordination in a sense, is a divine-human partnership made to further the work of God.

Ordination bestows a delegation of power and includes a vesting of authority. The word *investment* originates with the concept of "putting on vestments" (an investiture) like priests donning their royal robes before ministering before the Lord. The term later came to mean "the act of being invested with an office, right, endowment."[208] Investments are made with hopes for a return—a profit. Investing in women ministers clothes them with authority. Like the garments worn by the priests, it identifies and commissions them to serve as one of the body of believers who ordained them. With ordination, higher positions of service in the church are made accessible to qualified candidates. Other benefits may include tax credits, a housing allowance, and the opportunity to serve as chaplain.

When questioning the ordination of women, a pre-question must be asked: "Does God call women to preach, teach, and function in leadership positions in his church?" If the answer is yes, then the question of ordination should be simple. Ordination is a validation of the call God has placed on men and women to function as apostles, prophets, evangelists, pastors, and teachers. As such, they should be ordained to serve in their calls with all the authority the positions hold regardless of gender.

The only valid case against ordaining women would be a legitimate universal scriptural prohibition. Both the Old and New Testaments record women serving in offices for which men in today's church are ordained. If even one woman functioned as an apostle, prophet, evangelist, pastor, or teacher, a

SIDENOTE
from Juli Jasinski

Do not argue and fight but respectfully show the truth in the scriptures to those who enquire it of you. Be gentle with your response.[209]

—Juli Jaskinski
Author, Church Planter
and Prayer Coordinator;
Hollis, New Hampshire

precedent is established. As in a court of law, a precedent is a decision of a proceeding authoritative rule that can be used in the future in similar cases. Precedents found in Scripture were established and set by God's authoritative rule. What the Bible sanctioned in the early church should be allowed in the church today.

Early Catholic Ordination

The practice of ordaining women is longstanding, though not necessarily widely known. *The Apostolic Constitutions* (a collection of early Christian literature [375-380AD] that offered authoritative directions on church structure)[210] recorded the ordination of deaconesses. Specifically, it said, "Ordain also a deaconess who is faithful and holy, for the ministrations towards women ... the bishop shall anoint her head, as the priests and kings were formerly anointed."[211] It is important to note this practice was allowed in a church that had already adopted a patriarchal order (male headship or control) of the priesthood. Even in this restrictive culture, women were formally ordained into ministry to women.

Some have claimed these deaconesses were the same as the class of widows who were spiritually used in some capacity. However, in this same volume of *The Apostolic Constitutions,* the widows were instructed to be obedient to the deaconesses. These historic documents recognize a deaconess is in a separate classification than a widow. In fact, a preference was specified for a deaconess over a widow in assisting clergy.

The Apostolic Constitutions established the ordination procedure for a deaconess. In its preamble it stated the bishop "shalt lay thy hands upon her in the presence of the presbytery."[212] In their presence, he was to offer the following prayer:

"Eternal God ... who didst fill Miriam and Deborah and Hannah and Huldah ... who also in the tabernacle and the temple didst appoint women keepers ... look down now upon this thine handmaid who is designated to the office of deacon ... that she may worthily execute the work instructed to her."[213]

The ceremony of ordination differs in church organizations and has changed over time. Not only the rite has changed, but the qualifications of those being ordained. Men and women in the early church had no Bible school or seminary to attend. They did not have to pass written tests or write theses. This certainly applied in the case of the Twelve apostles as well as other early church leaders including Paul, Timothy, Priscilla and Aquila, and Phebe (see Mark 3:14; John 15:16; Acts 13:2–3, 14:23; Titus 1:5).

Education is beneficial, but it was the call of God on men and women who were chosen by the Lord and ordained by the church to serve.

Conclusion

The Lord designed women to be intelligent, spiritually-led, and fully capable. Without Eve, Eden was "not good." With her, it was complete. Although both Adam and Eve transgressed, God mercifully redeemed his purpose for humanity through the blood of Jesus. Today, all those who are "in Christ" are new creations, born of water and Spirit, one in him.

Throughout the pages of this book, we have seen that God used women in every era to do exploits for his kingdom. In the Old Testament and the New, faithful women prayed, judged, led worship, prophesied, and explained the Word of God. Jesus welcomed female disciples, and Paul affirmed women as his co-laborers able to teach, lead, and operate in the gifts of the Spirit. On the day of Pentecost, the Lord fulfilled his promise and poured out his Spirit on all flesh including his handmaidens or daughters. Since then women have played even greater roles in his kingdom. In revivals over the centuries, wherever the spirit of God moved, women served alongside—and sometimes led—men.

If the issue of women in ministry were straightforward, the church would have united on the subject long ago. Biblical concepts are best understood by balancing views through the "macro lens" of finite human understanding with the "wide angle lens" of the whole counsel of God. In the times our understanding of Scripture is foggy or indeterminate, as sincere believers we cannot pretend it is clear. When a passage's meaning cannot be conclusively determined (as in the case of missing correspondence or one-time word usage), wisdom dictates these verses should not be used to establish universal principles or create what could well be unscriptural barriers.

While biblical teachings and policies are important—especially pertaining to critical issues of salvation and eternal life—we must be careful not to build concrete doctrines on sand. The footings are simply not there to erect a pillar and fasten a Pauline ruling to it that he may not have made or that he did not specify should extend beyond a local situation. Every Christian must examine his or her beliefs against the Word of God and dismiss any augmentation—practices or precepts added along the way that restrict religious freedom.

Accepted interpretations and personal conclusions differ, and Christians should be respectful toward those who have differing beliefs. While we hold to our convictions, we should take care that we are not divisive. Jesus told his followers there would be places their ministry would not be received. In those times, they were to let their peace return to them and "shake off the dust" from their feet as they moved forward in the will of God (see Matt 10:13–14). Keep your peace and continue on your journey.

Jesus taught his followers that in his kingdom no competition for position or power was ever appropriate. So it should be today. It is in the best interest of the church to have as many passionate, qualified people as possible engaged in ministry. A called woman of God brings a unique benefit to the church. Her contributions in the pulpit and in organizational leadership complement the work of others and strengthen the body of Christ. Providing her a place to minister should not displace another. The kingdom of God is about expansion, not ladder climbing.

It's the Lord's prerogative to allow or disallow women from preaching, pastoring, or leading. In the biblical record we find no instance in which Jesus or other early church leaders restricted women from leadership positions based solely on gender. It seems logical Jesus would have plainly and directly expressed any prohibitions. And he would have transmitted such critical information to those he gave the keys to the kingdom.

Women not only bless the church in pulpit ministry, but their involvement in leadership brings an exciting dynamic to the work of God. Feminine aptitudes, instincts, and gifts are essential components to a healthy church body. In church organizations that license and ordain women, it is appropriate that opportunities should be open for women to serve at varying levels of leadership.

Women serving in ministry is not a part of a progressive liberal agenda, but a historic reality. If there was a Deborah or Huldah in the Old Testament—and a Junia or Priscilla in the New Testament—there can be a Crystal or Lindsay in God's church today. There can be a "you" functioning in whatever role God calls you to, regardless of gender, and regardless of the ratio of women we see ministering in the church.

All women are not called to preach, just as all men are not. The question each person must ask and answer is this: "Am I fulfilling the purpose and call of God in my life?" If the Lord calls you, you do not have to defend your call. Walk in the freedom of Christ who set you free. Stand. Find your place, and perform the work God has called you to do.

If you are in a position to support women called to ministry, I hope you will do what you can to equip and affirm them. A sister should help a sister, and a true Christian gentleman should hold doors open for the virtuous women of God. If the Lord has called you, woman of God, to preach, then preach like a lady.

While working on this project, I received a call from a woman minister who was discouraged by the lack of support in her district. I propped my feet up on the ottoman in front of me and closed my eyes as I listened to her pour out her heart. While she was speaking, an image came to mind. It was a vision of many women in row boats, and each was rowing out to a big ship that was out to sea. The big boat was turning to meet the ladies, but it was taking some time.

As the image played in my spirit, I felt impressed that the general acceptance of women in ministry by the church at large will take time, but when it is, the "ship" will be filled with women equipped and ready to serve. If the Lord is speaking to you, I encourage you to step into your rowboat. Push away from the shore in Jesus's name, and launch into the water. I hope to meet you there.

THE END

Appendix A

Competency Model for a Female Minister in the UPCI

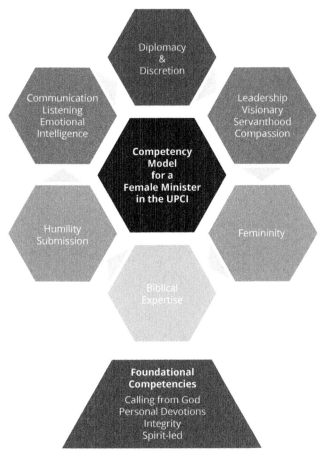

Diplomacy
&
Discretion

Communication
Listening
Emotional
Intelligence

Leadership
Visionary
Servanthood
Compassion

**Competency
Model
for a
Female Minister
in the UPCI**

Humility
Submission

Femininity

Biblical
Expertise

**Foundational
Competencies**
Calling from God
Personal Devotions
Integrity
Spirit-led

The *Competency Model for a Female Minister in the UPCI* is designed to help women identify the skills, knowledge, and behaviors necessary for the ministry. This process is called a skills gap assessment. Similar to a school's curriculum in which a student takes the required courses for a degree, a competency model provides a roadmap that aspiring professionals follow to reach their designated career choice. A woman who desires to be in the ministry can look at the model, assess which skills she is lacking, and then begin to develop those skills.

The "Foundational Competencies" (skills) shown on the bottom of the model in blue, represent the knowledge and behaviors that are building blocks for a female minister. For example, she must have a calling on her life from God and possess integrity. The colored clusters of competencies capture additional required skills, knowledge, and behaviors. For instance, after she receives her calling from God, a female minister should begin to develop her biblical expertise.

This competency model was a product of Carla Gray Weiser's (2015) research study on female ministers in the United Pentecostal Church International. The information in this model does not correspond with the organization's requirements to obtain ministerial credentials. For more information on the UPCI ministerial credentials, visit the UPCI Ministry Central website. For more on Gray Weiser's ministry, visit www.hopeacts.com.

Selected Bibliography

Alexander, Estrelda. *Black Fire: One Hundred Years of African American Pentecostalism,* Downers Grove, IL: IVP Academic, 2011.

Angell, Jeannette L. "Women in the Medievel Church: Did You Know," *Christian History,* Issue 30, 1991, www.christianhistoryinstitute.org/magazine/article/women-in-medieval-church-did-you-know/. Accessed 14 Nov. 2016.

Barfoot, Charles H. and Sheppard, Gerald T. "Prophetic vs. Priestly Religion: The Changing Role of Women Clergy in Classical Pentecostal Churches." *Review of Religious Research,* Vol. 22, No. 1, (Religious Research Association, Inc., 1980), pp. 2-17 Published by: Religious Research Association, Inc. www.jstor.org/stable/3510481. Accessed 26 Dec. 16.

Bauckham, Richard. *Gospel Women: Studies of the Named Women in the Gospels,* Grand Rapids, MI: Eerdsmans, 2002.

Belleville, Linda L. *Two Views on Women in Ministry,* Revised edition, Grand Rapids, MI: Zondervan, 2005.

Belleville, Linda. *Women Leaders and the Church*, Grand Rapids, MI: Baker, 2000.

Bernard, David K. *The Apostolic Church in the Twenty-first Century,* Hazelwood, MO: Word Aflame Press, 2014.

Bevere, John. *Breaking Intimidation,* Lake Mary, FL: Charisma House,1995, 2006.

Bevere, Lisa. *Fight Like a Girl,* New York, NY: Warner Faith, 2006.

Booth, Catherine. *Female Ministry, or, Woman's Right to Preach the Gospel*, New York, NY: Salvation Army Supplies Print. and Pub. Dept., 1975, 1859.

Bordin, Ruth. *Frances Willard: A Biography,* Chapel Hill, NC: The University of North Carolina Press, 1986.

Bounds, E.M. *Power Through Prayer.* www.ccel.org/ccel/bounds/power.I_1.html. Accessed 14 Jan. 2017.

Brengle, S. L. *The Soul Winner's Secret,* New York, NY: The Salvation Army Publishing House, New York, 1920.

Burgess, Stanley M., editor. *The New International Dictionary of Pentecostal and Charismatic Movements,* Grand Rapids, MI: Zondervan, 2002.

Butler, Alban. *Butler's Lives of the Saints.* 12 vols. Ed. David Hugh Farmer and Paul Burns. New full ed., Tunbridge Wells, UK: Burns & Oates and Collegeville, MN: Liturgical Press, 1995–2000.

Bullock, Noel. "First Timothy 2:8-15," *McMaster Journal of Theology and Ministry*, Volume 11, Hamilton, Ontario: McMaster Divinity College, 2009-2010.

Coffman, James Burton. "Commentary on 1 Corinthians 1:11," *Coffman Commentaries on the Old and New Testament*, www.studylight.org/commentaries/bcc/1-corinthians-1.html. Accessed 17 Nov. 2016.

Covey, Stephen. *7 Habits of Highly Effective People*, New York, NY: Simon & Schuster, 1989.

Cunningham, Agnes, S.S.C.M., *The Role of Women in Ecclesial Ministry: Biblical and Patristic Roots*, Washington, D.C.: United States Catholic Conference Publications Office, 1976.

Cunningham, Loren, David Joel Hamilton, David Joel, with Rogers, Janice. *Why Not Women?*, Seattle, WA: YWAM Publishing, 2000.

Danby, Herbert, D.D., *The Mishnah: Translated From The Hebrew With Introduction and Brief Explanatory Notes*, New York, NY: Oxford Press, 1933.

Deen, Edith. *All the Woman of the Bible*, San Francisco, CA: HarperOne, 1988.

Donaldson, James (translator). "Apostolic Constitutions," Book III, from *Ante-Nicene Fathers*, Vol. 7. Edited by Alexander Roberts, James Donaldson, and A. Cleveland Coxe, (Buffalo, NY: Christian Literature Publishing Co., 1886.) Revised and edited for New Advent by Kevin Knight. www.newadvent.org/fathers/07153.htm. Accessed 22 Feb. 2017.

Dupont, Florence translated by Hachette, France. *Daily Life in Ancient Rome*. Cambridge, MA: Blackwell Publishers, 1994.

Ellison, Robert H., editor. *A New History of the Sermon: The Nineteenth Century*, Leiden, Netherlands, Boston, MA, Brill, 2010.

Epp, Eldon. *Junia, the First Woman Apostle*. Minneapolis, MN: Augsburg Fortress, 2005.

Freeman, Nona. *What a Thing! The Story of Addie Williams*, Minden, LA: Nona's Book Sales, 1993.

French, Talmadge L. *Early Interracial Oneness Pentecostalism*, Eugene, OR: Pickwick Publications, 2014.

Gariepy, Henry. *Christianity in Action: The International History of the Salvation Army*, Grand Rapids, MI: Eerdmans Publishing, 2009.

Geller, Stephen A. "The Dynamics of Parallel Verse a Poetic Analysis of Deuteronomy 32:6-12," *The Harvard Theological Review*, Vol. 75, No. 1, Cambridge, MA: Harvard Divinity School, 1982.

Goll, James. *Lifestyle of a Prophet*, Ada, MI: Chosen Books, 2013.

Hallett, Judith P. *Fathers and Daughters in Roman Society: Women and the Elite Family*, Princeton, NJ: Princeton University Press, 1984.

Jasinski, Juli. *Step Up: For Lady Preachers Only*, Hollis, NH: Juli Jasinski, 2013.

Jeremias, Joachim. *Jerusalem in the Time of Jesus*, Philadelphia, PA: Fortress, 1969.

Kee, H. Clark. *The Origins of Christianity*, London: Prentice-Hall, 1973.

Keener, Craig S. *Paul, Women, and Wives: Marriage and Women's Ministry in the Letters of Paul*, Peabody, MA: Hendrickson Publishers, 1992.

Keener, Craig S. *Two Views on Women in Ministry*, Revised Edition, Grand Rapids, MI: Zondervan, 2005.

Klinedinst, Douglas C. "Spiritual Authority: The Example of the Centurion Servant," *Forward Magazine*, Vol. 47, No. 3, (July – September 2016), 7.

Koren, Daniel J., *He Called Her*, Hazelwood, MO: Word Aflame Press, 2016.

Lange, John Peter, D.D. Translated from German by Schaff, Philip, D.D. *A Commentary on the Holy Scriptures: Critical, Doctrinal, and Homilitical, With Special Reference to Ministers and Students,* Vol. 13., New York, NY: Charles Scribner's Sons, 1876.

Liardon, Roberts (compiler). *Frank Bartleman's Azusa Street: First Hand Accounts of the Revival,* Shippensburg, PA: Destiny Image Publishers, 2006.

Lightfoot, J. B. *St. Paul's Epistle to the Philippians,* London: Macmillan, 1894.

Lockyer, Herbert. *The Women of the Bible*, Grand Rapids, MI: Zondervan, 1988.

Maxwell, John. *Developing the Leader Within You*, Nashville, TN: Thomas Nelson, 1993.

McClintock, Jonathan. *Life Preaching,* Hazelwood, MO: Word Aflame Press, 2015.

McKnight, Scot. *Junia is not Alone,* Englewood, CO: Patheos Press, 2011.

McCray, Gerald. *God's Gals,* Mustang, OK: Tate Publishing, 2004.

McGraw, Barbara A. *The Wiley Blackwell Companion to Religion and Politics in the U.S.,* Chichester, West Sussex: John Wiley & Sons, 2016.

Miller, Calvin. *Preaching: The Art of Narrative Exposition,* Grand Rapids, MI: Baker Books, 2006.

Miller, Cindy. *Character Counts,* Dover, DE: Classic Publishing, 2010.

Murphy-O'Connor, Jerome. *St. Paul's Corinth: Texts and Archeology,* Collegeville, MN: The Liturgical Press, 2002.

Patterson, Eric and Rybarczyk, Edmund. *The Future of Pentecostalism in the United States,* Lanham, MD: Lexington Books, 2007.

Phipps, William E. *Assertive Biblical Women*, WJestport, CT: Greenwood Press, 1992.

Presbuteros, *Reply to a Priest of Rome*, Kensington: J. Wakeham Printer, 1868.

Pugh, J. T. *For Preachers Only,* Hazelwood, MO: Word Aflame Press, 2010.

Ramsay, W. M. "Historical Commentary on the First Epistle to Timothy," *The Expositor*, VIII (September 1909); Walter Lock, "A Critical and Exegetical Commentary on the Pastoral Epistles," *ICC,* Edinburgh: T&T Clark, rep. 1966.

Ramsey, W. M. *The Letters to the Seven Churches of Asia*, London: Hodder and Stoughton, 1904.

Ravenhill, Leonard. *Picture of a Prophet,* ravenhill.org. www.ravenhill.org/prophet.htm. Accessed 23 Feb. 2017.

Sanders, J. Oswald. *Spiritual Leadership,* Chicago, IL: Moody Bible Institute, 1994.

Scholer, David M. *Women in Early Christian History*, New York & London: Garland Publishing, 1993.

Spencer, Aida Besançon. *Beyond the Curse,* Nashville, TN: Thomas Nelson, 1985.

Spurgeon, Charles H. *Lectures to my Students,* London: Passmore and Alabaster, 1883.

Stanley, Andy. *Next Generation Leader,* Sisters, OR: Multnomah Publishers, 2003.

Strauch, Alexander. *Biblical Eldership,* Colorado Springs, CO: Lewis and Roth Publishers, 1995.

Sweet, Dr. Leonard. *I Am A Follower*, Nashville, TN: Thomas Nelson, 2012.

Tarn, W. W. and Griffith, G. T., *Hellenistic Civilisation,* 3rd Edition, London: Methuen, 1952.

Trout, Janet. *The Journey of Women in Ministry,* Dover, DE: Classic Publishing, 2009.

Tyson, James L. *The Early Pentecostal Revival,* Hazelwood, MO: Word Aflame Press, 1992.

Segraves, Daniel L. "The Battle of the Lexicons: Does 'Head' Refer to Authority or Source?," *Forward Magazine,* Vol. 47, No. 3, July – September 2016, 10.

Smith, Michael W. *It's Time to be Bold,* Nashville, TN: Thomas Nelson, 2003.

Wagner, Lori. *Gates & Fences: Straight Talk in a Crooked World*, Rochester Hills, MI: Affirming Faith, 2006.

Walston, Sharon Stoops. *A Woman's Place in God's Government,* House of Loy Books, Wilton, ME, 2001.

Warner, Wayne E. *Neglect Not the Gift That is in Thee*, Metuchen, NJ and London: The Scarecrow Press, Inc., 1986.

Witherington, Ben II and Hyatt, Darlene. *Paul's Letter to the Romans: A Socio-Rhetorical Commentary,* Grand Rapids, MI: Eerdmans, 2004.

Endnotes

Chapter 1

1 Mark Hollingsworth, "Divine Call to Preach or Man's Call to Preach," *Preachology*. http://www.preachology.com/divine-call.htm.

2 Gordan MacDonald, "God's Calling Plan: So What Exactly is 'A Call to Ministry?'" *Christianity Today: Leadership Journal,* (Fall 2003), 37.

Chapter 2

3 James Strong, *Strong's Exhaustive Concordance of the Bible,* (Peabody, MA: Hendrickson, 1988), s.v. "visions."

4 Daniel J. Koren, *He Called Her*, (Hazelwood, MO: Word Aflame Press, 2016), 171.

Chapter 3

5 Strong, *Strong's Exhaustive Concordance of the Bible*, s.v. "anoint."

6 W. E. Vine, *Vine's Expository Dictionary of New Testament Words, Unabridged* (McLean, VA: MacDonald Publishing Company, 1989), s.v. "anoint."

7 Ibid.

8 Ibid.

9 Smith, William, Dr. "Entry for 'Anointing,'" *Smith's Bible Dictionary*, 1901. www.biblestudytools.com/dictionary/anointing/. Accessed 13 Dec. 2016.

10 Cindy Miller quoted by Jonathan McClintock, *Life Preaching,* (Hazelwood, MO: Word Aflame Press, 2015), 247.

11 Dr. Leonard Sweet, *I Am A Follower,* (Nashville, TN: Thomas Nelson, 2012), 162.

Chapter 4

12 Edward Parsons Day, *Compiler, Day's Collacon: an Encyclopaedia of Prose Quotations,* (New York: NY: International Printing and Publishing Office, 1884), 93.

13 E.M. Bounds, *Power Through Prayer*. www.ccel.org/ccel/bounds/power.I_1.html. Accessed 14 Jan. 2017.

14 F. B. Meyer quoted by Chuck Swindoll, *The Church Awakening: An Urgent Call for Renewal,* (New York, NY, Hatchette Book Group, 2012), 4.

15 Integrity, Dictionary.com *Dictionary.com Unabridged*, Random House, Inc. www.dictionary.com/browse/integrity. Accessed 22 Dec. 26.

[16] Strong, *Strong's Exhaustive Concordance of the Bible*, s.v. "express image."

[17] Ibid.

[18] Susanna Wesley, *Susanna Wesley: The Complete Writings,* (New York, NY: Oxford University Press, 1997), 109.

[19] Roy B. Zuck, *The Speakers Quote Book,* (Grand Rapids, MI: Kregel Publications, 1997), 111.

Chapter 5

[20] Vine, *Vine's Expository Dictionary of New Testament Words,* s.v. "adoption."

[21] John Maxwell, *Developing the Leader Within You,* (Nashville, TN: Thomas Nelson, 1993), 47.

[22] Father Justin McCarthy, *Brother Juniper Strikes Again*, (New York, NY: Pocket Books Published by Hanover House, 1961), Cover.

[23] Stephen Covey, *7 Habits of Highly Effective People,* New York, NY: Simon & Schuster, 1989), 79.

Chapter 6

[24] Andy Stanley. *Next Generation Leader*, (Sisters, OR: Multnomah Publishers, 2003), 142.

[25] Janet Trout. *The Journey of Women in Ministry,* (Dover, DE: Classic Publishing, 2009), 28.

[26] Charles H. Spurgeon. *Lectures to my Students,* (London: Passmore and Alabaster, 1883), 173.

[27] Michael W. Smith, *It's Time to be Bold,* (Nashville, TN: Thomas Nelson, 2003), 132–3.

[28] Ibid.

[29] Richard S. Sloma, *No-Nonsense Management: A General Manager's Primer*, (Washington, D.C.: Beard Books, 2001), 13.

Chapter 7

[30] Addie Williams Quoted by Nona Freeman, *What a Thing! The Story of Addie Williams*, (Minden, LA: Nona's Book Sales, 1993), 35.

[31] Amelia Earhart, "Quotes," *The Amelia Earheart Official Website*, www.ameliaearhart.com/about/quotes.html. Accessed 31 Mar. 2017.

[32] Stanley, *Next Generation Leader*, 65.

[33] Covey, *7 Habits of Highly Effective People*, 106.

[34] Trout, *The Journey of Women in Ministry*, 27.

[35] John Bevere, *Breaking Intimidation*, (Lake Mary, FL: Charisma House,1995, 2006), 59.

[36] Omar Bradley quoted by Warren W. Wiersbe, *The Bible Exposition Commentary,* Volume 1, (Colorado Springs, CO: Cook Communications, 2003), 89.

Chapter 8

[37] Lori Wagner, *Gates & Fences: Straight Talk in a Crooked World*, (Rochester Hills, MI: Affirming Faith, 2006), 60.

Chapter 9

[38] Lisa Bevere, *Fight Like a Girl*, (New York, NY: Warner Faith, 2006), 109.

[39] Vine, *Vine's Expository Dictionary of New Testament Words,* s.v. "body."

Chapter 10

⁴⁰ Rev. Mildred Robinson, Personal interview, 5 Dec. 2016.

Chapter 11

⁴¹ Cindy Miller, *Character Counts,* (Dover, DE: Classic Publishing, 1998, 2010), 48.

Chapter 12

⁴² Strong, *Strong's Exhaustive Concordance of the Bible*, s.v. "modest."

⁴³ Craig S. Keener, *Paul, Women, and Wives: Marriage and Women's Ministry in the Letters of Paul*, (Peabody, MA: Hendrickson Publishers, 1992), 106.

⁴⁴ Perseus Digital Library, www.perseus.tufts.edu/hopper/text?doc=Perseus%3Atext %3A1999.01.0144%3Aspeech%3D1%3Asection%3D15. Accessed 12 Oct. 2016.

⁴⁵ Jonathan McClintock, *Life Preaching*, (Hazelwood, MO: Word Aflame Press, 2015), 280.

Chapter 13

⁴⁶ Shaffer, Bronya, "A Chat About Modesty," *Community News Service*, (June 11, 2009). www.collive. com/show_news.rtx?id=4005. Accessed 12 Oct. 2016.

⁴⁷ Calvin Miller, *Preaching: The Art of Narrative Exposition*, (Grand Rapids, MI: Baker Books, 2006), 17.

⁴⁸ J. T. Pugh, *For Preachers Only*, (Hazelwood, MO: Word Aflame Press, 1993, 2010), 97.

Chapter 14

⁴⁹ Leonard Ravenhill, *Picture of a Prophet*, Ravenhill.org. www.ravenhill.org/prophet.htm. Accessed 23 Feb. 2017.

Chapter 15

⁵⁰ Stephen A. Geller, "The Dynamics of Parallel Verse a Poetic Analysis of Deuteronomy 32:6–12," *The Harvard Theological Review*, Vol. 75, No. 1 (Cambridge, MA: Harvard Divinity School, 1982), 35–56.

⁵¹ See John 4:24.

⁵² Strong, *Strong's Exhaustive Concordance of the Bible*, s.v. "help."

⁵³ Strong, *Strong's Exhaustive Concordance of the Bible*, s.v. "meet."

⁵⁴ Francis Brown, *The Brown-Driver-Briggs Hebrew and English Lexicon* (Peabody, MA: Hendrickson, 2007), 617.

⁵⁵ *Septuagint*, (Internet Sacred Text Archive), www.sacred-texts.com/bib/sep/gen002.htm. Accessed 9 Feb. 2017.

⁵⁶ *LSJ*, (Greek Word Study Tool), www.perseus.tufts.edu/hopper/morph?l=%E1%BD%85%CE% BC%CE%BF%CE%B9%CE%BF%CF%82&la=greek, "ὅμοιος." Accessed 9 Feb. 2017.

⁵⁷ Vine, *Vine's Expository Dictionary of New Testament Words*, s.v. "like."

Chapter 17

⁵⁸ Wasson, Donald L. "The Extent of the Roman Empire." Ancient History Encyclopedia. Last modified January 05, 2016. http://www.ancient.eu/article/851. Accessed 12 Aug 2017.

⁵⁹ David Meager, "Slavery in Bible Times," Crossway Autumn 2006, No. 102, http://archive. churchsociety.org/crossway/documents/Cway_102_Slavery1.pdf. Accessed 12 Aug 2017.

[60] George H. Guthrie, "The Religious Background of the New Testament," Read the Bible for Life Leader Kit, (Lifeway Press: Nashville, TN, 2010).

[61] Judith P. Hallett, *Fathers and Daughters in Roman Society: Women and the Elite Family*, (Princeton, NJ: Princeton University Press, 1984). 77-79.

[62] Ibid.

[63] Mark Cartwright, "Women in Ancient Greece." *Ancient History Encyclopedia*. Last modified July 27, 2016. http://www.ancient.eu/article/927. Accessed 12 Aug 2017.

[64] Demosthenes, Speeches (English), Dem. 59.122, perseus.uchicago.edu/perseus-cgi/citequery3. pl?dbname=GreekFeb2011&query=Dem.%2059.122&getid=1. Accessed 25 Nov. 2016.

[65] Jerome Murphy-O'Connor, *St. Paul's Corinth: Texts and Archeology*, (Collegeville, MN: The Liturgical Press, 2002), 56.

[66] Jerome Murphy-O'Connor, *St. Paul's Corinth: Texts and Archeology*, 56–57.

[67] Douglas J. Moo (and eight others), *The NIV Application Commentary Bundle 7: Pauline Epistles*, (Grand Rapids, MI: Zondervan, 2015).

[68] Belleville, Linda L, *Two Views on Women in Ministry*, Revised edition, (Grand Rapids, MI: Zondervan, 2005), 45.

[69] Joseph H. Thayer, *Thayer's Greek English Lexicon of the New Testament*, Fourth edition. (Grand Rapids, MI: Baker Book House Company, 1977), s.v. "evangelist."

[70] Ibid.

[71] Herbert Lockyer, *The Women of the Bible*, (Grand Rapids, MI: Zondervan, 1988). www.biblegateway. com/resources/all-women-bible/New-Testament-Times. 11 Feb. 2017.

[72] Ibid.

[73] Ibid.

[74] Vine, *Vine's Expository Dictionary of New Testament Words*, s.v. "disciple."

[75] Joachim Jeremias, *Jerusalem in the Time of Jesus*, (Philadelphia, PA: Fortress, 1969), 375–76.

Chapter 18

[76] Strong, *Strong's Exhaustive Concordance of the Bible,* s.v. "assemble."

[77] Edith Deen, *All the Woman of the Bible*, (San Francisco, CA: HarperOne, 1988), 357.

[78] John Peter Lange, D.D., Translated from German by Philip Schaff, D.D, *A Commentary on the Holy Scriptures: Critical, Doctrinal, and Homilitical, With Special Reference to Ministers and Students*, Vol. 13., (New York, NY: Charles Scribner's Sons, 1876), 145.

[79] Ibid.

[80] H. W. F. Gesenius, Transcribed by Samuel Prideaux Tregelles, *Gesenius' Hebrew and Chaldee Lexicon to the Old Testament Scriptures*, 7th edition, (Grand Rapids, MI: Baker Book House; 1979), s.v. "Miriam."

[81] Paul Isaac Hershon (Compiler and Translator), *Talmudic Miscellany*, (London: Trubner & Company, 1880,) 283.

[82] Walter Brueggemann, *First and Second Samuel*, (Louisville, KY: John Knox, 1990), 21.

83 Judy Bolton-Fasman, "Hannah's Prayer: A Rosh Hashanah Story," *Jewish Boston* (2016). www.jewishboston.com/hannahs-prayer-a-rosh-hashanah-story/. Accessed 26 Mar. 2017.

84 Paulus Cassell, D.D., *Lange's Commentary: The Book of Judges*, (New York, NY: Charles Scribner and Company, 1872), 105.

85 Rev. Dr. Beth Jan Smith, Personal interview, 27 Mar. 2017.

86 William E. Phipps, *Assertive Biblical Women*, (Westport, CT: Greenwood Press, 1992), 85.

Chapter 19

87 Strong, *Strong's Exhaustive Concordance of the Bible*, s.v. "disciple."

88 Ibid.

89 Rev. Kevin M. Shaw, Personal interview, 19 Nov. 2016.

90 Eusebius of Caesarea, *Fathers of the Church*, Book 3. Chapter 31. www.newadvent.org/fathers/250103.htm. Accessed 19 Nov. 2016.

91 Strong, *Strong's Exhaustive Concordance of the Bible*, s.v. "kyrios."

92 Ibid.

93 Robert Law, "Elect Lady," *International Standard Bible Encyclopedia*, www.blueletterbible.org/search/dictionary/viewTopic.cfm?topic=ET0001150,IT0002949. Accessed 21 Nov.16.

94 Ibid.

95 Eusebius. *An Ecclesiastical History to the Twentieth Year of the Reign of Constantine, being the 324th of the Christian Era*, (London: S. Bagster, 1842), 141.

96 Strong, *Strong's Exhaustive Concordance of the Bible*, s.v. "abide."

97 W. W. Tarn and G. T. Griffith, *Hellenistic Civilisation*, 3rd Edition, (London: Methuen, 1952), 98–9.

98 Ibid.

99 W.M. Ramsey, *The Letters to the Seven Churches of Asia*, (London: Hodder and Stoughton, 1904), 324–35.

100 Coffman, James Burton. "Commentary on 1 Corinthians 1:11," *Coffman Commentaries on the Old and New Testament*, www.studylight.org/commentaries/bcc/1-corinthians-1.html. Accessed 17 Nov. 2016.

101 Donald S. Metz, *Beacon Bible Commentary*, VIII, (Kansas City, KA: Beacon Hill Press, 1968), 314.

102 John Trap, "Commentary on 1 Corinthians 1:11," *John Trapp Complete Commentary,* www.studylight.org/commentaries/jtc/1-corinthians-1.html. Accessed 17 Nov. 2016.

103 Daniel Whedon, "Commentary on 1 Corinthians 1:11," *Whedon's Commentary on the Bible*, www.studylight.org/commentaries/whe/1-corinthians-1.html. Accessed 17 Nov. 2016.

104 John Gill, "Commentary on 1 Corinthians 1:11," *The New John Gill Exposition of the Entire Bible*, www.studylight.org/commentaries/geb/1-corinthians-1.html. Accessed 17 Nov.16.

105 Florence Dupont translated by France Hachette, *Daily Life in Ancient Rome*. (Cambridge, MA: Blackwell Publishers, 1994), 103–5.

106 T. Hammer, "Wealthy Widows and Female Apostles: The Economic and Social Status of Women in Early Roman Christianity," in G. D. Dunn, D. Luckensmeyer & L. Cross (ed.), *Prayer and Spirituality in the Early Church: Poverty and Riches*, 5 (Strathfield: Paulist Press, 2009), 65–74.

107 Richard S. Cervin, "A Note Regarding the Name 'Junia(s)' in Romans 16:7," *New Testament Studies*, Volume 40.3 (Cambridge, MA: Cambridge University Press, 1994), 464–470.

108 Eldon Epp, *Junia, the First Woman Apostle*. (Minneapolis, MN: Augsburg Fortress, 2005).

109 John Chrysostom, *Homily on the Epistle of St. Paul the Apostle to the Romans XXXI*, (Oxford/London: John Henry Parker/J. Rivington, 1848), 489.

110 Epp, *Junia, the First Woman Apostle*, 34

111 David Noel Freedman, ed., *The Anchor Bible Dictionary*, (New York, NY: Doubleday, 1992), 1127.

112 James R. Beck, editor, Craig S. Keener, *Two Views on Women in Ministry*, Revised Edition, (Grand Rapids, MI: Zondervan, 2005), 212–13.

113 Strong, *Strong's Exhaustive Concordance of the Bible*, s.v. "en."

114 Thayer, *Thayer's Greek English Lexicon of the New Testament*, s.v. "among."

115 Ben Witherington II and Darlene Hyatt, *Paul's Letter to the Romans: A Socio-Rhetorical Commentary*, (Grand Rapids, MI: Eerdmans, 2004), 389.

116 Scot McKnight, *Junia is not Alone*, (Englewood, CO: Patheos Press, 2011), Kindle Locations 73–75.

117 Richard Bauckham, *Gospel Women: Studies of the Named Women in the Gospels*, (Grand Rapids, MI: Eerdsmans, 2002), 109–202.

118 Strong, *Strong's Exhaustive Concordance of the Bible*, s.v. "diakonos."

119 Edith Deen, *All the Woman of the Bible*, (San Francisco, CA: HarperOne, 1988), 231.

120 Strong, *Strong's Exhaustive Concordance of the Bible*, s.v. "prostates."

121 Aida Besançon Spencer, *Beyond the Curse*, (Nashville, TN: Thomas Nelson, 1985), 116–17.

122 Strong, *Strong's Exhaustive Concordance of the Bible*, s.v. "proïstēmi."

123 Booth, *Female Ministry, or, Woman's Right to Preach the Gospel*, 11.

Chapter 20

124 Loren Cunningham, David Joel Hamilton, with Janice Rogers, *Why Not Women?*, (Seattle, WA: YWAM Publishing, 2000), 13.

125 Ibid.

126 Daniel L. Segraves, "The Battle of the Lexicons: Does 'Head' Refer to Authority or Source?," *Forward Magazine*, Vol. 47, No. 3, July – September 2016, 10.

127 Ibid.

128 Thayer, *Thayer's Greek English Lexicon of the New Testament*, s.v. "strong."

129 Booth, *Female Ministry, or, Woman's Right to Preach the Gospel*, 8.

130 Ibid.

131 Catherine Booth, *Female Ministry, or, Woman's Right to Preach the Gospel*, 9.

132 Spencer, *Beyond the Curse*.

133 Herbert Danby, D.D., *The Mishnah: Translated From The Hebrew With Introduction and Brief Explanatory Notes* (New York, NY: Oxford Press, 1933), 447.

134 *The Greek New Testament,* Third Edition, United Bible Societies (New York, London, Amsterdam, Edinburgh, Stuttgart, 1975), www.greekbible.com/l.php?manqa/nw_v-3pad-s--. Accessed 20 Sep. 2016.

135 Interlinear Study Bible, classic.studylight.org/desk/view.cgi?number=5720&tool=grk, Accessed 20 Sep. 2016.

136 Cunningham, *Why Not Women, A Fresh Look at Scripture on Women in Missions*, Ministry and Leadership, 218.

137 Spencer, *Beyond the Curse* (Grand Rapids, MI: Baker Academic, 1985).

138 Vine, *Vine's Expository Dictionary of New Testament Words*, s.v. "silence."

139 Alexandrinus Philo, *Philo, Volume 2*, (Cambridge, MA: Harvard University Press, 1979), 131.

140 William E. Wenstrom, Jr., *De*, Wenstrom Bible Ministries, wenstrom.org/downloads/written/word_studies/greek/de.pdf. Accessed 17 Sep. 2016.

141 Vine, *Vine's Expository Dictionary of New Testament Words*, s.v. "authority."

142 Ibid.

143 Noel Bullock, "First Timothy 2:8–15," *McMaster Journal of Theology and Ministry*, Volume 11, (Hamilton, Ontario: McMaster Divinity College, 2009–2010), 81.

144 Ibid.

145 Gerald McCray, *God's Gals*, (Mustang, OK: Tate Publishing, 2004), 39.

146 Ibid.

147 Ibid.

148 S. L. Brengle, *The Soul Winner's Secret,* (New York, NY: The Salvation Army Publishing House, New York, 1920), 36.

149 Linda L. Belleville, *Women Leaders and the Church*, (Grand Rapids, MI: Baker, 2000), 165.

150 W. M. Ramsay, "Historical Commentary on the First Epistle to Timothy," *The Expositor*, VIII (September 1909); Walter Lock, "A Critical and Exegetical Commentary on the Pastoral Epistles," ICC (Edinburgh: T&T Clark, rep. 1966), 31.

151 Booth, *Female Ministry, or, Woman's Right to Preach the Gospel*, 13.

152 Ibid.

Chapter 21

153 Jeannette L. Angell, "Women in the Medievel Church: Did You Know," *Christian History*, Issue 30, 1991, www.christianhistoryinstitute.org/magazine/article/women-in-medieval-church-did-you-know/. Accessed 14 Nov. 2016.

154 Ibid.

155 H. Clark Kee, *The Origins of Christianity*, (London: Prentice-Hall, 1973), 51-2.

156 Joyce Ellen Salisbury, "Perpetua," *Encyclopedia Britannica*. (10 Nov. 1999), www.britannica.com/biography/Perpetua-Christian-martyr. Accessed 14 Nov. 2016.

157 Eusebius of Caesarea, *340 AD Church History*: Book 6, Chapter 41. www.documentacatholicaomnia.eu/03d/0265-0339,_Eusebius_Caesariensis,_Church_History,_EN.pdf. Accessed 14 Nov. 2016.

158 Johann Peter Kirsch, "St. Apollonia," *The Catholic Encyclopedia*, Vol. 1. (New York, NY: Robert Appleton Company, 1907). Accessed 14 Nov. 2016.

159 Ibid.

160 Clugnet, Léon Clugnet, "St. Catherine of Alexandria." *The Catholic Encyclopedia*. Vol. 3, (New York, NY: Robert Appleton Company, 1908), Newadvent.org. Accessed 14 Nov. 2016.

161 David M. Scholer, *Women in Early Christian History*, (New York & London: Garland Publishing, 1993), 310.

162 Alban Butler, Butler's *Lives of the Saints*. 12 vols. Ed. David Hugh Farmer and Paul Burns. New full ed., (Tunbridge Wells, UK: Burns & Oates and Collegeville, MN: Liturgical Press, 1995–2000).

163 Belleville, *Two Views on Women in Ministry*, 46.

164 Ibid., 45.

165 Strong, *Strong's Exhaustive Concordance of the Bible*, s.v. "elder."

166 Alexander Strauch, *Biblical Eldership*, (Colorado Springs, CO: Lewis and Roth Publishers, 1995), 16.

167 J. B. Lightfoot, *St. Paul's Epistle to the Philippians*. (London: Macmillan, 1894), 95.

168 J. Mark Jordan, "Abuse of Spiritual Authority," *Forward Magazine*, Vol. 47, No. 3, (July –September 2016), 15.

169 Strong, *Strong's Exhaustive Concordance of the Bible*, s.v. "diakoneō."

170 Philip Comfort, General Editor, *Cornerstone Biblical Commentary*, (Carol Stream, IL: Tyndale House Publishers, 2009), 75.

171 Charles John Ellicott, General Editor, *Ellicott's Commentary for English Readers*, (London, Paris, New York and Melbourne: Cassell and Company, Ltd., 1905). biblehub.com/commentaries/ellicott/1_timothy/3.htm. Accessed 17 Dec. 16.

172 Ibid.

173 Ellicott, *Ellicott's Commentary for English Readers*, Accessed 17 Dec. 16.

174 Agnes Cunningham, S.S.C.M., *The Role of Women in Ecclesial Ministry: Biblical and Patristic Roots*, (Washington, D.C.: United States Catholic Conference Publications Office, 1976).

175 Ibid.

176 Ibid.

177 Douglas C. Klinedinst, "Spiritual Authority: The Example of the Centurion Servant," *Forward Magazine*, Vol. 47, No. 3, (July – September 2016), 7.

Chapter 22

178 "Phoebe Palmer: Mother of the Holiness Movement," *Christianity Today*, www.christianitytoday.com/history/people/moversandshakers/phoebe-palmer.html. Accessed 26 Nov. 2016.

179 Ruth Bordin, *Frances Willard: A Biography*, (Chapel Hill, NC: The University of North Carolina Press, 1986), 87.

180 Barbara A McGraw, *The Wiley Blackwell Companion to Religion and Politics in the U.S.*, (Chichester, West Sussex: John Wiley & Sons, 2016), 179.

181 Frances E Willard. (1890). "A White Life for Two." *Illinois During the Guilded Age*, www.gildedage.lib. niu.edu/islandora/object/niu-gildedage%3A24224. Accessed 26 Nov.16.

182 Editors of the Encyclopedia Britannica, "Hannah Whitehall-Smith: American Evangelist and Reformer." *The Encyclopedia Britannica*, www.britannica.com/biography/Hannah-Whitall-Smith. Accessed 26 Dec.16.

183 Robert H. Ellison, editor, *A New History of the Sermon: The Nineteenth Century*, (Leiden, Netherlands, Boston, MA, Brill, 2010), 395.

184 Norman H. Murcoch, "The Army Mother," *Christian History Institute*. www.christianhistoryinstitute. org/magazine/article/army-mother/. Accessed 26 Dec. 2016.

185 Henry Gariepy, *Christianity in Action: The International History of the Salvation Army*, (Grand Rapids, MI: Eerdmans Publishing, 2009), 36.

186 James Goll, *Lifestyle of a Prophet*, (Ada, MI: Chosen Books, 2013), 232–3.

187 Ibid.

188 James L. Tyson, *The Early Pentecostal Revival*, (Hazelwood, MO: Word Aflame Press, 1992), 36

189 Tyson, *The Early Pentecostal Revival*, 45.

190 Marshall Allen, "Pentecostal Movement Celebrates Humble Roots," (15 Apr 2006), *The Washington Post*, www.washingtonpost.com/wp-dyn/content/article/2006/04/14/AR2006041401421.html. Retrieved 26 Nov. 2016).

191 Roberts Liardon (compiler), *Frank Bartleman's Azusa Street: First Hand Accounts of the Revival*. (Shippensburg, PA: Destiny Image Publishers, 2006), 57.

192 Stanley M. Burgess, editor, *The New International Dictionary of Pentecostal and Charismatic Movements*, (Grand Rapids, MI: Zondervan, 2002), 588.

193 Tyson, *The Early Pentecostal Revival*, 151.

194 Talmadge L. French, *Early Interracial Oneness Pentecostalism*, (Eugene, OR: Pickwick Publications, 2014), 67.

195 Wayne E. Warner, *Neglect Not the Gift That is in Thee*, (Metuchen, NJ and London: The Scarecrow Press, Inc., 1986), 146.

196 "Aimee Semple McPherson," *Christian History*, ChristianityToday.com. www.christianitytoday.com/ history/people/denominationalfounders/aimee-semple-mcpherson.html. Accessed 24 Mar. 2016.

197 Estrelda Alexander, *Black Fire: One Hundred Years of African American Pentecostalism*, (Downers Grove, IL: IVP Academic, 2011), 329.

198 "History," International Christian Education Association of the Pentecostal Assemblies of the World. pawicea.org/about/history/. Accessed 24 Mar. 2017.

199 Charles H. Barfoot and Gerald T. Sheppard, "Prophetic vs. Priestly Religion: The Changing Role of Women Clergy in Classical Pentecostal Churches." *Review of Religious Research*, Vol. 22, No. 1, (Religious Research Association, Inc., 1980), pp. 2–17 Published by: Religious Research Association, Inc. www.jstor.org/stable/3510481. Accessed 26 Dec. 16.

200 Liardon, *Frank Bartleman's Azusa Street: First Hand Accounts of the Revival*, 57.

201 Eric Patterson and Edmund Rybarczyk, *The Future of Pentecostalism in the United States*, (Lanham, MD: Lexington Books, 2007), 128–9.

202 Ibid.

203 Ibid.

Chapter 23

204 Pugh, *For Preachers Only*, 87.

205 Sharon Stoops Walston, *A Woman's Place in God's Government*, (House of Loy Books, Wilton, ME 2001).

206 David K. Bernard, *The Apostolic Church in the Twenty-first Century*, (Hazelwood, MO: Word Aflame Press, 2014), 87.

207 See Appendix A.

208 Investment, Dictionary.com, *Dictionary.com Unabridged*, (Random House), www.dictionary.com/browse/investment. Accessed 23 Mar. 2017.

209 Juli Jasinski, *Step Up: For Lady Preachers Only*, (Hollis, NH: Juli Jasinski, 2013), 3.

210 James Donaldson (translator), "Apostolic Constitutions," Book III, from *Ante-Nicene Fathers*, Vol. 7. Edited by Alexander Roberts, James Donaldson, and A. Cleveland Coxe, (Buffalo, NY: Christian Literature Publishing Co., 1886.) Revised and edited for New Advent by Kevin Knight. www.newadvent.org/fathers/07153.htm. Accessed 22 Feb. 2017.

211 Ibid.

212 Roberts and Donaldson, *Ante-Nicene Fathers*, Vol. 7, (Grand Rapids, MI: Eerdmans Publishing Company, 1988), 492.

213 Ibid.

Subject Index

CPSIA information can be obtained
at www.ICGtesting.com
Printed in the USA
BVOW06*2320150917

494730BV00005B/5/P